Sex, No Drugs & Rock'N'Roll

Memoirs Of A Music Junkie

By **L.E. Kalikow**

Art & Graphics by Aleks Rosenberg & L.E. Kalikow
for L.E.Kalikow LLC

Other Formats: This book is also available as an eBook, AudioBook, and companion Soundtrack Album, with additional information and sound samples available at www.LEKalikow.com

Copyright © 2016 by L.E.Kalikow LLC

ISDN: 978-0-9971319-0-1

SEX, No Drugs & Rock-N-Roll

Memoirs of a Music Junkie

Part 1
The 50's & 60's

L.E. Kalikow

Please note that this autobiographical story, although based on true life, includes altered names, personalities and events, both for artistic and legal reasons and should, therefore, be considered a creative re-creation.

Copyright© 2016 L.E. Kalikow

Sex, No Drugs & Rock'n'Roll
Memoirs Of A Music Junkie

Part 1: The 50's & 60's

I. (1950-53)
(Age 3-6, The formative years)

I was oversexed before I could talk. Playing "tent" under my mother's dress, I'd stare at a "Ring Around The Rosy" coloring book for hours, trying to picture what the little girls would look like without their clothes on. Next door to us on Stanley Street in Schenectady, lived a Polish family and a little blonde named Karen. We were about four years old when I began pulling her pants down under the elm tree beside our house. One afternoon her grandmother threw a bucket of ice water from the second floor window yelling something about what they did to dogs in the old country. To this day I hate cold showers.

As a matter of fact, I don't like showers at all. I like the smell of sweat. I love feeling a woman perspire in my arms and all the aromas that go with sex. Standing in each other's breath, if you try, you can just make out the scent of her wetness. Then there's the excitement of running my hand under her dress, up her thighs, and into her panties to a full soft cushion of pubic hair... and the moisture on my fingers. That is, if she hasn't covered it with powder and feminine hygiene spray.

'Madison Avenue' has done a pretty good job of convincing women to buy plastic holders for their breasts, fill their hair with guck so that you can't get your fingers through it, and to shave every inch of body hair so as not to be mistaken for human beings. The female body is gloriously attractive. I love the curves and motion and form of a woman. I have

never, however, found her genitals to be especially attractive. When picturing a woman stretched out naked on the bed in front of me, with arms and legs open and inviting, there is something much more sensual about a mound of pubic hair hiding the mysteries within, than a thin arrow pointing out in which direction I am supposed to insert my dick.

It's amazing how much more children perceive than we adults acknowledge. I understood everything going on around me but just couldn't tell anyone. I created a 'best friend' for myself named Giggy because it was the only word I could say at the time. Whenever a lamp mysteriously fell off a coffee table or a telephone cord was pulled out of the wall, "Giggy did it."

We all have our Giggys. We just get more sophisticated in creating them as we get older.

There are certain vivid memories that stand out from Stanley Street: Hopalong Cassidy stickers on the bags of Wonder Bread that "built strong bodies twelve ways;" Jumping off of the living room chair with a big "S" on my undershirt and a towel on my back *(It was during these flights I saw quite a bit of Giggy.)*; The magician that lived down the street who had dead bodies buried in his garage; A horse-drawn cart that sharpened knives with a spinning grindstone that sparked; Riding the merry-go-round in the park so I could throw up afterwards *(It's a wonder I didn't end up bulimic.)*; and the first time I saw black people. Negroes weren't called "black" back then, they were "colored." And no "colored" people lived on Stanley Street.

I must have been about six years old, on a park path that led to the municipal pool. In the distance coming toward me were a group of 'Boogie Men' with dark brown bodies and white shiny teeth. "The better to eat me with," I thought, as my heart pounded into the bushes to hide...

I guess it's instinct that human beings tend to fear anything new or that we don't understand. "Instinct" is the word we use for animal behavior we can't explain (and take for granted). Sex is an instinct. "Instinct" is a non-secular way of saying "God did it"... Which is very close to "Giggy did it."

Anyway, where was I? Oh yeah, Stanley Street... We had a bully on Stanley Street. Alfred was a freckle faced redhead whose mother and father beat on each other, then turned on him, who in turn came over and turned on me. One day I decided it was my turn... I had my mother call Alfred's house and invite him over to "make up and be friends." As Alfred came smiling up the back steps I darted out, smashed him in the head with a sock of marbles, kicked him in both shins, and pushed him down the steps. I was so proud of myself. Unfortunately, mom was not especially pleased with my diplomacy. The end result was one of the most humiliating experiences in my young life. Right then and there I was forced to return to Alfred's house and apologize to him and his family for what I considered perfectly justifiable behavior. If nothing else, however, I learned an important lesson ... never let my mother know what I was up to.

As a matter of fact, never let anyone know what you're doing or planning to do. First of all, it allows you the luxury of being able to deny it; Secondly, it precludes any pressure to alter or stop whatever it is you've decided to do; and most importantly, no one can be judgmental about you or your morality if they don't know what the fuck you're up to! Then of course, there's the "mystery factor." There's romance in the unknown. When a woman pictures Zorro in mask and cape, sweeping her into the bedroom, I don't think she really cares who made him Zorro. And no matter how attractive he is in reality, he can never match the fantasy of what lies behind the mask.

Imagination is always more powerful than reality. In later years, when I worked on staff at a singles country club, we found it much easier to sell memberships before the club was actually in operation. We sold people on their own imagination of what would be. This is not dishonest. There is an important distinction to be made here... it comes down to motivation. Keeping something to yourself because you have a right to some secrets or even because you hope it will stimulate your partner's imagination takes on a different meaning if you are ashamed of the secret or are afraid of the effect it might have. Keeping part of yourself private is not the same as hiding the truth.

As I entered first grade dad was transferred and we moved from the tree-lined houses of Stanley Street to a temporary brick apartment in Hartford, CT. This was a bit more urban than I had been used to but I learned how to make flying saucers out of Popsicle sticks and that the new kid on the block is an outsider. I also learned that the best thing to do when someone pushes you to fight is to turn away like it doesn't bother you... then turn back and hit him in the face as hard as you can. Suddenly you have friends and you're not an outsider anymore.

By the time we moved to our new home in the suburbs of West Hartford I was a good two *Dick and Jane* books behind the rest of my second grade class. Reading was a chore. Always trying to catch up meant a lot of "face punching." Kids in the suburbs would push each other ten times before either one threw a punch (and then never in the face). My technique was devastatingly successful. In no time everyone wanted to be my friend, even if I couldn't read.

My fascination with females also continued. I even fixed my uncle up with my second grade teacher. You see every time he took me out I'd pick out the best-looking woman. So when I told him my teacher was worth a date, he did. I don't know exactly what he did, but she smiled a lot after that. Meanwhile, I was pulling down the pants of every little girl in the neighborhood. Giggy made me do it. It was instinct, mixed with a heavy dose of curiosity. I just loved seeing and touching the places on little girls that weren't supposed to be seen or touched. Never hiding behind the subterfuge of games like 'house' or 'doctor,' we hid behind the bushes and played my game... 'touchees.' The rules were simple. The little girl would pull up her dress and then either she or I would pull down her underpants. Sometimes my pants would come down first, depending on how trusting (or scared) she was. She could touch my thing once for every two touches of hers. That was because I had more to touch and besides... it was my game.

I would daydream about little girl's cunts all the time, even noticing that when I bent my leg, the fold at my knee looked just like the hairless slit between a girl's legs. Playing Clark Kent in class I'd undress every girl with x-ray vision *(a habit I have never outgrown)*. The real fun though, was talking them into it. First timers would sometimes take hours of convincing. Occasionally I would even let them have a free look at mine... just to show my sincerity. After the first time, it got easier. One little girl used to come over regularly and show me hers and let me touch it without having to take my pants off at all. Sometimes it was a dare. Others would do it because their girlfriend already did (even though each promised to keep it a secret).

> *Again, a valuable lesson... When a girl tells you she can keep a secret, that means she can keep it until she feels she doesn't have to anymore.*

For months I went about teaching touchees to every little girl I could tutor. Then one summer afternoon, with my fingers between the legs of Ivy Cartrosse, her mother called out from two houses away. Moving too fast, the zipper caught her skin and her cry punctuated my first cold sweat. Thank God Ivy realized the gravity of our situation and regained her composure. We needed a story, quick... She told her mother that we were climbing a tree when a branch stuck through her jeans. The next afternoon, mom and dad took me out to the back porch. Apparently the parents of every little girl in the neighborhood had been on the phone threatening legal (and illegal) action to curtail my extra-curriculum activities. I believe some also suggested curtailing certain parts of my anatomy. Relieved to see that dad still had his belt on, my mind began racing for a list of possible excuses. Nothing seemed to work. I was too old for Giggy and too young for God. Who else could I blame? What could they do to me? Would we have to move again?

At first nothing was said. We just sat there. The silence was deafening. Then, in an amazingly soft voice, dad began with "When two people love each other..." For the next two hours I learned, in graphic detail, the mysteries of the universe and what it meant to get laid.

By the beginning of third grade, like a gunfighter on TV, my 'face punching' reputation preceded me. Even when I tried to pick a fight, the other guy would back down. Bored with kids my own age, I set out to meet Mark Razini. Mark was three years older and the neighborhood juvenile delinquent. He had this cool way of folding his little league hat with three creases in the visor. Only his friends could fold it that way. My visor got three folds the day I learned how to play tackle football in Razini's backyard.

All the players were fifth and sixth graders and here I came, this little wise-ass from third grade that wanted to play. I didn't know the rules but this kid with mud in his hair explained that the object was to stop the guy with the ball... any way I could. So when they pushed me out into the field and this giant sixth grader came running toward me with the ball ... I punched him in the face. Right then and there, I became Mark Razini's friend.

> *Everything is relative. Mark was really a pussy but to our middle class white suburban neighborhood he was frightening.*

Mark smoked cigarettes and swore a lot, wore black leather and had a gravity knife that clicked open with a flick of his wrist. When he wasn't wearing his trademark baseball hat, his hair was slicked back in a 'D.A.' which stood for "Duck's Ass" because that's what it looked like from behind. Mark was cool.

The fact that I was his friend simply added to my mystique and by fourth grade I was almost a God to my classmates. There was also something else... I could sing. Encouraged by my former second grade teacher *(the one getting laid by my uncle)*, I sang *"Kisses Sweeter Than Wine"* at the Fourth Grade Dance for five dollars. My first professional engagement was a resounding success, placing me in heavy demand at birthday parties thereafter. Singing, however, was not as important to me as my fighting reputation because this was the 50's 'B.P.'(Before Presley). My heroes came from Saturday morning TV. There was Wild Bill Hickok, Sky King, Captain Midnight, and Roy Rogers (who sang occasionally but only in the 'mushy' parts of the show).

It's worth pointing out here that although I couldn't play touchees anymore for fear of losing my life (or worse); I never stopped thinking about naked girls and sex. It wasn't just little girls either. Every weekend I'd run across the street in the morning to help Mrs. Huther with her laundry. What does that have to do with sex you might ask?

> *Now here's a good example of how imagination can be much more powerful than reality. If I were to stop writing right now, your imagination would take over. As a matter of fact, you might have already started to expect some perverted scenario...no such luck.*

Mrs. Huther was a young newlywed with reddish brown hair and freckles all over her body... well, almost all over. She always did her laundry wearing nothing but a sheer nightgown. From my vantage point on the floor in front of her, helping sort clothes, her breasts would sway back and forth in front of my eyes when she leaned forward. I noticed how the freckles faded on her chest. Her breasts were large and milky white but with dark, well defined nipples. From directly in front of her, if she leaned over far enough, I could see all the way to her red pubic hair. Whenever possible I'd accidentally reach up with an article of clothing and rub my hand against anything I could. She was oblivious to it all... I think.

I love large breasts and big nipples. I'm not sure why. As a matter of fact I'm not sure why most men find breasts so exciting. I've heard it suggested that men associate the breast and nipple with nursing and mother. But girl babies nurse too. No, I think it's because tits are something women have that we don't (reverse penis envy). Also, psychologically we know that a woman's breasts are very much tied to her sexuality. Here's instinct again. I may be wrong but I believe that the human female is the only creature with nipples that get hard from sexual arousal or even sexual thoughts. It doesn't happen to a cow.

Then there's also the 'forbidden factor.' Men are taught that it's OK to be aware of her tits but not to look at them. And don't ever touch them! You can hold her hand or her arm or even kiss her, but don't touch her tits. It always amazed me that I could park with a girl and pull her body up close; feel our mouths open in a passionate kiss; stick my tongue in and out; feel my cock moving against her thighs. Then all I had to do was reach for a breast and that was it... "What kinda girl do you think I am?"

And the ones that 'advertise' the most usually feel the least. After hours of putting on makeup, a push up bra, black stockings and a revealing dress, she'll complain that "All men want the same thing." Then there's the 'head trip' that any guy she allows to touch her should cum in thanks... 'Head Trip', those are two words that together or apart conjure up an amazing array of images.

II. (1954-56)
(Age 7-9, The elementary years)

Fourth grade was a significant year. For the first few months my godliness was taken for granted by my classmates. Then the first challenge to my heretofore unchallenged face punching reputation came in the form of Allen 'The Eyes' Eisemann. Three months into the school year, Allen moved in from South Philadelphia. Word around school was that he had killed one of his former classmates by bare-handedly ripping out his throat during recess and as a result his whole family had to leave the state of Pennsylvania.

It would be an understatement to say that 'The Eyes' and I did not see eye to eye. From the first day he showed up it was obvious that the school wasn't big enough for both of us. The funny thing was that even though I really hadn't had to fight anyone in two years, I had actually come to believe my own hype.

So did Melvin Spivak and Sherman 'The Tank' McNaughton. Melvin was about my size, with straight black hair, beady eyes and a high pitched voice that always seemed to be there, even when he wasn't. Sherman was about twice my size and I imagine today is either a truck driver or an interior decorator. Together we made an awesome trio. On the other side, 'The Eyes' soon developed a following and henchmen of his own. As we moved into winter, it was obvious that a confrontation was coming.

Despite the fact that Mark Razini had moved on to Junior High, he was more than happy to contribute his advice and consultation in planning the big 'Fourth Grade Rumble.' *"Blackboard Jungle"* had recently been a hit movie and street gangs, rumbles and rock 'n' roll were now in style. By the second week in December, the snow was more than a foot high and the challenge was issued for a secret after-school snowball fight between the two warring factions. The stage was set. All week there was whispering in the hallways, marbles and baseball cards changing hands, and rumors of secret weapons and outside muscle being flown in from Philadelphia.

Having not yet experienced any substantial pain or injuries in my life, the whole thing was a terrifically exciting real life TV show. Each day after school, Sherman, Melvin and I would meet to plan strategies, practice maneuvers and build up each other's confidence.

> *Make note...another human instinct, our inborn fascination with conflict, power and violence. You'd think we'd outgrow this type of behavior as we get older but instead we just get better at it (or worse, depending upon how you look at it).*

The night before the big fight, Melvin was filling his family freezer with ice balls. Mark coached me in the fine art of crotch kicking, and Sherman was at home doing push-ups. That morning the fresh-waxed school corridors looked unusually shiny. I had never been to school early before. It seemed much bigger with no one there. I went to the window and looked down to the snow-covered playground behind the gym, then went to the bathroom. As I sat on the toilet the bathroom door opened and someone entered the stall next to me. Whoever it was, was in a hurry. A tremendous fart was followed by a gush of diarrhea. It was The Tank.

By eight o'clock our classroom had pretty much filled. Melvin was late. The ice balls had frozen together and he couldn't get them out of the freezer... so much for planning. Across the room The Eyes was watching me. Actually he was staring at me without blinking. The second hand on the clock was inordinately loud as it clicked twice for every unit of time. It was almost unbearable to imagine that I was going to have to go through a whole day of this.

Lunch time marked the first stage of the battle. Both sides headed for the playing field behind the gym where, with the precision of racing squads we built snow forts and stocked them with ammunition for the coming conflict. Spivak brought out a pail of water to dunk our snowballs. We would have ice balls one way or another. Meanwhile I noticed one of their guys head back to the school and return with something hidden under his coat. What were they up to?

The Eyes had a sardonic smile as the bell rang and we headed back to class. Could all the stories about Allen be true? What if they had chains, or knives, or a gun? I could see it all now... We'd get up to throw our ice balls and they'd shoot them out of our hands... I went to the bathroom again.

A light snow had begun to fall when the final bell rang and the whole school held its breath. The teachers knew something was up but they didn't know what. All day I had tried to find an opportunity to sneak down and see what was hidden behind their fort, but every time I turned around The Eyes was watching me.

The plan was that we would all go home and wait an hour for the teachers to leave, then return to do battle. Time sped up and a half-hour later Melvin, Sherman and I headed back only to find The Eyes and his crew busy at work behind their fort with no less than twenty spectators bundled up around the perimeter of the field of honor.

As I write this I can't help but think again...how childish... and how grown up.

It started innocently enough with plain old-fashioned snowballs. Then suddenly we found out what they were hiding... It happened just after Melvin and The Tank had thrown the first of our ice balls. We decided that this long distance stuff was bullshit and with two aluminum garbage can covers we brought as shields, we were going to charge. Our pockets filled with ice balls, prepared to go over the top, the first of their 'Black & Whites' hit... The 'white' was snow and the 'black' were sharp triangular pieces of gravel. The first Black & White caught Spivak squarely in the forehead and it took everything inside him to keep from crying as a thin trickle of blood started over his eyebrow. In what was more panic than bravery Sherman and I found ourselves yelling and running with the garbage can covers up in front of our faces, unable to actually see where we were going, throwing our ice balls as we ran. Before we knew what had happened, Sherman literally crashed through the wall of their fort and it was hand-to-hand combat.

I saw The Eyes pick up a handful of gravel and heard the splatter of stones crash against my aluminum shield. With typical Saturday morning TV bravado, I threw down my cover and tackled him football style in the snow. Unfortunately from then on The Eyes refused to go along with my script. You see on television, only women scratch and bite and scream... men duke it out. Not The Eyes. Suddenly his fingernails were cutting into my face. He wasn't punching, he was scratching and kicking and screaming and biting... NO FAIR! This was dirty fighting! His arms and legs and finger nails and body were all flailing in every direction while at the same time he was screeching at the top of his lungs and his eyes were bugging out of his head. All other fighting stopped and out of the corner of my consciousness I could feel the spectators pull back like a rodeo crowd from a wild bull. All I could do was hold on for dear life.

We rolled over and over in the snow and I thanked God for the thickness of my leather gloves as his teeth almost bit through. In time we were tangled up in a snowy heap against the school wall and neither of us could move. Now what? The adrenaline stopped pumping. I could feel the sweat on my forehead grow cold and felt my fingers and toes both tingling and becoming numb. I dared not let go, at the same time not knowing how much longer I could hold on. Was I the winner? After all, I was on top. But he also had me. Gradually every cut and scratch began to throb. I could almost hear my pulse. "Give Up?" I asked. The Eyes said nothing. He just kept holding on, breathing heavily into the snow beneath us. The audience began to close in again. I prayed for a teacher or somebody to break us up, but nobody came. And the onlookers did nothing but look on.

Was he just waiting for me to let go so he could go crazy again and rip out my throat like his last victim in Philadelphia, or was he just as tired as me? Was The Eyes really just Allen Eisemann, a fourth grader like me? Then, at the last minute of my strength, a divine inspiration... I simply announced myself the winner, for all to hear. "I'm gonna let you go now Allen," I said as if I were doing it on purpose. Pulling my arms free, which by this time had no feeling, I magnanimously offered my lifeless hand, "let's shake." If he hit me again now with my hand extended in peace, he'd be branded a coward forever. On the other hand, what difference would it make if I were dead? For an endless moment of uncertainty I waited for his answer. He didn't move. What was he thinking? What would he do?

Like a snake uncoiling from a winter's sleep, The Eyes stretched open to face me and hissed with a pointed finger, "It's not over yet!" Give me a fuckin' break! I didn't even have enough energy to stand up again, let alone fight. I sat there in disbelief as he rose to his full height. Then to my astonished relief, The Eyes turned and left me there hunched over in the snow.

The story of the 'Great Fourth Grade Rumble' snowballed with each telling forever writing my name into the history of King Philip Elementary School. Now I was not just a god to my classmates, like Davy Crockett... I was a legend. For the next two years, I was elected President of my class and President of the student body. Nature, however, was about to play an ironic trick on me in payment for this glory.

> *Over the years I've come to believe that our existence is a giant cosmic game. Life is the gift of time we're given to play. Although the starting point and rules may be different for every player, the basic premise is that for every positive there is a negative. Sometimes we get to choose whether we wish to pay the price, while other times we simply have to play the cards we're dealt.*

In gym class toward the end of fourth grade, as we all lined up according to height, I found myself at the end of the line...the joker! Even though this was only fourth grade and it wasn't important yet, it would be.

There was one other event that took place in fourth grade that not only had a profound effect on me, but also changed the lives of every teenager in the country (and eventually the world)... One Saturday afternoon Melvin Spivak invited me over to hear a new record. With rock 'n' roll in its infancy, radio was pumping out the Carvel soft ice cream music of Perry Como, Patty Page and the Lemon Sisters. It's hard to put into words the culture shock of *"Heartbreak Hotel"* and Elvis Presley. It was the sound of sex personified at a time when you couldn't say the word "pregnant" on television. Everything about it was exciting... the beat, the echo; the breathy growling raucous delivery... none of us had ever heard anything like it before.

Collecting every fan magazine, record and picture, I learned all the lyrics and spent hours mimicking his groans. Elvis was the symbol of youth and rebellion. Parents and teachers and ministers and politicians spoke out against him as I tried desperately to make my hair straight with hot metal combs and gobs of Brylcream. All over the country, teenage collars went up and side burns grew down. Pants got tighter and my lip began to curl when I sang. Radio broke wide open with the Rockabilly music of Carl Perkins, The Everly Brothers, Buddy Holly, and Jerry Lee Lewis... and for the first time in my life, the fact that I could sing became important.

III (1957-58)
(Age 10-11, The age of innocence)

Our family rented a house every summer at Chapman Beach. Cary was bigger and stronger than any other kid on the beach and looked and talked and dressed like Elvis. No one did anything on the beach without Cary's permission. She was 'the leader of the pack' ten years ahead of her time. Cary didn't like anybody and ignored me. If I could just get her alone and sing for her. The problem was that wherever Cary went she attracted a crowd. You see if you weren't with her, you were against her.

There could be another instinct at work here. Whether its team spirit, patriotism, or organized religion, we humans have an uncanny knack for finding excuses to identify with a group so that we can beat up on those that don't belong. It's probably ironic that years later, Cary would find herself an outsider.

Every year my parents would bring a different teenage girl with us to watch me, my two younger brothers, and my sister. The one I remember best was Jeanie. She was probably 16 or 17 and the image of innocence. The first night my parents left us alone however, this sweet young thing turned into *"The Bride of Frankenstein."* After forcing me to bed a half hour early, she sat in front of the mirror with hairspray and makeup to complete her transformation. Luckily the opportunity would soon present itself to exorcise her of her demons. I felt it was my moral obligation (and besides, she pissed me off!).

You see my baby brother Barnett had an annoying habit of getting up in his sleep and banging his head. Understand that this wasn't light taping in rhythm. He would arise on all fours and smash his forehead into the headboard so hard that the crib would literally loose its screws. If you woke him, he'd turn over, fall asleep for ten minutes and then get up and start again. Imagine how frightening this could be to a teenage baby-sitter watching over an infant for the first time, especially considering that mom and dad had forgotten to tell her about this little idiosyncrasy.

They probably expected me as the oldest, to assure my protector that everything was alright... no way, José. Shortly after my banishment, the familiar banging began. I crept to the edge of the stairway to watch. As Miss Hairspray opened the baby's door it was obvious she couldn't quite make out what was going on in the darkness. Then her eyes gasped, dropping her hairbrush as she dashed into the room. I could imagine her standing next to the crib with her hand between the baby's pounding forehead and the wooden backboard not sure what to do next. She probably then woke Barnett, who would most likely open his eyes briefly, drool down his chin, roll over, put his thumb in his mouth and innocently fall back to sleep. I pulled back as emerging from the room, she glanced up the stairs, probably debating whether to come up and wake me. I giggled to myself knowing that in ten minutes the banging would start again.

Jeanie literally fell out of her chair when the next crash rang out. It took considerable self-control not to laugh out loud at the sight of her half teased hair sticking up in every direction as a cloud of makeup became a jet-stream. When she emerged this time, amidst the wreckage of combs, brushes, lipstick and makeup powder, Little Miss Monster looked like she had just seen a ghost. With the pitter patter of mice feet back to bed, I covered my head with the blanket. Sensing her standing over me, waiting for just the right moment, when the light switch clicked, I leaped... got her! A blood curdling scream and I screamed back, faking fright. My brother and sister then came running in, took one look at Jeanie's mascara running face and hair raising bouffant, and they started screaming. Now everybody was doing it and I was having the time of my life.

After assuring my siblings that this black-eyed screaming monster was actually our baby-sitter and it was safe to go back to sleep, the banging began again. Now I was in control. "There's something wrong with the baby," she whimpered as she clutched my hand on the way downstairs. Sure enough, there was Barnett smashing his forehead full blast into the headboard. The crib had now come away from the wall and Barnett was literally knocking it across the room. "You see?" she trembled, waiting for me to tell her that this was normal and not to worry. "Gee," I said, "I've never seen him do that before."

When mom and dad came running into the house after having received a less than coherent phone call, they found Jeanie cowering in the corner with Barnett in her lap. Out of the goodness of my heart, I stayed up to offer my moral support.

> *Here was another example of adults underestimating the perceptual maturity of a child. Even at eleven I knew they felt guilty. When I said that I assumed Jeanie had been told about Barnett's 'head trip' and that what I meant was that I had never seen him knock the crib across the floor before, they bought it. This explanation by the way, was another of those last minute inspirations that to this day continue to save my ass. There are various names for this ability... To a performer, it's 'stage presence;' To a punk, it's 'street smarts;' If you're a lawyer, it's called 'talent;' A used car dealer says it's 'salesmanship;' To an ambassador, it's 'diplomacy,' A politician calls it 'honesty;' Otherwise, it's generally known as 'Bullshit.'*

All that summer I tried to catch Cary alone but someone always seemed to be around. Then one rainy afternoon toward the end of the season when most families had migrated home, I was alone out on the rocks, crabbing... I just realized that 'crabbing' could have a couple of meanings. In this case it meant dangling a broken black-shelled sea mussel, with protruding orange meat, on a length of twine, into the rock crevices at the water's edge. Every so often a giant blue crab would venture out. Once committed, like a lonely lover holding on to a relationship, its claws firmly affixed to the object of its desire, the crab could easily be pulled all the way out of the water. Before it knew what had happened, it would find itself in the bottom of an empty pail. The challenge was luring them out and getting them to commit and then the skill of sweeping them out of the water. That was the fun. Once I had them, I didn't know what to do. I didn't want to eat or own or hurt them... I just wanted to catch them. So I'd throw them back.

Cary had come up behind me. She spit on the rocks, combed back her D.A. and with her black hair in silhouette against the rain clouds, I could have sworn she was really Elvis. All summer I had been practicing what I'd say and now I was stage struck. It all gets a little vague after that, but much of my memory is a series of photographs and film clips. One such picture was a rainy afternoon at the end of the summer on the rocks by the sea where I sat across from Cary and sang *"Love Me Tender."*

Back at school for the next two years in gym class, it seemed I had to look up higher every week to see the kid next to me. Even Melvin's voice began to change. Meanwhile what was later to be known as 'The Establishment' launched the musical career of the 'Anti-Presley,' Pat Boone. He was the symbol of what every mother wanted their son to be. His clean-cut white smile matched the color of his shoes, his sport coat, and his music. It was Wonder Bread music and I was embarrassed to admit that I actually liked some of it. I was going through an identity crisis.

Everything was turning inside out. Despite my gunfighter reputation, I was now the shrimp of my class. No one dared to challenge me and I still believed in my own invincibility, but it was disconcerting to bump into a wall only to look up and realize that it was one of my classmates. The girls all stopped playing touchees too. Annette was growing tits on the Mickey Mouse Club and all around me training bras began to pop up. It was like they all shared the apple of knowledge at once and were no longer interested in playing with the snake. I didn't fit in anymore. Maybe I never did, but before I was having so much fun it didn't matter. Now things were changing and the biggest change was yet to come...I was almost reading at a sixth grade level when dad was transferred to New York and we moved again.

Our new home in White Plains was in a development built around a small private lake. Along with the painted turtles and frogs were giant red carp, often over a foot long, that traveled in schools and dotted the water like a Cézanne painting. There was no swimming as the bottom was also home to massive, prehistoric snapping turtles that could literally break off the end of a broomstick with one violent chomp.

To this day I have trouble skinny dipping for fear of dangling lunch in front of such a creature.

Among my earliest memory of White Plains, was waking up every morning in a sunlit baby blue bedroom with a hard-on. My voice still hadn't changed but my cock was very mature for its age. Laying on my stomach and rubbing it against the mattress felt great! I had no idea that this could lead to blindness or stunt my growth.

In retrospect, maybe that's why I stayed so short.

It didn't take long to make the connection between sex and masturbation. The thought of a naked girl and my penis sat up to be petted like a wirehaired puppy. Afraid my messy sheets would tip mom as to what I was up to *(an appropriate choice of words, don't you think?)* I tried turning over and pulling back the covers at the last minute. This would either splatter the wall or worse... the constant fear of someone walking in to see me shoot myself in the eye *(which was humiliating enough even if no one came but me)*. It was much safer to keep everything under the covers and let mom deal with it.

A musty smell of wooden beams permeated the attic adjacent to my room. Fiberglass insulation, and a torn cardboard box covered with ice skates and old draperies hid dad's stash of *Playboy* magazines. *(Here was that 'forbidden factor' again.)* Oh, the hours I spent staring at the airbrushed blonde bunnies with no cunts and perfect breasts, dreaming of the day that I'd be able to touch a real woman.

Entering my new sixth grade class, still a legend in my own mind, it was important to pick a fight with someone as soon as possible to establish 'an image' for myself. In Connecticut we were told horror stories about New York schools, so there was also the anticipation of astounding them with my reading ability. I astounded them alright.

My teacher looked very much like the actor Dean Jagger. His bald head, strong jaw, and bony index finger soon made it painfully clear that I had a good deal of "catching up" to do. Then there was Howard Gutman, a clumsy, likeable kid that had no idea why I was insulting him into a 'showdown' after school. The white tiled boy's room was a little smaller than I expected, which made Gutman appear even bigger. As he looked down and good-naturedly questioned my sanity, I went for my famous face punch. Barely reaching the top of his chest, it did however, get his attention.... Humiliation is perhaps too small a word to explain what it felt like to be literally stuffed in a trash-can and thrown through the bathroom window. As if this weren't enough, my Niagara Falls container continued to roll down a grassy slope to the front driveway where the last school-bus was waiting. The next thing I saw were the four legs of Dorothy Baxter, the most beautiful girl in school, as the trash can came to its final resting place between the fender and the curb. Flashing on the Stanley Street merry-go-round, I displayed my lunch to the crowd... quite 'an image' for my first day at school.

Returning the next day was as difficult as my trip to Alfred's house back in Schenectady. Fingers followed me through the hallways and into class, where the whole room actually began laughing. From the moment Howard Gutman placed me in that white metal trash can, everything was turned upside down. Until that moment I still really believed I was a god. Each day thereafter I sat alone in the back of the class, determined that next year, junior high would be different.

My brother Steve helped teach me algebra that year even though he was only in third grade. Years later we discovered that Stevie was severely dyslexic, slightly autistic, and a mathematical genius.

Growing up with Steve was a learning experience for the whole family. He would take the milk out of the refrigerator and the chocolate powder out of the closet to make himself chocolate milk, then return the milk to the closet and the chocolate to the frig. As a result, normal things were often found in the most unusual places around the house... wet shirts in the dishwasher, dirty dishes in the clothes drier, etc.

Most of my waking hours at home were spent torturing Stevie. When we slept in the same room, I'd wait for him to dose off and kick him out of bed, tie his shoe-laces together and glue his money into his wallet. There were water balloons over the door and fresh shoe polish on his bicycle seat. Eventually, when I raised my arm Stevie would twitch. This was because I was a god. By the end of sixth grade however, I stopped teasing Stevie.

IV. (1959)
(Age 12, Moving to junior high)

Eastview Junior High was a large red brick building in the heart of downtown White Plains. Homeroom was an assemblage of every color and shape... and I was still the smallest. Although racially mixed, a segregation system called "tracking" was used. The theory *(or excuse)* was that students would learn better if grouped with others of their same approximate IQ. Those in the "S" group had tested superior, "M" was for the medium, and "E" students needed extra help.

> *I would spend the rest of my life trying to prove to myself (and the rest of the world) that I was something more than an "M."*

Homeroom and gym were the only places we were all allowed to mix. Charlie Post sat next to me in homeroom. It was the first time either of us had been so close to another race and we didn't quite know how to interact. It's funny though, how simple proximity can lead to bonding. As I watched him run faster and jump higher and hit a ball farther than anyone else in school, I truly came to understand what Melvin and Sherman must have felt like when I was a god. My most vivid memory of Charlie Post was yet to come however...

Rainy weekend afternoons were often spent in the balcony of double feature movie theaters watching Steve Reeves as *"Hercules"* or Vincent Price poking out eyeballs. I loved the sticky floors, the smell of popcorn and the anticipation as the room went dark and I was drawn into fantasy fear. There were two main theaters in town that competed for our $2.50 with gimmicks and giveaways. One such come-on was an experiment at The Loews Theater for a movie called *"The Tingler."* It was shot in black & white except for the red blood. To carry the suspense one step further, the movie-house advertised that they had actually wired some of the seats to provide a mild electrical shock at appropriate times throughout the picture and required that every patron sign a release form before entering. I couldn't help but imagine what a great job that would be...pushing the button.

On this particular Sunday afternoon, the audience was rowdier than usual. It seemed that every wise-guy in the county had to prove that he was brave enough to attend. Extra police were actually brought into the theater for the occasion. I noticed Charlie a few rows behind me and waved to him. Then I heard, "we got a nigger lover here." To my immediate right sat the white cast of *"West Side Story,"* complete with cigarette packs folded into each t-shirt and enough grease in their hair to run a service station. For an instant the irony of this 'B' movie cliché taking place in the fantasy house itself didn't register. Then there was the flash of metal and the point of a switch blade under my chin. Out of the corner of my eye, Charlie was literally flying through the air like superman. I saw the blade cut into his hand. How red the blood looked in contrast to the dark brown of his skin.

In seconds police were everywhere and Charlie was in handcuffs. "No! No!" I tried to explain as the original trouble-makers fled through the exit doors. It was like yelling in a dream where no one could hear me. "He was only protecting me... please somebody listen ..." but nobody would. As the police wrestled Charlie out of the theater and warned me to "sit down and shut up!" it just didn't make sense. These were the years when we believed in the police and the government and the law and truth. Something was terribly wrong with this picture. The scar on Charlie's hand Monday morning evoked a mixture of guilt and embarrassment. I didn't know what to say. He just shrugged it off and said it was "no big thang." But it was... and we both knew it.

The world outside my own existence began to seep in. Francis Powers was shot down on a U2 flight over Russia while Adolf Eichman was captured in Argentina. I laughed at the funny African names of Lumumba and Kasavubu on the evening news while politics became a spectator sport with the first presidential debates. Then a dashing young Catholic from Massachusetts was elected President and the world's stomach began to rumble in places like Algeria and Cuba and Vietnam. There was something unsettling about the two all-white schools in New Orleans being desegregated and the funny name 'Lumumba' wasn't so amusing when he was murdered. It was OK though because he was a Communist, and besides...that was Africa.

Squirt-gun season started about a month into the school year. Even though they were strictly against school policy and would be confiscated if detected, everybody had one. They weren't always filled with water either. (You would especially try to avoid those that squirted yellow.) Although most squirt-gun fights took place in the hallways, my favorite targets were girls who sat in class with their legs open. In all honesty, half the time I just watched the targets without shooting, hoping to get even the briefest glimpse of pubic hair. There was always this inner fight, weighing the joy of watching her legs open against the thrill of hearing that little squeal when I hit the target.

Mr. Faraci strutted in front of science class with greasy black hair and a streak of gray, like a skunk spraying any male student who incorrectly answered his questions from an arsenal of appropriated weapons. Each squirt was accompanied by a wisecrack and an implicit dare. He especially liked to force students to sit still and be soaked by their own gun whenever he confiscated one. Our relationship was established the first time he asked me something in class…

"From your reading last night, please tell us all the meaning of 'osmosis.'" Unfortunately I had cut the center out of my science book as a home for my new gun. "I'm sorry Mr. Faraci; my grandmother accidentally ate my homework." The splat landed squarely in the center of my forehead. "I see intelligence runs in your family." "At least I know who my family is," came out of my mouth before I realized it. There was dead silence… "Excuse me, what was that sir..." Here was another test of my stage presence... "I said at least I know what a mammary is," rhyming my statement as closely as possible before extending my tongue toward the girl's chest sitting next to me. There was the exhilaration of a narrow escape as she smacked me in the head. That was until Faraci requested that I turn to page thirty-nine to read out loud the definition of 'osmosis.' How could I tell him I no longer had a page thirty-nine? The teacher made his way toward me. "What page was that?" I stalled. There was that obnoxious smile coming ever closer, "Perhaps you need your ears washed out." There was no way out now... I couldn't believe how long he stood there with his mouth open to my squirt-gun, like an arcade clown. The swagger washed from his face in a self-conscious instant of role reversal before he shot back. The air was suddenly filled with lines of water from every pistol in class. Giant hairdos began screeching for the door as homework papers dripped to the floor and the hallway filled with spectators. Mr. Faraci would never forget me.

Desperate to be accepted, I would do anything for attention. My seventh grade English class laughed as I loosened the screws in the chair and wooden desk of Mrs. Small. We held our breath when all 300 lbs. of her waddled into the room and stood at the blackboard scribbling out the day's lessons. She leaned back and a soft wooden creak was accompanied by an audible collective gasp. You could see the creases in her print dress become more pronounced as she shifted her weight further back. The anticipation was almost too much... Would it give way before she moved? The tension in her dress loosened as she leaned forward. Would she make it to her chair? If she did, would the chair hold, or give immediately? As the massive print dress rotated in our direction, Jennifer Bettes raised her hand. She was going to tell. But Mrs. Small didn't like questions until she was ready. Then came another mental snapshot for my memory book.... framed by the giant print dress were wide frightened eyes unable to extricate themselves from the world collapsing around them. When it all came crashing down, nobody laughed.

Sometimes when you try too hard for something, you just push it away. Even today, on those lonely horny nights, I'll never meet a girl. It's only when I'm not looking that it happens.

The harder I tried to be liked, the less likeable I became. It's ironic that the one place I found acceptance was with Charlie Post and the colored kids that used to hang out after school and sing a-cappella in the hallway. They didn't care about my height or the color of my socks or how much money my father made, they just liked the way I sang. After the bells and bustle and buses had gone, the fresh buffed floors echoed *"In The Still Of The Night"* against the stairwell and the music was magic and made total strangers feel like friends.

V. (1960)
(Age 13, Learning how to play)

Summer camp would give me another chance to start over with a fresh slate. Based on past performance however, my parents felt it wise to send me to an all-boys camp. Camp Crystal Lake in Maine was situated on a glacial body of water formed by the melting snow of the surrounding mountain range. Learning to swim in that environment was supposed to make a 'man' of me. *(You know how much I love cold water)*. Unfortunately, one dip and the only manly thing on my body shriveled up so small I couldn't find it to pee.

As a reward for three years of Sunday morning trumpet lessons with Mr. Benedetti (to the aroma of simmering tomato sauce and Sicilian mob slayings in the basement), was the honor of becoming Camp Bugler. This meant getting up in the dewy dark of pre-morning; trying to move my hands fast enough not to get caught by the snaps clicking open my felt-lined imitation leather instrument case; and warming up a silver mouthpiece between my palms before screwing it into place *(a practice I would later find useful, along with my tonguing techniques)*. On the way out to the baseball diamond, with wet grass soaked sneakers, I'd finger the sleeping valves of the horn. There was a distinct smell of metal as I became a brass rooster. Next was flag rising at assembly (where I'd miss half the notes). Later came flag lowering at dusk (when I'd miss the other half), and taps for 'lights out' each night. This daily routine made me a target for water balloons, practical jokes and a central 'camp personality'... it also made me someone special again.

On the mantel in the camp dining room were a row of plastic trophies. These would go to the winners of the Olympics that closed the season. God, how I wanted to be the best at something again. I wasn't big enough to compete in anything physical and my singing didn't mean shit to these guys. My counselor Brad was archery and riflery instructor and even though I enjoyed the concentration of riflery and the eye-hand co-ordination of archery, I'd never be the best. Then there were the horses. There was something amazingly powerful about sitting on top of an animal ten times my size and forcing it to do exactly what I wanted. This wasn't a piece of machinery, but a massive living creature with muscles that rippled beneath my hands and a will that was there to be challenged. And it didn't matter that I had to stand on an apple crate to reach the stirrups.

A horse is probably not as bright as your average dog, but like people, they have personalities, differences in intelligence, and moods. If you pay attention to his ears and idiosyncrasies, you can practically sense what he's thinking. Much like a dog will love its master even if he's a mass murderer; a horse will follow its rider practically anywhere as long as he believes that the creature on his back knows more than he does. A decisive pull on the reins accompanied by a swift kick in the side and all that power was at my command. I loved horseback riding. I began to spend all my free time around the horses; brushing and riding and shoveling and listening to the experience of Jason Perkins, the camp riding instructor. Jason was a tall blonde Tennessean who grew up around horses and had generations of knowledge to impart. At meal times I would sit near the plastic trophies and picture my name on the one that read "Camp Crystal Lake – 1st Place - Horseback Riding."

The Camp Olympic finals came down to six riders and as we moved around the track, Jason watched our form and control. One by one my competition was eliminated until it was down to me and Elmer Bernstein. The butterflies in my stomach were talking. "Keep your toes in and your heels down," they were saying... "it's almost yours." The final round seemed to go on forever and I could see Elmer's thick glasses fogging up and his pudgy body bouncing on the saddle in front of me. But his form was good and Jason couldn't decide between us. We'd have to change horses and compete in a 'sudden death' runoff. Perkins gave me Mr.Ed, an English riding horse with double reigns and Elmer was put on Sundown, with a Western saddle and single reign. It didn't matter to me. I knew both these horses and could ride either style. As we took off around the ring,

Elmer was bouncing in his saddle and with the final turn to the finish line I knew I had won.

When Jason announced my disqualification for "neck reining" a 'Strictly English' horse, the words made no sense. "Ignorance is no excuse," Perkins answered to the crowd rather than to me. This couldn't be happening. Everyone in camp knew I was the best rider! How could I lose to Elmer Bernstein? As the tears welled up, I ran and kept running deep into the woods where no one could see me crying. How could my teacher disqualify me for something he never taught me? It just wasn't fair! A virgin at betrayal, I was ashamed by my cherry red eyes. What a wimp! How could I go back now to play assembly for the whole camp to see the 'little loser cry-baby.' Careful not to be seen, I snuck back to my cabin. But Brad was there waiting. When he put his arms around me, as much as I tried not to, the crying started again. At first his words made no sense. So what if Elmer's father was rich? What did tips have to do with the Olympics? Jason Perkins was a counselor and my teacher. At assembly, everyone in camp seemed to know what had happened. It turned out to be the only time in my life that I actually enjoyed hearing an audience 'boo.' Jason made his way half way up the hill, then turned and went back to the stables. My trumpet had no trouble hitting every note as the flag came down.

At some point during the next school year I just said fuck it! If I don't grow another inch and I can't make any friends, tough shit! Someday I'll be a star and if no one likes me now, fuck'em... and a funny thing happened.... it was like a religious revelation... the 'theory of trying too hard' also worked in reverse. The less I tried, the more I got. The less I said, the more people listened. The less I sought acceptance, the more I received. I suddenly knew how to play!

Meanwhile, the virus of human stupidity began to cause the whole world to choose up sides. Kruschev and Kennedy played macho man with each other and the term 'brinkmanship' was born. It was 'us' and 'them' just like back in elementary school but now the 'adults' were playing. The Russians were beating us in the 'space race' but we set up the Peace Corps. Headlines screamed as the USSR continued nuclear testing in the atmosphere then barely noticed that our allies, the French, were doing the same thing. The British were called in to protect Kuwait from their neighbor Iraq and overnight the Berlin Wall went up. As governments were overthrown in the Congo, the Dominican Republic and Vietnam, we tried to figure out which ones were the good guys. Then, just when we thought we had it straight, we got caught in the Bay of Pigs trying to invade our neighbor's little island. Eichman was sentenced to death while I watched "Judgment At Nuremberg" in the movies and "West Side Story" sang and danced to the theme of racism and murder. My neighbors were building fallout shelters and Ernest Hemingway shot himself in the head. The whole world was going crazy. We actually had atomic bomb 'safety drills' in school diving under our desks to cover the back of our necks with our hands. Give me a fuckin' break!

Whether it was the times or that time in my life, the meaning of both time and my particular life became important. In bed, in the dark, I'd hear my own breathing. With fingertips on the veins in my neck and the realization that someday all of this would stop, I'd logic myself to sleep thinking: 'What will it be like after I'm gone?....The same as it was before I was born.'

I can't convince myself that there is an all-powerful human type being sitting up there in the sky watching. In fact I have trouble with most 'organized' concepts of God and religion. We humans are conceited creatures to think we're the last rung on the evolutionary ladder.

In a high school poem I'd later write:

Life is the coastline that circumscribes it all
   Fringed by the sands of time
Life is a wheel that rolls ever forward
   With no reason or rhyme?
Each generation, each death and each birth
   Carries on a perpetual climb.
Where is the end, the summit, the halt
   What lies beyond the sea?
This cycle cannot persist forever
   And on through infinity
There must be an object, a terminus, a goal
   No matter how far it may be
Or else why am I living, why am I here
   And most of all
Why am I me?

Each human being to flourish on earth
   Is a single grain of sand.
His bit of knowledge, no matter its worth
   Adds on to form an island.
And from that island, a continent a world a galaxy a universe
   And who knows what then
Is it possible we'll reach a point were we'll stop
   And start over again?...
No, there is a purpose, somehow it must be
  But we are mere sand
And unable to see.

VI. (1961)
(Age 14, Becoming a teenager)

After a period of hibernation, my libido began to come back to life. Daddy's *"Playboys"* weren't enough anymore as I discovered such potential Pulitzer Prize periodicals as *"Screw Magazine," "Gent,"* and *"Blow Jobs International"*(*or reasonable facsimile thereof*). These were a bit more graphic in their detail and deserved a special place in the attic, where no one else could possibly find them. Adjacent to the main floor were a series of parallel beams where I was warned on numerous occasions never to walk. One false step on the insulation between them and my foot could easily plunge through the ceiling of the master bedroom below. No one would ever be fool enough to venture out there... it was perfect.

On one of those special afternoons when no one else was in the house, my hard-on made it all the more difficult to crawl from beam to beam to the plywood cubby hole I had created in the far corner of the room. With intense concentration, each hand was placed firmly on a hardwood plank. Then ever so slowly bringing my knee forward, careful not to let my toe penetrate the insulation paper, my penis pointed the way.

> *More than half the excitement came from the 'forbidden factor.' I've come to believe that 50% of sexuality is seeing what you're not supposed to see, touching what you're not supposed to touch, and doing what you're not supposed to do. The other 50% is ruled by Giggy.*

In the corner, the trick was then to find a position in which I could both touch myself and turn the pages without damaging either. Considering that all this was being attempted on a two foot square of plywood made it all the more challenging. Actually this was one of the few times that being four-foot-three was an advantage. First I shuffled the magazines, to add variety. It didn't matter though, I knew every picture 'by hard,' as the index finger on my right hand gently moved up and down the little bump in my pants. Flopping open to a smile of recognition in my memory book was the glossy scene of a woman masturbating, her legs wide open and her other hand grasping a man's erection inches from her mouth. Fixating on details like the pubic hairs surrounding the finger, my zipper came down with fingertips now touching the underside of my penis through white cotton "Fruit Of The Loom's." Erect nipples and tongues, and a large cock with a woman's hand wrapped around it and my hand was doing the same. Back to the finger inside her cunt and her hand on my dick and I could see everything with my eyes closed.

She got up from the bed and spread her legs in front of me. She took my hand and continued to rub my cock. Her pubic hair surrounded my finger and her nipple was in my mouth... She was squeezing my penis ... I could see it...I could feel it...Sticky milk was shooting everywhere, splattering the page... and the wall... and my underpants... and a car door slammed in the driveway... So did my left foot, right through the floor! Talk about getting caught with your pants down. There I sat with cum dripping from my hand, my leg through the ceiling, and my mother coming up the front walk. Plaster and dust was dropping through the hole in the floor on to the powder blue bedspread below. The various punishments I received were nowhere near as severe as that instant of embarrassment. I was never allowed in the attic again.

As a carry over from the 50's there were still basically two types of teenagers: The 'collegiates,' that combed their hair with a neat part, wore madras jackets and penny loafers; or the 'greasers,' with skin-tight stretch pants, black socks and pointed Tom McCann shoes. Both sides wore jeans, but never to school... it was against the dress code. I tended to lean toward the latter, especially when I hung out with my cousin 'Burnout' Bernard. He was two years older, with shocking red hair, a substantial nose, an obvious stutter, a gregarious personality, and most important... a driver's license (actually only a learner's permit but that didn't stop us). They lived on the Mount Vernon/ Yonkers border, in three rooms above an Esso gas station.

Bernard spent more time under cars than he did in school. It must have been all that carbon monoxide that burned out Bernard's mental bearings, hence the name. He always believed it referred to the way he drove.

With Burnout, there were push-button, automatic, green Dodge Saturday nights, leaving rubber to the shrieking sound of neighbors saluting us with fingers and fists. Then there was that winter night on Pelham Parkway in the Bronx, when we decided to try and 'pick up some babes.' Burnout's friend Jocko said that even in the winter there were girls out there... just waiting, and to my amazement... they were. Neon lit fishnet high heels strutted, breathing smoke at snowy storefronts with siren red fingernails beckoning us to slow down. It was too surreal to be real, and it was both. Jocko rolled down the front window to 'make conversation,' and freezing air whispered into my ear, "How the fuck can they stand out there like that?"

The girls giggled and gaggled, but refused to come over to our car, preferring we guessed, the relative safety of the grocery doorway. This was too good to be true. There were three of us and three of them. We were virgins and they were.... obviously not. Our little heads soon convinced our big ones that decisive action was required, but as we opened the car doors, everything changed. Suddenly there were leather jackets everywhere, with sticks and knives and hammers and chains. I tried to slam back the door, but somebody was pulling from the other side. The rear window shattered behind my head in thousands of perfect little square pieces of plastic glass. Blood streamed down the side of Jocko's face as Burnout gunned the engine, but the wheels just spun on the icy pavement and the smell of burning rubber filled the back seat. Jocko bit a hand reaching through his window. There was vomit in the back of my throat as I kept pulling on the door, but someone was very strong on the other side. Burnout threw the car in reverse and then gunned it again. This time the tires caught for an instant and then skidded wildly. The car fishtailed across the street and did a 360, slamming into the side of another car. As gang members were thrown in every direction, a metal pole came flying through what was once the back window. It missed Burnout but hit the steering wheel and the horn began to blare. There were feet on the hood again and then a blunt smashing sound...the ceiling light shattered as the roof almost caved in. The tires squealed once more and then took hold. As we pulled away, Burnout tried to yell "Fuck You" but his stutter wouldn't get past the "F..F.." blowing wind and spit at the blaring horn and the shrieking neighbors saluting us with fingers and fists.

> *For each of us, the problems of our immediate lives are very real and can sometimes seem overwhelming. And yet, how insignificant those problems might appear to someone living in a different reality. That night in the Bronx, only a few miles away from where I grew up, was a very different realty. In my world, guns shot yellow water.*

Jocko's best friend Felix, had a rock group that was the back-up band for Joey Dee and The Starlighters. They could get ANYTHING. Jocko always talked about getting 'skin flicks.' We didn't know exactly what they were, but we knew we weren't supposed to see them (another example of my sex philosophy). In the attic (yes, the very same attic), was an eight-millimeter silent projector for home movies. The problem was arranging a time so as not to get caught with my pants down again. Eventually an opportunity arose, when left alone for a weekend to 'study for finals.' I must admit, it wasn't easy opening that attic door, even though the rest of the family was in Massachusetts.

After more than an hour with the shades drawn in the living room trying to thread the damn machine, Burnout was so desperate he was feeding the film to a flashlight. But 'necessity is a mother,' and somehow the obviously overused celluloid began to fumble through the sprockets and flicker on the coated screen. At first it looked like Charlie Chaplin standing on a ladder as a girl with heavy eye makeup entered the room. When she pulled down his pants it was obvious this was not Charlie Chaplin. The guy's cock was so big it looked like a special effect. None of us knew how to react. The room filled with macho jokes about the giant prick's public pubics probing precariously on the projection screen *(Now that was a 'PP'!)* As 'Eye Makeup' climbed the ladder and put it in her mouth we were all so embarrassed by our own hard-ons there was literally a moment of silence when the film snapped.

> *The whole 'Titty Bar' mentality, making sex a spectator sport, doesn't make sense. I understand the excitement of watching a naked woman prancing in front of me with erect nipples signaling to Giggy. But to do it in public, with a bunch of guys around me, all staring at the same woman, not able to touch her or ourselves... how fuckin' frustrating! There's also that woman standing in the spotlight, knowing that every faceless man in that room is staring at her... wants her... needs her... is fantasizing about her. But they really aren't. What they want are her tits and her ass and her cunt and her sex, but they don't want her.... And she knows that too. It's all a dehumanizing contradiction. Commercialization of basic instincts is not by definition a perversion. We have no problem paying for food or water or a place to sleep. But sex and love are not as objectively measured or satisfied. While we're on the subject of sex and bars... I wonder who came up with the word 'cocktail' and how they ever got it accepted into the English language?*

Our next feature was called "*Superdog.*" I'm sure you can imagine what that en-tailed. Suffice it to say, without going into de-tail, my sexual horizons were broadened.

VII. (1962)
(Age 15, My voice stops changing)

That summer, too old to be a camper and too young to be a counselor, I was sent off to Camp Thunderbird in Vermont, as a camper-waiter. From the outset there was something basically unfair about working three meals a day and paying for the privilege. At the same time, I went with a definite objective… to get laid. The cabins were built on stilts with a crawl space under each. My first hour in camp was spent cutting the bathroom floorboards into a secret trap door.

The camp owners, a heavyset woman named Beatrice ('Aunt Bea') and her much older husband 'Uncle Martin,' had obviously recruited heavily in the Bronx and Brooklyn. The staff all looked like they could easily have been members of the gang on Pelham Parkway. Among my cabin-mates were 'Spike,' David, and 'The Leach' (so named because he was always sucking up to the other two). Along with their blue collar upbringing came a tradition of unions and the power of workers united. This was going to be an interesting summer.

There were two CIT's (Counselors-In-Training) that caught my attention. Kelly Byron was a short sultry black-haired girl, with a touch of acne, who's every movement exuded sexuality through her skin tight over-worn jeans. Kelly loved to flirt with a hint in her eyes that she was available under the right circumstances and was aware of the power that unsaid promise had over boys. She proudly held her small perky breasts to be noticed and sat with legs invitingly open. Tara Weil, on the other hand, was a very tall, brown eyed brunette with a quiet sexuality. She almost tried not to be noticed but couldn't avoid standing out in a crowd. Tara had a subtle way of touching her tongue to the center of her lower lip when we talked and a dimple that smiled when she did.

Not quite sure how to meet either one of them, when Kelly auditioned for the camp production of *"My Fair Lady"* so did I. Unfortunately, as much as she loved the spotlight, she couldn't sing for shit. Life has a funny way of constantly changing the rules as you play the game. Winning or losing, like everything else, is relative. Cast as Henry Higgins, I found my failed means to an end become an end in itself. During rehearsals new faces appeared at the windows everyday as performing on that empty wooden stage turned out to be more of a rush than anything I had ever experienced on horseback. At times I'd finish a scene or the last lines of a song to dead silence, as if everyone in the room had been hypnotized...BY ME...it was magic... and deep in my subconscious awoke memories of being a god.

Often our own self-perception is based on the reflection in the eyes that surround us. Until we know ourselves without looking, it's almost impossible to tell when the mirrors are distorted. All we can do is go on what we see. Each time I sang, the reflections became brighter. Like a plant withered from years of darkness, I flourished in the light and could actually feel myself beginning to grow.

It was deja vu with a twist as fingers pointed and talked behind my back. In the dining room, all the little girls wanted me for their waiter and flirted with innocent eyes that hadn't played touchees yet (and some that had). Unlike the rest of the waiting staff, the unbearable workload didn't bother me at all.

Every morning, before camp assembly, we had to clean the kitchen and dining room and set up for breakfast, then line-up at the Totem Pole for assembly, at attention, in our waiter's whites. Next came breakfast service and clean up before we were allowed to eat... standing up in the kitchen, since the dining hall was needed for camp activities. This was all followed by our choice of a rest period or one morning activity before returning to the dining room to start the entire process over again for lunch. There were two activity periods between lunch and dinner, and at night a curfew with 'lights out' at 10:00 PM. Meanwhile each of our parents were paying the camp $350 for teaching us the meaning of slavery.

'Spike' either got his name from the way he spiked a basketball, the way he spiked a football, or the way he once spiked an umpire. On the other hand, maybe it had nothing to do with sports. Suffice it to say that when Spike spoke everyone listened. His suggestion of a waiters' union and list of grievances was met with a resounding "All for one and one for all!" This all would probably have meant one hell of a lot to me if I wasn't preoccupied with my plan to sneak out that night after curfew to meet Kelly by the lake.

Since the counselor-on-duty each night checked all the beds with a flashlight on irregular intervals, my sleeping bag had to be stuffed carefully before sneaking into the bathroom. After flushing, I pushed the bathroom door back open before dropping through my escape hatch, hopefully giving the impression to anyone still awake that I had done my business and headed back to bed. The night's condensation heightened the scent of pine needles. Fallen leaves and anticipation mixed with the mystery darkness and crackling twigs under my sneakers. With hands up to protect my eyes, searching for the path that the moon wasn't full enough to reveal, came the doubts... 'Was Kelly really going to sneak out to meet me or was this all for nothing? Even if she did, look at the trouble I was having, how would she find her way? What if she was there already waiting for me? What if she heads back before I get there? What if I don't make it at all?.. Where the fuck was I anyway!' A brief moment of panic set in along with the terrible need to take a piss. Standing motionless in the dark, punctuated by the pattering of a steaming leaf, was the welcome sight of a painted wooden finger pointing to the beach.

I sat by the lake until it became obvious that Kelly wasn't coming. There was a feeling of relief fingering the rubber in my front right pocket. After a year forming a ring in my leather wallet it probably wasn't any good anyway. The mental image of skinny dipping with Kelly and making love on the Senior Life-Saving raft in the center of the lake faded. Besides, how would I have brought my protection? With these thoughts and more, I stood up to leave and took a deep breath when an animal or something rustled in the bushes. Oh my God... it was Kelly! From within the trees she came talking toward me in her trademark jeans but the words didn't register, just the shock of actually seeing her lipstick lips moving in my direction. Holy shit, this was really gonna happen! It took a few extra heartbeats to notice when she stopped talking that I was still fingering the prophylactic in my pocket. In a reflex action, my hand jerked out, accidentally taking the condom with it. A bullfrog belched somewhere nearby (probably hit in the head by my Trojan). Neither of us knew what to say or do next so we held hands and walked out on the pier. Kelly's heavy makeup included a layer of acne cream that smelled like a combination of Calamine lotion and mothballs but my dick was so hard I would have kissed the damned frog at this point.

Touching was tentative until Kelly actually leaned back and pulled me up on top of her and I came in my pants. As it turns out, I don't get soft after climaxing and in fact, can cum eight to ten times over a period of hours with a hard-on. It was many years later that I discovered this was not normal. As we kissed more intensely, Kelly's tongue began probing and so did my hands. Every time they got near her tits though, she would block me with a shoulder and take my hand in hers and kiss me all the more passionately. After two or three such interceptions I decided to change the play, rolled to my right, and slid my hand into her jeans. For a split second my fingers touched down into her panties when she changed position and countered by wrapping her legs around me. All the bumping and grinding was fun for a while but it wasn't lovemaking. It was more like masturbating with a partner. And there was something else.... she wasn't really feeling anything. It was all fake, like her makeup. She was kissing passionately without passion, moving sexually without sex and acting a part without part of the act. A little girl playing dress-up, using me for the mirror. I began to get a stomach-ache. Out of frustration I went for a double play... one hand reaching for her tits while the other tried her pants. Kelly got up and went home. The mystery had definitely gone out of the night as I made my way back through the woods with an empty ache in the pit of my stomach, wet soggy sticky pants, and the aftertaste of lipstick and Calamine lotion mixed with mothballs in my mouth. This was not what I expected.

Early the next morning Spike, David and The Leach presented our list of grievances to Uncle Martin during his morning ritual washing of Aunt Bea's yellow Volkswagen. Uncle Martin spent no less than half of every day washing, polishing and admiring 'The Bug,' complete with its full color replicas of Camp Thunderbird's Totem Pole on the doors. Both the Totem Pole and The Bug were treated with the reverence of religious artifacts, as were Aunt Bea and Uncle Martin, which is why it was almost unthinkable that a slave should have even approached Uncle Martin during the morning baptism. After assembly that morning, the waiting staff was asked to stay for a moment.... and that was all it took for sweet loveable Uncle Martin to make it very clear that any of us who weren't happy at Camp Thunderbird could pack our bags and leave. So much for collective bargaining.

A secret meeting was called during afternoon activity period in the tractor shed behind the stables. This time Dave did most of the talking. Dave Miller was tall for his age but a little awkward with a short blonde flat-top that didn't quite fit his personality. Even though he was probably a virgin, the second or third word in every sentence was "fuckin'," often emphasized by pointing with the unlit cigarette that usually sat in his ear. His father, who was head of the local printer's union in Yonkers, raised his son on the values of Sinclair Lewis and Jimmy Hoffa. With Spike standing behind him and The Leach shaking his head as if he understood the deeper meaning of every word, the human tendency to form an 'in group' rallied around the slogan "All for one and one for all!" We had to do something dramatic to make it clear to Aunt Bea and Uncle Martin that a slave revolt was at hand.

That night amazingly, we were all able to sneak out of the cabin without being noticed. Dave and a few of the other guys headed for the lake while Spike led the rest of us, a few at a time, across the open field, past the Totem Pole, and into the underbrush next to Aunt Bea and Uncle Martin's cabin. There nestled safely under the car-port was The Bug.

There was quite a commotion the next morning before reveille as a police car pulled into camp and a somewhat hysterical Aunt Bea stood on her cabin porch pointing to the empty car-port below. Giggling with anticipation, we all ran to the scene. Uncle Martin was chewing on the end of his thumb for some strange reason while pacing back and forth behind Aunt Bea. 'If this is how they're reacting now... wait 'til they get to the lake!' I thought to myself. In no time the entire camp was standing around asking each other what was happening when the waterfront counselor came up the beach path in his converted golf cart and stopped to talk with the police. He didn't quite know how to tell Aunt Bea and Uncle Martin what he had seen. So all together, the whole camp, led by the waterfront counselor, the two police officers, Aunt Bea and Uncle Martin, everyone headed for the lake. This was the most exciting happening at Camp Thunderbird since the year a bear came by to scratch his back on the Totem Pole.

Those of us that knew what was waiting below jostled for position. As the curtain of trees opened half way down the path, Aunt Bea opened her mouth wider than her face and fainted dead away. At the same time, Uncle Martin practically bit off the end of his thumb and started ping-ponging back and forth, not sure whether to help Aunt Bea or run down to the lake where, out in the very center of the water, bobbing up and down on the Senior Life-Saving raft... was The Bug.

The two police officers found themselves in the awkward position of trying to stifle their own laughter while dealing with these two hysterical old people, one of whom was just coming out of a coma while the other was going into one. When Spike joked about finding out whether Volkswagen's could really float, Uncle Martin went berserk and began firing everybody, including the police. At Totem Pole that morning, with his thumb wrapped in gauze, kindly old Uncle Martin was spewing saliva. Spike was already packing his bags. "This is my camp and I can fire whoever I damned want. If anyone out there doesn't like it, you can pack up and get the..." (catching himself)... "go with him!" The poor little campers stood there in shock. Uncle Martin had never yelled at the staff in public before. In their own protest that morning, Dave and The Leach piled their breakfast trays full of dishes and 'accidentally' smashed into each other in the center of the dining room. When the noise ended, so was their employment. It now fell to the rest of us to decide whether "All for one and one for all" was just for the *Three Musketeers*.

After a tense day and an evening of the peer group pressure that causes soldiers to give their lives for each other, all of our bags were secretly packed, ready for a walk-out the next morning. It's not as if our grievances were so extreme. All we wanted was that the janitorial staff clean the kitchen; staggered shifts so each of us could have some time off occasionally; the right to be able to sit down and eat our meals either before or after the rest of the camp; and to have the counselors clean-up after their own kids. But that wasn't the point. This was all about power. It was also my first real confrontation with authority and my 'coming out party' as an adult.

The next morning as Spike, David and The Leach exited the cabin with their suitcases and headed for the Totem Pole, Uncle Martin and Aunt Bea waited in smug satisfaction. With the campers lined up in formation for the execution, we watched our comrades make their way across the field on their own before, one by one, each of us filed out of the cabin in their footsteps. By the time we were finished, a pile of suitcases reached more than half way up the Totem Pole and the king and queen were in check.

With the silent time clock ticking Uncle Martin hesitated on his next move when Aunt Bea decided to take the initiative and officially fired us all proclaiming that, until replacements could be hired, the counselors would take over our responsibilities. This did not sit well with the counselors however, who vocally announced their opposition to this plan. In a blind rage, Uncle Martin lost it again, and fired everybody. As the counselors left the playing field to pack their bags, the campers started running off in every direction. Aunt Bea and Uncle Martin stood there yelling. The pile of suitcases toppled over in front of them. With all this liberation taking place, I thought it would be a nice touch to free the horses. So I did. Now there were kids and counselors and horses running in every direction. Aunt Bea and Uncle Martin retreated to their cabin. In a flaming finale, Spike doused the Totem Pole with gasoline and set it on fire. The sirens and flashing lights of the police and fire cars coming up the driveway completed the cacophony.

After an hour of anarchy, the announcement horn blew, signaling assembly at the smoking stump that was formerly the Totem Pole. With the charred remains of the camp symbol smoldering behind them, Aunt Bea and Uncle Martin were leaning on each other and crying. I flashed on the eyes of Mrs. Small when her chair collapsed and the guilt that accompanied her fall. Now Aunt Bea and Uncle Martin were no longer the slave-masters. They were just two old people we had managed to hurt very deeply. The rest of the day was spent in negotiations and in the end the camp was ours.

Knowing Kelly was just a cock-teaser still didn't prevent me from getting hard, but the smell of Calamine lotion slapped me back to my senses. On the grass in front of our cabin, a girl's field hockey game was in progress. It was easy to spot Tara standing on the sidelines a foot taller than the others. A brief glimpse of recognition was interrupted when Kelly was suddenly back at my side, jabbering about nothing. And so it went for the rest of the day. At dinner that night though, while holding my hand, Kelly began opening her legs to Spike. We both knew what was happening when I excused myself for the bathroom. Kelly and Spike's laughter filled the dining hall when Tara came out of the front door, not at all surprised to see me standing there.

Tara was so easy to talk to, I almost forgot she was a girl. There was no agenda, just thoughts and ideas that generated new ones that we couldn't wait to tell each other. Each time we laughed or she did that little thing with her tongue and lower lip the air smiled until, for no reason we both stopped talking at the same time. The kiss just happened. It wasn't sex, it was… magic.

Aunt Bea and Uncle Martin had delegated control of the camp to the Head Counselor, Uncle Milt. Milt in turn, was sure that if he did anything to cross Spike, he would be nailed to what was left of the Totem Pole. By the third day, camp was starting an hour later and half of the waiting staff had the day off, including me. Tara skipped out on her normal duties and, with a box full of food from the kitchen; we snuck off camp grounds together into the woods. Everything we were doing was against the rules, which of course made it all the more exciting. Tara was so tall that if we walked with my arm around her, I'd be holding her ass. So we held hands.

Throughout rehearsal that night, all I wanted was to finish and be with Tara. But everything ran late, and it was 'lights out' by the time we left the stage. Security had lightened up and the full moon made it easy to sneak out through the woods to the CIT cabin on the girl's side of camp. Peering through the screens for a glimpse of Tara, the enormity of what I was attempting began to set in. This was a cabin full of semi-naked girls that I was about to enter through the bathroom window, years before Joe Cocker would sing the song. Tara said the bathroom window would be open. What she didn't tell me was that it was six fuckin' feet high.

A discarded tire noisily ground pebbles as it rolled. Then, even on tip-toes on top of the tire it wasn't enough. After a half-hour of scavenging a pile of junk half way up the wall, my sneaker caught on the edge of a broken folding chair before I leveraged into the square black bathroom and down on to the toilet seat below. Allowing my eyes to adjust, I stood motionless on the seat. The bathroom door creaked as it opened into the main room where my first impulse was to freeze against the wall. Directly in front of me a girl's bare leg stretched out from under the sheets. Could that hint of black between her legs be pubic hair? Straining for a closer look another restless sleeper snapped me back into a statue. Tara told me her bed was along the bathroom wall, out of sight from the front door, but I couldn't move for two reasons: First, I really wanted to see if the naked thigh in front of me had panties on; and second, I was scared shitless!

The first of these problems was solved when the leg found its way back under the covers. As for the second, I was now more horny than scared. Tara was sound asleep. Her long legs and sprouting breasts were mine to awaken with a Sleeping Beauty kiss...by me, a little boy standing in the dark, reeling in the contradiction of this self image and fantasy. Ever so carefully I removed the cotton blanket from her chin and folded it down to uncover a pink flannel night shirt with small pearl-white buttons. Tara nestled to her side and my penis pointed at her sheer pink panties with wisps of pubic hair protruding around the borders. One at a time my fingers freed the pearl buttons while the thought of sliding my hand into her panties fought with the effort to see the dark nipples just inside her blouse. Sleep sounds rustled randomly in the background as Tara changed position again. Simultaneously she stretched her legs wide open while the flannel top shifted to reveal her right breast. In the blink of an eye my zipper was down, pants and shirt on the floor and prick in the air. Her nipple stared at me while I watched her open crotch and leaned forward touching my erection to her sleeping hand as it rested on her stomach. Then, to my utter amazement, the hand gently turned over and wrapped around my ego. As her grip tightened, Tara's eyes opened with a smile to watch me spurt. (Perhaps it wasn't a coincidence that *"Sex And The Single Girl"* by Helen Gurley Brown was the #1 best seller at the time.) A pool of cum filled her belly-button. Tara's hand began rubbing it in a circular motion before moving down into her own panties. With her fingers running in small fast circles underneath the pink material, her other hand was squeezing my cock. Each time I reached to pull her panties down for a better view, she would stop and push my hand away. It didn't matter... nothing mattered.

Climbing back out of the window that night, I was so high I forgot how high I was until the folding chair half way down the pile of junk reminded my head it was there. The ensuing racket even scared me into the woods, virginity still intact but with the overwhelming sense that my libido had definitely been fucked.

The next day lasted a week anticipating the night to come and replaying images of the previous night. With Parent's Weekend four days away, *"I've Grown Accustomed To Her Face"* suddenly took on new meaning. The drama counselor even commented that my Henry Higgins was "showing maturity." No wonder actors fuck around so much. After lying awake in the cabin for what seemed like hours, and jumping over now familiar potholes and branches in the dark, it was a relief to find my junk pile still intact against the cabin wall. I couldn't put my finger on it, but there was a different energy in the room that night. No protruding body parts, no erratic sleep sounds. But I didn't give a shit. I just wanted to get naked with Tara.

On the third night, heading for my trap door, from the bottom of the last bunk before the bathroom, a hand grabbed my leg… it was The Leach. His girlfriend, Nancy, was in the same cabin as Tara. His weaselly little pointed nose and glasses square danced in the dark, gesturing that he would turn me in if I didn't take him with me. Reluctantly guiding him through the woods, there was some compensation in the whooshing sound of branches flashing backwards into his face. I also enjoyed the dull thud that followed moments after jumping over a familiar pothole. By the time we reached the girls' cabin, The Leach wasn't so sure this was such a good idea. Once inside, it turned out that Nancy felt the same way.

Within minutes of our arrival, my clothes were in a rumpled pile at the foot of Tara's bunk. Even with my cock against her naked thigh, it was difficult to ignore the pantomime wrestling match taking place across the aisle. The silent movie was accompanied by muffled giggles from the phony sleeping room. We could barely make out the pushing and shoving taking place as Nancy struggled desperately from beneath her covers to keep The Leach from getting his hands between her sheets. Trying to get back to the business at hand (so to speak), I put Tara's nipple in my mouth but her laughing made it hard to concentrate. God, how I hated The Leach! Nancy was now getting a little more violent in her opposition until suddenly there was a spotlight catching the two of them in a freeze frame. The head counselor's flashlight looked like a film projector from the front door. The Leach never stuffed his bed and they were on to us.

Using all of his self-control, in an effort not to wake the entire cabin, Uncle Milt stormed in as the flickering sheriff in a silent movie and grabbed The Leach with both hands. Tara pulled the covers over my head and scooped up my clothes from the floor. Milt's flashlight began searching the room to the thumping sound of Tara's heart in my ear. Ever so slowly I tried to slip down next to the wall. Then it happened… in suspense movies there is always a scene when the music stops to create tension until, when you least expect it, a sudden jolt and a scream knocks you out of your chair… my belt buckle fell off the bed and hit the floor. The scream came from Uncle Milt as he picked up a shoe and threw it at my head. In that instant the room was suddenly full of girls screaming, pillows streaming, lights gleaming and, Uncle Milt on the floor underneath it all, steaming. Meanwhile, with my clothes in one hand and my balls in the other, the last thing he saw of me that night was my bare ass jumping out the window.

To my amazement the next day, even though we were caught 'red-handed' (in every sense of the word), nothing happened. At first I thought it was our union, which was probably part of the reason. By now the camp had degenerated from well structured activity periods to general 'playtimes' where the campers took part in whatever activities the counselors felt like teaching that day. We didn't see much of Aunt Bea and Uncle Martin anymore and mealtimes had basically become a series of food fights. But it was David who explained the real reason that the police hadn't been summoned to place me in protective custody. Tomorrow was 'Parent's Weekend.' What would happen, he explained, if the parents of the CIT girls found out that waiters had been sleeping with their daughters? And besides, without me there would be no *"My Fair Lady."*

Sleeping was not easy that night, what with thinking about Tara, Uncle Milt's flashlight checking in every fifteen minutes, and something else I'd never experienced before…opening night jitters. It was almost like years ago when I'd lie in bed and think about death. Now it was thoughts of opening my mouth on stage and nothing coming out or forgetting my lines and standing there in a puddle of yellow water. By Saturday night I was a nervous wreck. Then the magic happened again…. once on stage, the spotlight literally blinds you and everything disappears. In that twilight of unreality, my electronically enhanced voice made me a god again. When the final wave of applause ended, I knew in what place my grain of sand was destined to land.

VIII. (1963-64)
(Age 16-17, The Folk Movement begins)

Back in the real world, Peter, Paul & Mary were *"Blowin' In The Wind"* at *"The First Family,"* as lovingly portrayed by Vaughn Meader. Meanwhile, it felt like our entire country was running parallel to my life experience and adolescent self-awareness. After the trial-by-combat of WWII, like 'The Great Fourth Grade Rumble' of King Philip Drive, we as a nation believed that 'The Eyes' of the world saw us as 'defenders of the right.' For more than fifteen years we believed our own hype, failing to realize that the rest of the world was growing up around us.

Everything was black & white, and we were 'white'....and that was part of the problem. On our new color television, as I entered high school, Walter Cronkite tried to explain why James Meredith was surrounded by gray German Shepherds snarling into the shaky camera images of trampled bodies under the feet of federal marshals when he tried to enter the University of Mississippi. This was serious shit and we were now old enough to understand that white was not the presence of all colors.

Tara and I wrote to each other for a few months, but she lived in Connecticut, ironically close to King Philip Drive, and that was a very long way away. Greenwich Village was much closer.'The Village,' where turtle necked beatniks once banged on bongos and spouted poetry, a new generation was now playing songs about magic dragons. Finding it difficult to understand the words through the mouthpiece of my trumpet, a guitar instruction picture book showed me where to put my fingers to sing along. Although it had taken a year to get a decent sound out of my trumpet, within hours and a few chords, I was 'playing' the guitar. There was no need to learn music, or theory, or notes and Allen Sherman's *"My Son, The Folk Singer"* went to number one.

Monday was "Hootenanny" night in The Village. Since none of us were old enough to drink, there were 'coffee houses' lining the streets of Bleecker and MacDougal that catered to the ant stream of teenage troubadours carrying guitars from hole to hole. At each stop you would first put your name on a list to sing, and then come back later to see how long a wait there was before your turn on the 'open mike.' The best talent was cherry picked by the club owners to perform later in the week for real...no money...just real. One such hole in the ground was The Gaslight, a narrow brick-walled basement in the middle of MacDougal Street. The owner, Sam Hood, was notorious for having thrown Bob Dylan out because "he couldn't sing for shit." Sam eventually became a bit less judgmental, especially after Dylan sold a million records.

On one particular night there, amidst the faint smell of marijuana and a heavy cloud of cigarettes, I watched a tall, young but already toothless colored man in a gray mohair sweater humbly wrap himself around a beat-up guitar. While complaining to the waitress about having to pay 50 cents for a glass of water, clinking restless undercurrents were overpowered by acoustic guitar waves bouncing off the red brick walls. On stage, the brown skin of the performer's elbow peaked through his frayed sweater as fingers flailed over the guitar mouth so inhumanly fast and hard that a second hole had been worn away in its face, now sweating with beads of perspiration dripping from the dark furrowed forehead above it. He didn't make chords with his fingers but rather laid his oversized thumb across the neck of the guitar and strangled it while incessantly attacking the strings with his free hand. And the room shook. The hypnotic rhythm began to rise and fall on the wooden stool beneath him and we all became one with the movement. Old gravel in a young voice then lisped into the microphone, ironically giving new life to *"Maggie's Farm"* (a Bob Dylan composition). On the last chord of the séance no one applauded... no one even moved... momentarily paralyzed until the inevitable exhale of applause. None of us had the balls to get up and sing when Richie Havens finished that performance. A comic named Carl Waxman took the microphone and began his routine about cockroaches doing the backstroke in his toilet. I skipped my turn and headed home to practice

The guitar is easy to play but hard to play well (there's that word 'hard' again). The left hand supports the neck, always aware of where fingers are placed. While holding the guitar up against your chest, the curve of its body rests on your thigh, your arms wrapped around it and right hand fingering in front of its hole. Sometimes gently plucking, but often using your entire hand, shaking it up and down, violently trying to get the most out of the instrument. It's not just putting your fingers in the right place (which isn't always easy), but continually finding that spot, and then doing it in rhythm... both hands simultaneously working on different tasks... but together. If you bend and squeeze the strings just right they'll cry for you and each place on the body makes a different sound when you tap it. Some players use plastic or metal extensions on their fingers... I liked to feel the strings.

White Plains High School was a sprawling, college type campus, covering literally acres of property with playing fields, tennis courts, and its own driver training course, complete with control tower. The glass buildings and corridors were in stark contrast to Eastview Jr. High's five stories of bricks and pavement. The dark echoic stairwells were replaced with bustling dress code students clicking shoes in the glass hallways rushing past their reflections to reach chrome and wooden classrooms on time. The shoes were primarily collegiate penny loafers with a minority of basketball sneakers and, every so often, a pair of pointed Tom McCann's or work boots. I was never especially comfortable in any one type of shoe but walked with renewed confidence (although still only 5 feet tall) and the knowledge that grown-ups were fallible.

Luckily we all had no idea how fallible, since we as a nation were still staring into the spotlight, unaware that Kennedy and Khrushchev were in the process of blowing up the theater. Thirty years later we discovered that the *"Missiles Of October"* were nuclear phalluses that almost climaxed prematurely.

Miss Parris was a tall fiftyish woman whose long pointed nose and chin both jutted precariously far from a white witch face and thin red lips. Her totally black wardrobe matched the tight beehive hairdo that tottered when she wobbled into class on black patent leather pumps. In contrast to this striking appearance, Miss Parris loved poetry with a passion. Tenth grade English was a daily deluge of rhyme and meter. And even as we laughed at her occasional blush under the white cake makeup, her love of words was contagious. It's kind of a pleasant thought to imagine that somewhere out there Miss Parris might be reading this right now (although she probably burned this book after the first page of 'colorful' language). Anyway, if anyone out there knows Miss Parris, tell her how much she meant to me. On second thought, I just realized how long ago that was... She's probably tutoring Marilyn Monroe today. Now there's an image... I can almost see them in stark black and white, sitting on a giant feather bed. Like *'The Tingler'* the only color in the picture is a large red book of poetry between them and perhaps their matching red lipstick, legs swinging in iambic pentameter... Tenth grade was also the year that Marilyn Monroe died.

Under the influence of Miss Parris' constant encouragement my first poem was published and awarded a notice of special merit by the National High School Poetry Association. Following John Glenn into space, astronaut Wally Shirra orbited the earth in the Mercury space capsule when I wrote:

Towers of Babble are these streaking rockets
  Set to puncture the curtain of space and time
And unmask the face of the 'Almighty Divine'

Man's outstretched hand and dissatisfied mind has groped for a deity, a holy sign
  To answer questions of both the alert and the blind
And forgive one's trespasses or justify his crimes

Martyrs to 'Him,' so many have died
  'In God's Name' is the song that the hypocrite cries
As he plunders and enslaves for the color of one's eyes

If the curtain is opened it's then we may see
  That God, SHE'S COLORED!
And doesn't look like me.

Meanwhile, The Village was night school on the weekends with teachers like Tom Paxton, Pete Seeger, Tom Rush, Phil Ochs, Eric Anderson, and Buffy Saint Marie. While Chubby Checker was doing *"The Twist"* all over the radio, I was sitting in the dark at The Bitter End listening to Dave Von Ronk sing about *"Cocaine"* (which was something hobos used during the depression). There was a youthful innocence about The Village then. We still cut our hair and believed in the government and associated hash with corned beef. But the *times were a changin'*.

Charlie Post was now the fastest athlete in High School and an Olympic hopeful, but we were farther apart than before we met. Every five minutes Martin Luther King, Roy Wilkins, Malcolm X, The Ku Klux Klan, and Governor George Wallace were telling us how different we were. If the years following WWII were our nation's elementary years of blissful invulnerability, the sixties marked the onset of our teens. Nothing seemed to fit anymore. After standing up every morning with my hand over my heart reciting "One nation, under God, indivisible, with liberty and justice for all" the TV mirror in my living room reflected something else. We weren't "one nation." We were still a North and a South (not to mention East and West). The Supreme Court struck down prayer in the schools, so there went "under God." When federal troops were sent in to Birmingham to fight the Governor and state militia, it seemed to indicate that perhaps we were "divisible." And to this day "liberty and justice for all" has proven to be the biggest lie of all.

At the same time, television itself was coming of age. Even though Edward R. Morrow's courageous commentary on the McCarthy hearings of the 50's had set the standard for TV journalism, the Korean War went by practically unnoticed by everyone except the soldiers who died there. This would never happen again. The new

Telstar satellite (immortalized by an annoying hit record) now let us see events while they were happening all over the world. As Johnny Carson took Jack Paar's place on *The Tonight Show* and the country was laughing at *I Love Lucy* and *The Beverly Hillbillies*, the most compelling drama on TV was the *Nightly News*. On it we watched a Buddhist monk in South Vietnam set himself on fire at our dinner table as the smoke rose from mom's roast beef. Then the flames enveloped a church in Georgia and a cross in Mississippi and fire hoses were turned on people in the streets of Alabama. The blood soaked bodies of dead civil rights workers looked sticky as dad poured maple syrup over his bread pudding.

Meanwhile I still wanted to get laid. Unfortunately girls were sent home from high school back then if their skirts were more than ¼" above their knees (which was where I wanted to be). On an early morning in the summer of 1963, three yellow school buses left White Plains. To my left sat Reverend Davidson (whose son John would later become the 'Pat Boone' of the 70's) and an elderly Negro grandmother with a little girl in her lap. Directly in front of me was a blonde with ironed hair and Janie 'Big Tits' Weissberger (the main reason I was along for the ride). Just walking down the school hall, Janie caused Pavlovian male reactions that involved involuntary hand gestures and animal noises.

Janie was active in the National Conference Of Christians And Jews (NCCJ) and when the Rev. Dr. Martin Luther King Jr. called for his first March On Washington, this presented a terrific opportunity. Knowing that good luck is 50% planning, there I sat at six o'clock in the morning on a bus full of every conceivable type of stranger planning for good luck with Janie Weissberger. It would probably be interesting to go back through history to figure out how many momentous events were directly as a result of the mating dance between male and female. Would Napoleon have conquered the world if not for Josephine? Would Rocky have beaten Apollo Creed if not for Adrian? Would I have gotten up with my guitar to sing *"We Shall Overcome"* if not for Janie 'Big Tits' Weissberger? In a study of the migratory habits of the red-winged blackbird, a group of scientists marked some of the birds with red labels to track them. What they didn't realize was that in so doing, they made those particular birds more attractive and the marked birds got laid twice as much. This comes to mind with the bouncing memory of my open guitar case on the seat next to me, lined in red felt

When Janie turned around it took an amazing amount of will power not to stare at her tits. Forcing myself to look into the eyes of the people around me so as not to give away my secret agenda, something unexpected happened. Each set of eyes became a face, and each face, a person and each person found their voice until the whole busload of eyes became a marble box of people singing in unison. Behind each voice was a human being just like me... and not like me at all. In the gentle eyes of the grandmother were memories, perhaps of sitting in the back of the bus, and wet with obvious love for the wide eyes of wonderment on her lap. The Reverend was singing with pride in the glory of God allowing this moment to happen as the blonde threw back her hair trying desperately to look like Mary Travers. This wasn't lost on the suited salesman two seats ahead, next to an unassuming housewife, who probably had two kids and a dog in her white picket home that employed the grass stained Negro gardener singing in my ear.

Like a smile, music has a way of transcending barriers. It allows us to experience universal emotions with people we've never met. Years later, on the desert coastline in Egypt, I sat by the Gulf of Aqaba one night and picked on my guitar. Then one by one, lights went on in campsites around me and soon there was an African drummer and a Swedish guitarist, and a flute player from Japan, and an accordion from France and none of us could speak to each other... but we could play in perfect harmony. And so it was on the bus that morning. Even though we were all from the same country, we really weren't. And even though we all spoke the same language, we really didn't. But we could sing *"We Shall Overcome"* in unison. At the outskirts of Washington, the arteries leading to the heart of the city were clogged with every manner of vehicle and lined with streams of people pouring through. Our buses pulled up on the grassy shoulders of the road and flipped open their yellow tongues for our little instant family to dribble into the flow. As luck would have it, Janie Weissberger ended up walking next to me, and the Reverend was the only other person trying not to stare at the loose fitting blouse designed unsuccessfully to hide those giant breasts. Meanwhile, it was deja vu joining the procession of marchers to the towering Washington Totem Pole on the hill. Nothing I had experienced up to now though, could have prepared me for the breathtaking sight of some two hundred thousand people standing together as Dylan and Baez and Martin Luther King proclaimed "We will not be satisfied until justice rolls down like water and righteousness like a mighty stream." And God listened as he spoke and the skies opened with a mighty stream of righteousness that brought forth Janie Weissberger's nipples... and it was good.

The day was a patch-quilt of images; Sitting on blankets, the smell of grass, strangers sharing food, superstars rallying the crowd, black & white hands clenched together, tears and hugs, the sheer power of numbers blending into an impressionist canvas. From a pragmatic view, it was a massive exercise in group-dynamics. Starting with the early morning bus ride of strangers connected by music and a common cause; to marching with thousands to the heart of the nation with the symbols of power as a backdrop; to the feeling of community as we huddled together under the emotion of Martin Luther King's 'Dream;' to the bus ride home, knowing that we had just taken part in an historic day in American history. On a personal level, as the bus pulled into the driveway at White Plains High, Janie Weissberger was asleep with her head in my lap, unaware that for the last half-hour my hand was holding her breast... *"Who could ask for anything more?"*

High school was structured to teach the 'three R's' but increasingly it was TV (now in capital letters) teaching the fourth ...'R'eality. The Nightly News expanded its coverage to 30 minutes to try and explain why Buddhist monks were burning themselves and students my age half way around the world were protesting against their own president. For some unexplained reason, we had US troops there in

Saigon backing the guy even though everybody, including the Secretary General of the UN, was denouncing him. Meanwhile a 'sit-in' taking place in Boston over something called 'de-facto segregation' didn't seem that important when compared to the bomb that went off on a quiet Sunday morning in Alabama, killing four little Negro girls. At the same time the Senate was trying to pass a nuclear test-ban treaty so we could stop building fallout shelters and ducking for cover under our school desks and, as if all this weren't enough, a hit man named Joe Valachi was actually testifying that gangster movies were real.

Considering all this shit going on, even with an ulterior motive for attending the NCCJ meetings, I couldn't help but begin to understand that there was more to life than sex and music. On the other hand, Janie Weissberger had great tits. Then one night in the rectory of the First Lutheran Church after a meeting, everyone had gone and we were talking about prejudice and being judged on appearances when something in Janie's eye's implied that she was trying as hard as I was to ignore her breasts. In that moment of revelation she almost cried out with relief and then she did... and we did. With her sobbing in my arms, the sexuality was overpowered by her simple need just to be held, like mom would hold me when I was sick. Everywhere she went people stared, making verbal and silent comments. Boys (like me) saw walking tits; and girls... a freak or a threat or a shame... but no one saw Janie. It was prejudice and it hurt... more than she could say.

Then, as quickly as it had disappeared, the sex came rushing back with her wet cheeks turned up, her mouth open for a kiss of such passion and need it even scared me. Jesus looked down on us from the wall as one of her breasts came flopping out from under the bra my hand struggled to undo. When it wouldn't come apart I pulled on the under wire until the whole contraption flipped up under her chin and both monstrous mammaries were *"free at last...free at last... thank God Almighty!"* Everything pent up inside her came flooding out. With her legs wide open a wet spot formed on the white panties now visible from beneath her plaid woolen skirt. She was holding me so tight I couldn't move but could feel myself cumming over and over again, staring at the large pink nipples glistening with her tears and my saliva and our sweat. Every inch of her was quivering and grasping and it was all I could do to keep from suffocating between her tits... (Ah, but what a way to go). While managing to extricate my head far enough to encompass her nipple in my mouth, my free hand slid down between her thighs, wet with her excitement. It was instantly inside her panties and inside of her. This wasn't like making out with Tara, Janie had completely lost it and I was trying desperately to find it. Sprawled out on the floor in sight of The Father, The Son and The Holy Spirit, I did.

Janie stopped coming to meetings and wouldn't see me again after that night. For over a month she refused my phone calls or even to acknowledge me in school. Then one fall Friday in the hallway we stopped in front of each other... but before we could speak an alarm went off... not an allegorical one... a real alarm...followed by an announcement on the public address system. Big Brother told us to return to our classrooms immediately.

There was something surreal in the words "The President Is Dead." Assassination happened to Lincoln in history books, but Kennedy lived in Camelot. He was the vibrant symbol of what we all could be someday. Even as we watched the news footage in class and saw the motorcade pull away with Jackie kneeling on the car hood, we believed that JFK would somehow pull through. Over and over, we saw the same blurry images, waiting for word from the hospital, that *Ben Casey* had stepped in to save the day. But when Walter Cronkite glanced back at the clock before turning to tell us that it was over, he had to remove his glasses and wipe his eyes. Up until that very moment the news never cried, and the hero never died on TV. The bullets that shattered the president's brain that afternoon also blew out the magnificent spotlight that surrounded him and house lights came on that evening in denial and uncertainty.

Our family was abnormally normal. A throwback to *"Ozzie & Harriet"* of the 50's, with mom up every morning cooking breakfast and each night we circled around the dinner table, dad at the center, directing or inducing conversation. But that evening we all sat in silence, staring at the TV, to the scratching sound of forks and knifes. It just didn't make sense. We lived in America for Christ's sake!

The unreality of it all continued through a Thanksgiving weekend that wasn't. A droopy faced vice-president raised his right hand as we held each other's. Then, just as the enormity of what had happened began to set in, a baby-faced assassin was gunned down in our living room. The magic box made its final transition and stared back at us in disbelief. This wasn't just life imitating art… it was the end of innocence. I don't think we realized how deeply the razor had cut until the bleeding began (more bleeding than we could ever have imagined). Deep emotional ligaments had been severed and America would never use its muscles the same way again.

Our elementary years of self-perceived invulnerability were suddenly over, symbolically marked within months by a second British invasion. With the spotlight no longer in our eyes we looked for someplace to run and returned to our English womb and the naive energy of the working class 'Fab Four.' Practically overnight the Beach Boys and Chubby Checker were replaced on our radio by The Beatles. Up until now, music was rock 'n' roll and rock 'n' roll was American. The Beatles had taken our music and turned it back on us with a new twist. The basic rock beat was there but the harmonies were strange and discordant… much like our emotions at that particular time in history. And it clicked, like a revolver, and another shot was heard 'round the world.

Once the stage door opened, The Beatles were followed in by the likes of The Dave Clark Five, Dusty Springfield, The Rolling Stones, Peter & Gordon, The Hollies, The Animals, and the list went on. In stark contrast to this pop phenomenon, Greenwich Village had also lost its virginity. Lenny Bruce was jailed for obscenity and there were no more folkies digging up our musical roots and replanting them. Now pot planting poets replaced the old folkies. If nothing else though, the folk movement had changed the American public's perception of popular music. The non-traditional singing styles of songwriters performing their own compositions broke down the established distinction between creator and performer and allowed our collective ears to accept a wider definition of 'singing.' A lyrical change was *"Blowin' In The Wind"* as wide pupiled poets were our teachers and we accepted the new sounds coming out of England as part of that evolution.

Like everything else, radio then began to factionalize. Some 'loyal Americans' still wanted to hear The Beach Boys, Jan & Dean, Elvis Presley and Bobby Vinton. While the civil rights movement also had its effect and Little Stevie Wonder reaching out with *"Fingertips"* while The Supremes pointed the way for Marvin Gaye, The Temptations, The Four Tops, and Martha & The Vandellas, who told us there was in fact *"no where to run and no where to hide."*

It's astonishing to look back now and see how much was going on around us at the same time. Bloated with bureaucracy and self-indulgence, our country's wasteline was now showing and our cloak of confidence didn't cover it anymore. The left hand of the government was tearing at the civil rights seams while the right got its fingers stuck in Southeast Asia. Examining everything through the TV lens, we could actually see the fabric disintegrating but were powerless to stop it.

Nothing made sense anymore. Why couldn't we wear blue jeans to school and let our hair grow like The Beatles... Fuck the rules! Who made them anyway? Everyone lied to us. Everything we were told from the time we were little kids was bullshit. This wasn't a free country unless you were white. We didn't have a government "by the people and for the people." We had a big eared, sour faced, Southern bureaucrat that nobody elected acting as President. School wasn't teaching us anything about life. School wasn't teaching us anything at all. And besides, the way that adults were running things, we weren't gonna be around that much longer anyway. It was time for the campers to take over the camp again.

With practiced stage presence and knowing how to play the game (which meant keeping my mouth shut until everyone asked for my opinion), I was elected president of the NCCJ youth chapter. Our first battle was against the school dress code which, we argued, discriminated against poor families that couldn't afford 'proper attire' and was also unconstitutional, restraining our right to free expression. It started with a petition. Ironically, the only kids that wouldn't sign it were the 'student leaders,' afraid it would hurt their chances of getting into a good college. With over a thousand signatures, including such notables as Alfred E. Newman, F.U. Seekay and Kent A. Lingus, the petition was presented at a meeting of the school board. Vice-Principal Anderson politely agreed to take our suggestions "under advisement." Some two weeks later, with my hair now growing out over my ears like the new 'bad boys' of rock, The Rolling Stones, I was sent home from school in an illegal pair of used blue jeans. Mom and dad were not happy. They also wanted me to get into a good college (if they only knew).

The Board of Education building in White Plains was the remains of a colonial estate, complete with giant pillars and guarded by 'Little Black Sambo' statues (in white face to be politically correct). As the heavy wooden doors opened, a thin red carpet led the way across shiny hardwood floors to a flowered desk that all seemed to be set up to make me feel uncomfortable in my jeans. This was a plank I would never have walked if not for the manicured hand of Harriet Stern on my shoulder, the Executive Director of the New York chapter of NCCJ. Her quick witted blue eyes were accented by over-colored red hair, a sharp lined business suite, and a short tailored skirt, specifically designed to show off well shaped nylon legs. When finally summoned into the Superintendent's office, Harriet, who completely understood *"The Feminine Mystique,"* made a point of crossing her legs in front of the master of the house. He didn't give a shit what I was wearing… there went the dress code.

On another battle front, my 5'2", 125 pound frame made me too small for anyone to hit cleanly on the White Plains High School Ice Hockey Team. But there was tremendous exhilaration in smashing the legs out from under giant defense men. My stick handling and shooting was for shit, but the coach loved to use me as a kamikaze. The coach was a story himself. Actually, he wasn't really a coach. Mr. Whitehead was a science teacher who couldn't skate but was asked to 'sit in' when the real coach retired. He understood the physics of skating, it was the practical application he had a problem with. He did so much unexpected 'sitting in' that we changed his name to 'Whitebottom.' At times he'd start yelling about something and fly by like a runaway bumper car, usually on his ass, barking commands over his shoulder as he careened off in the opposite direction. Then there was the time he came running out on the ice, completely forgetting that he had skates on, and somersaulted into the Zamboni machine.

Old Whitebottom was no dummy though. He knew, for example, how much I hated the cold. During games he'd keep me on the bench freezing my ass off, until I'd kill anybody just to get in. Actually, that's how I made the varsity. We were playing Montclair, New Jersey, and just looked flat. After a period of no scoring, Whitebottom threatened to replace the captain with 'someone from the junior varsity' if they couldn't make something happen. Two minutes into the second period you could hear laughter when the coach actually called out my number and popped me into the pinball machine. To the stands it apparently looked like the team mascot was jumping over the boards to replace the captain. Oblivious to everything but the fact that my fingers were freezing, my internal guidance system targeted the biggest, ugliest face it could find. He didn't know what the fuck hit him! Amazingly, as Dumbo flew off his feet, my stick accidentally hit the puck and scored. The next day *The Reporter Dispatch* called me 'Mighty Mouse.'

Ice hockey is a fast moving game with all the players on the ice constantly in motion along with the puck. Even substitutions are made 'on the fly.' When you first start to play, it seems like you are making split second pressure decisions every time the puck comes near you. Gradually though, as you learn to feel the game and understand where the other players are moving, based upon your position and place in time, everything begins to slow down. You make decisions before you receive the puck so that by the time that little hard piece of rubber hits your stick you know what your options are. You don't necessarily have to do something right away. Sometimes the longer you maneuver, the more options open. On the other hand, when an opportunity presents itself, you'd better take your shot. It's amazing how much life is a hockey game.

Getting knocked to the ice isn't necessarily a negative either, unless you break something and can't get up again. One night we were playing New Rochelle at the Playland Ice Rink when our key defense man was thrown out for punching the ref in the face. His backup then got knocked out on the ice when a third heavyweight had gone into the back room for stitches. Defense men are usually the biggest guys since it's their job to bodyguard the goalie. Whitebottom needed someone just to go in long enough for one of our defense guys to regain consciousness... here comes Mighty Mouse! Even I thought this was pretty amusing until three seconds later when the puck came skipping along the boards and their right wing was barreling down in my direction. What were my options? Turning toward the puck meant Mighty Mouse would be Peking Duck. On the other hand, trying to block the right wing, now traveling at the speed of sound, would result in Moo Goo Gai Pan. So I improvised and fell on my ass. But as the wing sliced by, my white bottom was suddenly up smashing him into the boards. The crowd went crazy! "Here I come to save the day" and Mighty Mouse posed, unfortunately failing to notice the left wing sailing around the net behind him... the audience then saw Mighty Mouse fly... at least that's what I was told when I woke up.

There were a number of life lessons in this little episode: Down does not mean out. Never underestimate an opponent. A negative can become a positive. Think before you act. Vanity comes before a fall. And of course, never turn your back on a flying wing.

Meanwhile, following our success with the Board of Education, Harriet Stern arranged for me to attend a "Leadership Training Conference" for high school students at nearby Briarcliff College.

To be honest, the only reason I attended was the ego massage, and of course, to meet girls. After an initial presentation we broke into groups and were instructed to list our preconceptions about each other. When they were read aloud it led to some 'lively discussions.' A heavy set Italian girl from Brooklyn, for example, cured me of associating her accent and weight with stupidity. The initial sting of her lightning crack wit was a revelation.

The emphasis was on accepting our differences and realizing that we are in fact not all created equal. We learned about group dynamics and how simple things like the arrangement of chairs in a room made a difference in our interaction. There was an amazing demonstration; starting a story at one end of the room, each whispering it to the next until, by the time it was repeated at the other end, it was a different story. (No wonder the bible is so 'colorful.') Then there were games like standing blindfolded in the center of a circle and allowing yourself to fall, trusting the group to catch you; or identifying each other's faces with just fingertips. The humanity was contagious.

That summer the civil rights movement was picking up momentum. It was June 1964, when our neighbor's son, Andrew Goodman, disappeared with two other civil rights workers someplace in Mississippi. Suddenly mom and dad decided to send me off on a own freedom march of their own... far away from New York, Greenwich Village, color television and the NCCJ.

IX. (Summer,1964)
(Age 17, Finding my voice)

Shoved somewhere up in the mountains of Pennsylvania, Camp Mayfield was run with military precision. There would be no unions here. I couldn't fuckin' believe it! This was sixth grade all over again. Just as I was becoming a leader... it was off to Siberia. And just like sixth grade, I managed to offend everyone around me. It might have been the combination of refusing to change clothes, cut my hair or wash, coupled with such anti-social behavior as knife throwing in the cabin and pissing out the window. But as hard as I tried, they wouldn't send me home. It looked like I was destined to be a camp waiter the rest of my life.

The other anti-social character in camp was Jed Longfeather, the riding instructor. Jed was a well-marinated combination of American Indian and Irish Catholic. With greased black hair, cured in the scent of Camels and Jack Daniels, Jed was a throwback. He loved Elvis Presley, his handmade 1950 Ford and girls (not necessarily in that order) and was a perfect antidote for my radical TV withdrawal. We hit it off the day I passed the 'Thunderbolt Test.'

Thunderbolt was a big old chestnut-brown mare with a white lightning streak running across her face and another devilish streak running just below. As soon as she sensed inexperience, she'd balk. You could hit her, kick her, smack her upside the head... nothing worked... she'd just stand there. Then, when least expected... a ten-yard bolt and a polite drop of her head to allow the rider an easy exit. If you managed to stay on and then beat the crap out of her, she'd never do it again. Otherwise, she'd remember. Many a rider was able to stay seated, but only a few would teach her who was boss. That day, I was in no mood to take any bullshit, especially from a horse. When Jed saw me neck reining her backwards and bending Thunderbolt to my will, he knew we could ride together. A few bars of *"You're The Devil In Disguise"* on my guitar, and the bond was complete.

There were immortal summer nights galloping through the darkness with a hand up in front of my face as protection from the dirt and pebbles flying off the hooves of Jed's horse on the path in front of me. His usually half-crocked silhouette tottered precariously back and forth in the saddle while yelling at the stars, arms waving to his ancestors. It's amazing how drunks somehow don't get hurt when they fall...even off a horse. It scared the shit out of me, but Jed would just laugh out loud and roll over in the leaves. Sometimes a campfire of flaming marshmallows and hot dogs on sticks reflected the red man in his skin when he spoke of dreams and how important they were to his grandfather. Then he'd take another swig of Jack Daniels and pass out as a thin line of tobacco smoke wisped up from the cigarette still lodged between his fingers and joined the ancient smoke from the fire that crackled into the clouds. Jed was a trip.

The camp itself was full of suburban white kids and a few coloreds trying 'to pass.' Everyone had short hair and listened to The Beach Boys or Gerry & The Pacemakers. The Beatles were considered radical. The only news we got was about camp Color War... nothing about the real one. Giggling virgins hung out at the stables to watch Jed sweat with the horses or work on his car. I began to learn little techniques like how to undo a bra with one hand.

Teenage girls are more curious than sexual, with little pink nipples that are sensitive but not completely orgasm circuited. This coupled with the fear of losing control and a heavy dose of guilt training made it practically impossible to get laid. It's an ironic joke of nature (instinct, God, Giggy, whatever...) that keeps us from fucking all the time by making a man's sexual prime age 17, when girls don't want it, and girls' at about 37, when men first start to learn the meaning of prostate.

Jed felt it was both his Irish and Indian responsibility to 'get me some pussy.' Time warped as we pulled into Johnny's Truck Stop just off the Jersey Turnpike in Jed's dark blue 1950 Ford. The submarine shaped metal diner's screen door slammed us in to a world of green plastic plates, mismatched metal forks and truck drivers. The patrons either looked like ex-marines, cowboys or

Elvis, all eating together in a fake neon painting. Donna came dancing out from behind the counter with a yellow pencil sticking out of her teased up hair and smacked Jed with a kiss. She would be off work in about 15 minutes and we were all going to meet her younger sister Jessie, who took care of the kids while Donna and her parents worked.

Driving up the dirt road to a small wooden farmhouse, it was a scene from *'Lil Abner'* when Jessie pushed open the screen door. With a little one in her arms, another pulled at the cotton dress that almost didn't cover her amazing figure. Jed and I just sat there with our mouths open. "Trying to catch flies?" Donna quipped with an edge as she slapped Jed and straddled him at the steering wheel, setting off an alarm for the chickens in the yard. The front door opened directly into a gray linoleum kitchen. To the right was a room filled with comfortable torn Salvation Army furniture facing a 19" black & white Zenith, flashing on a floor full of crayons, dolls, dominoes and Tinker Toys. A fluffy blonde cat curled up on the sofa ignoring the three dogs running back and forth to the TV greeting..."Th..th.. the..th.. That's All Folks." In the center of it all stood fourteen year old Jessie, like the Statue of Liberty in a wind storm.

Jessie was taller than me, with long thin reddish blonde hair and a lightly freckled complexion. Her permissive control of the household reflected both her innocence and experience. As the four of us fell into relaxed conversation, she managed unobtrusively to keep tabs on the kids and animals. Meanwhile, the very things that set me apart at camp, including my filthy jeans and gamy scent, made me right at home on the farm. To compete with her beautiful younger sister it was easy to understand Donna's overly outgoing personality and possessive concentration on Jed's inner thigh. This combination soon led them to the back room and an awkward moment when Jessie and I suddenly had nothing to say. It was time for my guitar.

Rusty, the fluffy cat I later discovered was named after Jessie's jealous boyfriend, finally changed position as my fingers began teasing the guitar strings. Jessie turned down the sound on the TV, and with *"Heckle And Jeckle"* romping silently on the screen behind them, she and the two children politely sat on the floor to listen. Then came that wonderful moment of surprise as they glanced at each other in amazement when I began to sing. Suddenly this was more than just a nice boy sitting in their living room. And then, the ultimate compliment... Jessie actually reached back and turned off the TV (probably for the first time since they got it). With a hint of self consciousness her hazel eyes no longer made direct contact with mine and her body language became almost nervous. God how I loved to sing!

In *"North By Northwest,"* Hitchcock's got a great scene with Cary Grant on a long empty country road before he's attacked by a sinister bi-plane. There was exhilaration in the freedom and adulthood of a similar road that led to Jessie's house on my next day off. Lush green corn fields waved at the golden wheat across the road and dive-bombing barn swallows crop dusted just barely over the stalks of corn and then swooping back into a clear country sky. Jessie waved from the window as the two little ones bounced out to greet me along with the dogs and chickens, all accompanied by a cow somewhere groaning at my arrival.

Jessie would someday marry her boyfriend, Rusty, but when I sang something happened. After twenty five choruses of *"Puff The Magic Dragon"* and a round of *"Row Row Row Your Boat,"* the kids were tucked in for their afternoon nap and she hesitantly sat next to me on the sofa. *"Love Of Life"* silently unfolded on TV as she told me about Rusty. I sang *"Love Me Tender"* before leaning over to kiss her. At first she wasn't sure. Taking advantage of her infatuation.... Giggy made me do it. Gradually her mouth opened as did her legs and she turned toward me on the sofa. Jessie was not at all self-conscious about her body or sexuality and once she made the decision to let go, she did.

This was all new for me. Tara's passion had been controlled curiosity and Janie's a cathartic cry but Jessie was just freedom. She stood up, pulled her dress over her head, right there in the open living room, a naked child woman, innocently laughing, pulling off my pants. There was no foreplay, just play play. As soon as my underpants came down so did Jessie. No girl had ever done that to me before. I saw my penis between her lips and watched her breasts squeezing against my thighs and immediately came in her mouth. She laughed and threw back her head as she sat up further and I could see the mound of reddish pubic hair glistening up and down on me while squeezing her breasts with both hands, her nipples tightening as she moved faster. Afraid to cum inside, I tried to pull back but Jessie just jumped harder, throwing her hair back and forth, sweat sweeping across us. My entire cock was now visible each time she rose. There it was in plain view, sliding into her ... it was gonna cum again... it was cumming.. no...no....I reached down and squeezed tightly. Milk splattered everywhere. Jesse kept moving as if I were still inside her, desperately rubbing her open legs against my thigh. "Put it back...Put it back" she whimpered, pulling away my hand. And then the warmth... In a gentle motion, placing her nipple in my mouth, her palm cradling my head, it felt like all of me was inside her again, and again, and again

That night I was staying for dinner to meet her parents who had been hearing about my singing for the past week. Her mom got home first. A cashier at the local Woolworths, Mrs. Cerrington was short, thin and dark like Donna, but very quiet and old for her age. Together, we all watched the six o'clock news while waiting for Jessie's father. It was an unexpected reality check. In the short month I had been away, LBJ signed the Civil Rights Act; Senator Barry Goldwater was nominated to run against him under the slogan "Extremism in defense of liberty is no vice;" Which also seemed to justify the Negro riots taking place in New York; South Vietnam was becoming another Korea; and for me the most shocking revelation that the three civil rights workers who disappeared, had in fact been tortured to death in Mississippi. Somehow, I didn't feel like singing. As it turned out, I didn't have to.

A pickup truck pulled up in the front yard but it wasn't Mr. Cerrington and Rusty was not there to hear me sing, unless perhaps as a soprano. Rusty had a pretty strong voice of his own, accompanied by the heavy metal crash of a tire iron bouncing off the front wall and the sound of chains being dragged from the bed of his truck. Suddenly I was living a ballad called *"Come A Little Bit Closer"* when Bad Man José returned to the cantina and our hero jumped through an open window into the darkness. Breathlessly squatting in the center of the cornfield, the searchlight moon peaked in through the rustling stalks. This wasn't camp, this was real. Afraid to pee for fear of giving away my location my underpants felt like a wet diaper.

The original plan was for Mr. Cerrington to drive me back to camp after dinner. Now what? After twenty minutes worth of hours it was time to stand up just enough to see if the grim reaper was in the vicinity. Even though Rusty's truck was no longer visible in the Cerrington yard, my imagination could see it silently waiting somewhere down the road. At least it seemed safe enough to take off my underpants. Carefully draping my wet jeans and Fruit Of The Looms over a sturdy cornstalk, my balls were shrink-wrapped by the night air. A gentle wave of my Levis in the moonlight, with senses keenly awake, brought out the scent of foliage and urine and sex and horses and topsoil, and the realization that I really wasn't a little boy anymore. There was no reason to go back to camp. If I could hitchhike to Johnny's Truck Stop, I could hitchhike home.

Stepping down out off a diesel cab in North White Plains the next afternoon, I could have sworn Charlie Post either didn't recognize or ignored me as he drove by my thumb in a gold Cadillac with chrome covered headlights and shiny wire wheels. Then again, mom didn't recognize me either, coming up the driveway, especially since Camp Mayfield probably hadn't noticed I was missing yet. My unexpected metamorphosis from a butterfly to an earthworm was a bit much for the family to assimilate. The next year proved to be a practical lesson in tolerance, understanding and compromise, on many levels.

X. (1965)
(Age 18, Graduating high school)

Greenwich Village had lost its smile. There were no more magic dragons to slay now that the killing was real... and so was the dragon, even though we didn't know it yet. Our collective paranoia about communist Russia and the possibility of nuclear holocaust flickered on in *"Dr. Strangelove," "Fail Safe"* and of course, *"From Russia With Love."* But as James Bond lived, Ian Fleming died. It was both the 50's and the 60's at the same time. Most of America still had short hair, parted to the right, and believed in the government. Broadway seemed oblivious to the race riots in New Jersey while looking for meaning *in "Fiddler On The Roof."* Carol Channing sang *"Hello Dolly"* across the street from *"Funny Girl"* Barbra Streisand. Meanwhile, The Beatles now held the top five records on the *Billboard* charts as *"A Hard Day's Night"* frolicked on to sold-out movie screens across the country... and the band played on.

Senior year in high school meant focusing on the most important next step of my life. Getting into a good college would mean the difference between begging in the streets (there was no McDonalds to work at yet) or possibly becoming President of The United States. Much of this, in turn, rested on the outcome of the SAT's. After a year of review books and practice exams and studying the percentages of filling in little boxes with a number two pencil, it all came down to a grueling day of guessing and praying, followed by another few months worth of the same, waiting for the results. Meanwhile, I enrolled in every extra-curricular activity possible. Along with ice hockey and the NCCJ, there was the choir, the drama club, the tennis team, even forming the school's first advertising club and electing myself president. To be honest, the pressure wasn't nearly as bad for me as it could have been. Getting into a 'good school' was more an ego thing since I was gonna be a star. But mom and dad wanted me to get a 'good education' and they were paying. Besides, it kept me out of the army.

Everyone signed my high school yearbook, but no one really knew me. There were only a few of us with hair out over our ears, which for me was a sign of empathy with the colored kids who were just beginning to assert their independence. Cassius Clay changed his name to Muhammad Ali in what looked like another of his publicity stunts and for the first time we heard colored people referring to themselves as 'black.' The Black Muslims were a group of radical separatists with a fiery Malcolm X preaching contradictions like black was good and white was bad. There was no gray in his philosophy... just red in his eyes. The intensity of his stare and match stick tongue set off brush fires that licked at the heels of the non-violent movement of Martin Luther King. What scared us most was the truth that laced his rhetoric, pointing out our 'white devil' propensity for genocide.

Cassius Clay was the Jackie Robinson of the 60's. A phenomenal charismatic athlete who's bravado replaced Robinson's humility in capturing the imagination of the nation. We all laughed at his braggadocios poems and tuned in to watch Sonny Liston make him eat them, then sat astounded when he actually did "float like a butterfly and sting like a bee." Clay came to symbolize the new Negro in America, no longer seeking acceptance, but demanding recognition. He really believed he was beautiful and 'The Greatest' and wasn't afraid to get up and yell it. When he became 'black,' so did a generation that identified with him.

That generation, however, did not include Charlie Post. Charlie never made it to the Tokyo Olympics. He was too busy spending the money and 'gifts' being thrown at him by college and pro scouts. He didn't need school anymore either, except to show off his new car, and bright clothes, and diamond rings and gold filling smile. When Charlie made the local papers for the last time he looked like Sammy Davis, Jr.... with a drug dealer's bullet in his head. No one even noticed the small scar on his right hand.

We all breathed a sigh of relief and smiled at the memory of Khrushchev's threatening shoe, when he got the boot from some new guy in Russia. Meanwhile our parents got sucked in to Lyndon Johnson's landslide over the madman Goldwater who wanted to blow up the world (at least that's what Johnson's TV commercials said). Television was no longer just showing the news, now it was shaping it. There was also something basically wrong with a system that offered only these two alternatives for President of The United States. Things were definitely getting fucked up.

But not me... I couldn't get fucked up because I was too young to drink. To be honest, that's a cop out. It was fear, fear of losing control. There was nothing moral in my refusing to drink or do drugs. It was an obsession with control and its power. Actually that's a contradiction too, since obsession means the loss of both power and control. But having learned how to play the game, I was afraid to put down my cards, even for an instant, for fear of losing my place.

The power to control the actions and reactions of others is first based on observation. Every animal exhibits body language, but the human animal displays an infinite number of physical cues to intellect, mood, personality, etc. A simple thing like hand movement or the lack of it; whether it's fluid or choppy; how deftly the fingers move; the roughness of complexion or fingernails; gestures that indicate peer group influence or ethnicity; the strength and speed; whether the gestures accompany speech or punctuate it. Each of these little cues tells you about a person, even from a distance, and that's just sleight of hand.

A good actor is, by definition, a master of observation. Changing the meaning of a line with a simple inflection or raising an eyebrow. But real power comes in acting on your observations to shape the behavior of others. Sitting across from a girl on a train, her eyes, expressions and body language will indicate her complexity and degree of self confidence. Her clothes and mannerisms tell me about her background, hygiene and attention to detail. If she's shy or unsure (two different things) but knows she has good legs, she'll avoid my eyes when she crosses them. But she will cross them.

Staring at her legs though, will tell her that I'm just another shallow asshole. Barely noticing or 'seeing' all of her, avoiding the obvious, will touch her curiosity. These were life lessons that required attention and sobriety. Besides, I hated the taste of alcohol. Why try to acquire it.... to end up looking like the people who did?

Getting laid, on the other hand, seemed to enhance my lesson book. Here there were two basic problems: First, there was no place to do it. Oh, the afternoons lost exploring dead ends and dirt roads for a private place to park with a potential paramour. A deflated air mattress laid waiting in the back of the family station wagon, its hard rubber nipple ready to be used with the Trojans hidden under the maps in the glove compartment. The second problem... who the fuck would I take? This was before 'the pill' and free love, when all the girls in high school were virgins (except of course Janie Weissberger, and she'd never do it again). It all came down to Lillian Renaud. Everyone in school knew that Lil 'did it,' but how to get her to do it with me? We never even met. She wasn't in any of my classes, her homeroom was at the other end of the school, but she did play flute in the high school orchestra... and I was soloist for the choir.

It was a rainy Thursday when Lillian opened the garage door that led into their partially renovated basement. A week of anticipation lost its edge in the humidity of her loneliness. Wood paneling warped away from the cement walls. A photo of her mother had faded with Lillian's memory of her. On a plaid covered foam rubber couch, words stumbled, a pale plaid in contrast to the lush dark memory of Janie Weissberger's dress. This was not what I expected. Lil was a small quiet willow with dirty-blonde hair and false smiling eyelashes. She told me we were alone and that her father wouldn't be home for hours. It wasn't clear what that really meant. Why couldn't we just go upstairs?

It was weird... here she was, right in front of me, with the hairs of her blonde cunt rubbing inside jeans that would come down if I could just ignore my conscience. Moments strained between gaps in conversation until there was nothing else to do but touch. Lillian responded to a need that had nothing to do with me.... Giggy was not happy. He wanted to come out and play... but this wasn't play.. and it wasn't fun. Groping at each other's guilt, making believe it was all something else. Sex made my dick hard even as my stomach turned in the opposite direction. There was no music when Lillian arched her back to pull off her pants, just the awkward sound of clothes wrestling, accompanied by the wood-frame couch straining on the concrete floor. Her thighs were anemically white, except for bruises from some previous encounter. There was no warmth or excitement. It wasn't even masturbation, which implies fantasy or feeling or emotion. It was the empty pail at Chapman Beach and Lillian was the blue crab, clutching at my muscle. When it finally shot, the wetness went cold. The temporary insanity that wins murder cases passed and every inch of me wanted to deny my part in the crime. This was prostitution and it felt like shit. But Lillian refused to let go, clinging to a lifeboat in some fog of her own. A small black spider in the corner spit out a lifeline in intricate patterns while its legs danced on a tightrope of its own making. How the fuck was I gonna get outta here?

The light from outside that had been peaking through the cinderblock windows retreated into dusk but Lillian held on and then shuddered as a door slammed upstairs. Her father was home. Holy shit! I tried to get up and reach for my pants but she wouldn't let go. Jesus Christ, she was gonna get me killed! Heavy feet thumped across the ceiling as a truck driver voice began yelling out her name. I could feel her wince in the darkness and suddenly knew where she had been and why. A crack of yellow light shot down the stairs as Lillian called back that she had fallen asleep and would be right up. "Make it quick," her father grunted, and the heavy feet pounded off. This was her sanctuary, and he would never come down, but she would have to go up and serve him. There was nothing sexy about shivering naked in the darkness, dressing in silence, avoiding each other's shame, before the garage door led me back into the rain.

The thumping sound continued outside as Lyndon Johnson ordered air strikes against targets in North Vietnam while he proclaimed "we seek no wider war." Only a few of us didn't believe him, huddled in the sanctuary of educational institutions, as thousands were quietly being called up to serve him. Meanwhile streets in Selma, Alabama, were overflowing with Negro protestors herded into jail with white cattle prods and clubs. Blood red letters announced the assassination of Malcolm X. (Thank God he was killed by a black, we said to ourselves). The pressure cooker lid of 'national security' covered an American sponsored coup in the Dominican Republic to surgically prevent the birth of another Cuba. White noise news commentaries were so deafening we didn't even hear the brown velvet voice of Nat King Cole whisper goodbye or see Stan Laurel silently scratch his head for the last time. Within a month, Dr. King was marching again, 25,000 strong, from Selma to Montgomery. Ironically, we now had just about that same number of 'military advisors' in South Vietnam. The 'truth' had become a matter of semantics... and Edward R. Murrow died.

The hills were alive with *"The Sound of Music"* at the Academy Awards while we dropped Napalm on Vietnam and 10,000 Students For A Democratic Society (SDS) protested on the White House lawn. President Johnson happened to be in Texas at the time. Actually, ever since the death of Kennedy the entire country was in a state of denial. *"Bonanza"* was still the most popular show on television, followed closely behind by *"Gomer Pyle, U.S.M.C."* It was the British invaders who made us deal with our feelings, searching for answers in *"Yesterday,"* reminding us that *"To Everything There Is A Season,"* demanding *"Satisfaction,"* along with a cry for *"Help!"* All in counterpoint to the innocent relief of *"Mrs. Brown's Lovely Daughter,"* married *"Over And Over and Over Again"* to *"I'm Henry VIII."*

It's hard to imagine now, but very few guys, black or white, had long hair back then. It was not yet a fashion statement, only a political one, and not very popular at that. For me it was more personal. Constant demands to cut it just strengthened my resolve to let it grow. But again, everything has a cost. Along the waterfront in Rye, were ruins of what was once a public pool and amusement arcade. There, under the watchful eye of a laughing clown, with half its face blown away by a demolition ball, the moon complemented the other half and made a place for me to stand. On a boardwalk that once led parasolled ladies and men with handlebar moustaches to the beach, seahorse arches still framed the ocean view. There's something about the eternity of the sea that helps me put things in perspective... an independent universe of creatures fighting and dying just out there under the surface. The energy of the tides and the wind and the smell of the salt water coupled with realizing that body of water was here long before mine and will be, long after I am gone.

At the end of the pier a window flickered in blue and red neon. The Sea Shanty Bar spawned images of Humphrey Bogart and Charlie Chan. A last vestige of the midway I never intended to visit. Then one night, the station wagon wouldn't start and there was no place else to go. Barely eighteen, it was one of the first bars I ever stepped into (and boy did I step into it). The greasy haired bartender took one look at me and politely suggested, "Get the fuck outta here and get a haircut you little piss-ass commie freak!" Explaining that I just wanted to use the phone resulted in a gracious chorus of obscenities from the assemblage. At the bar a Budweiser tee shirt waved proudly above a protruding stomach, color coordinated with the yellow teeth of a skinny weasel crunching peanut shells on the next stool. 'Deep down inside these were really not bad people,' I told myself, 'with a little understanding they would end up treating me like their own son'... and they did.... they beat the crap outta me. Big Stomach used the old face punching trick. I hadn't seen that for years, and didn't see it this time either. The Weasel emphasized his position with a bar stool. Amidst songs of "love it or leave it" helping hands tossed me back into the night pavement.

A wounded animal lying in a stream of consciousness, dripping from my nose and mouth, the taste of salt coated tar pebbles tore my shirt and tongue. Disjointed thoughts came in waves of sporadic breathing, nausea and pain. Doubled over in the fetal position touching my own mortality for the first time since lying in bed at night as a child. A spinning red light danced in from stage left, then reflected off black leather boots and the words 'To Protect And Serve' ... Thank God.... A firm reassuring hand reached down from the merry-go-round and helped me stand. He asked if I needed an attorney. A doctor maybe, but a lawyer? All I wanted was to get home, without the added aggravation of bringing charges against anyone. A nightmare laugh snapped metal handcuffs behind my back. The charges were against me! For "causing a public disturbance and provocation to violence" as reported by the upstanding taxpaying citizens of the Sea Shanty Bar.

The red brick police station looked closed from the back seat of the patrol car. A seat that had probably held rapists and murderers and was now bringing me to justice, for offensive hair. Somewhere out there Arlo Guthrie was eating a late night snack at Alice's' Restaurant when they held me down in an avocado room and shaved my head to 'clean my wounds.' But the wounds would never be clean again.

I don't remember much about high school graduation except dancing with Allison Pines at the senior prom with a hat to cover my embarrassment. We were Sonny & Cher with my nose placed firmly in her navel as the Supremes sang *"Stop! In The Name Of Love."* That night LBJ committed our first combat troops in Vietnam. The next morning, still haunted with the Nazi image of uniforms shaving my head, I would write:

I've come to realize that we've been socialized
   by a hypocritical civilization
As TV massacred the American Indian
   admiring the cowboy who destroyed a nation

My first toy was a gun, learning young
   it takes courage to beat up your neighbor
If he strikes you then hit him back or hit him first
   but God forbid... don't run

It's bravery to die for what you believe
   or to kill the non-believer
You're right if you win and wrong if you lose
   for victors decide the rules after the game is over

Indians forced on reservations were sent infested blankets
   This history books choose to hide
But Jews burned in concentration camps
   was the heinous crime of genocide

And medals are given to those that kill
   and degradation to those that cry
You're a coward or a commie not to kill for your country
   and a hero if you die

But somehow someone has slipped up somewhere
   for suddenly students are asking why

XI. (1965-66)
(Age 19, Starting college)

Freshman camp at Indian University was two weeks of indoctrination into the life affirming joy of becoming a 'Hoosier.' Those of us from other pagan states who had chosen the path of enlightenment through the limestone portals of Indiana, gathered for two weeks in the woods of Brown County to literally learn to sing the praises of 'Old IU.' In the camp song cabins, with upper class counselors, camaraderie was encouraged to make the transition to our new lives as college freshman. For me Indiana offered the advantages of a world famous music school in a large University set in the heartland of the United States... and the girls were fuckin' beautiful. That included Diana Mendenhill, the counselor in charge of the camp talent show who was obviously out of my class (or so they thought...)

On show night, the social distance that separated campers and counselors held for the first three bars of *"Hang On Sloopy,"* then it was everybody's ball game. Midway through my strip routine on *"Twist & Shout,"* the paternal glue holding together the pussy and the cat in Diana's eyes disappeared... and both wanted me... God, I love performing! The audience becomes an emotional wave, driven by music's gravity. Superimpose my image bathed in multi-colored light, and the power was addictive.

A good performer can control that power on stage, but very few can carry it off (no matter how you interpret this). That's charisma. And performance is not necessarily art. Art is the more inclusive... the creation of something lasting designed to elicit an emotional response as opposed to the act of presentation. In this case music is the art. The creator is the artist. The presenter is the performer. For me the presenter is not a true artist unless he brings something unique to the art, thereby contributing to the creation. To be artistic is to display the ability to create art, even if what you are doing is not art at all. Now that you are completely confused, suffice it to say that artistic performers get laid a lot. By the time I reached my dorm room for the first time, there were invitations from every fraternity on campus (and a few sororities). It was my face-punching reputation with a new twist, and once again I was on my way to becoming a god.

IU's home town of Bloomington once survived on limestone mining, so the nickname 'cutters' attached to the locals who referred to us in other earthy terms. The campus architecture ranged from gothic gargoyles and ivy to limestone monoliths and glass. It was the first year they dared to experiment with coed dorms. In Indiana that meant one building for women attached to another for men, sharing a dining hall. My dorm was appropriately named McNutt (probably after the idiot who dreamed up this public relations gimmick). My McNutt roommate was Bailey Links from Fayetteville, North Carolina. Bailey warned me, every night unopened books sat on my bed.... He warned me every morning I dragged in to wake him at his desk.... He warned me at the urinals as he went off to class before I went back to sleep.... He warned me in the hallway in front of the bulletin board where our grades would be posted at the end of the semester....He warned me that this was not high school.

An elaborate bus system required a monthly pass for unlimited use. Bailey was pleased on the afternoon he found me at my desk... until he discovered I was copying his bus pass, trying to match the pastel pink with a set of Woolworth watercolors. He warned me.... It pissed him off the next morning to see me flash past the bus driver. I'm not sure what it was about Bailey that inspired me to annoy him. Maybe it was his constant scratching, or that he referred to colored people as 'coons,' or the way he picked his nose and ate it.

Confident in my future stardom, I chose not to major in music or anything that would require math, science, or classes before 10:00 o'clock in the morning. By process of elimination, that left English, even though I still couldn't read for shit. But after a lifetime of school bells, the freedom to choose was exhilarating. This was definitely not high school.

A twinge of fear with every flash of the phony bus pass reinforced my new invulnerability. Another test was the mystery girl on the 9:30 bus, always in the same rear seat, shrouded in long black hair, usually hiding her amazing green eyes and perfect turned-up nose. A week of my most creative attempts at conversation only once brought the slightest reflection of a smile. Half concealed in that same bus window was a book cover with an address, in reverse, carefully written in block letters: "Charlotte Hamilton...Briscoe Dorm, North Bldg."

The small town Indiana accent on the phone that night didn't seem to fit the image I had created. Each time Charlotte hung-up on me, Bailey dug deeper into his books (and nose). When she finally agreed to talk on the bargain that I not call back again, Links stormed out of the room... And he warned me... The simple distrustful voice on the phone was surprisingly needy. An hour later Bailey puffed back into the room and Charlotte agreed to talk to me again some other time.

Meanwhile, invitations kept arriving from every fraternity on campus. The early 60's in Midwest Indiana felt more like the late 50's everywhere else and the frat system still reigned supreme. High school students throughout the state were shipped in and sized up a year ahead of time, each hoping to become one of the chosen few to pledge their lives to The Greeks (Not to be confused with the geeks, who were often rejected for having the wrong letters in their names). Now they wore colored beanies and flittered around like eunuchs, while the fraternity jacket 'brothers' extolled the virtues of their particular house with white smiling hands. Then there was Beta Alpha Kappa. When the brothers at the BAK House sat down for dinner and began throwing mashed potatoes at each other, I decided that next semester this would be my home.

Back at McNutt, other than Bailey, half my floor was made up of the freshman football squad. These were the biggest fuckin' human beings on earth! Like neckless 'Mas' Masowski, who got a kick out of passing... me... in the air... down the hall... in a tight spiral. It was like King Philip Elementary School again when everyone kept growing but me. Now King Kong hands wrapped around my chest and suddenly I could fly. Then came the smell of Speed Stick as the receiver tucked me into his armpit for the run-back. Even gods must learn humility... especially from bigger gods (another lesson from the Greeks).

The anti-war/civil rights movement had not yet reached Indiana as my hair began to grow out again. No one paid any attention to the additional 50,000 troops shipped to Vietnam that summer or the race riots in Watts. Not in Indiana, where the Imperial Wizard of the Ku Klux Klan sat a few miles away in Martinsville. It's a common misconception that The Klan is rooted only in the Deep South when, in fact, it flourishes in 'border states' like Indiana. At first my long hair was written off as a musician's fashion statement.

When Charlotte Hamilton turned and stared full faced with those amazing green eyes offset by the ink-black hair that spilled down the length of her back, she was astoundingly beautiful. But her sadness took weeks of trust building late night phone calls to penetrate. Apparently, her fiancé was killed in a motorcycle accident three days before their wedding. So college was her escape. This was my first brush with real life tragedy and an ego challenge. For me, dancing was just another means of becoming the center of attention. The urban jumps and splits mastered in New York were revolutionary to white Midwest Indiana. Charlotte, on the other hand, loved to dance just to get lost in the music, oblivious to the audience that would inevitably encircle us in hand-clapping rhythm. Like a sock turned inside out, her gray exterior personality would transpose to a bright flourish of movement and color. Dance is another art form, and what might have seemed like intricate practiced routines were actually spontaneous reactions, like the magic of musicians playing off each other. When the music stopped, Charlotte was always surprised at what we had just done.

Each such exhibition would also attract other girls and, like high school, I still needed a place to get laid. The 'coed' dorms were not exactly conducive (with nose picking Bailey and football farting

Masowski). The answer came with an invitation from 'Fireman Bill' to his private off-campus apartment one night when I had one too many girls and he just had one too many. Bill Krane was the 'Singing Fireman' host of a children's TV show on Channel 4 in Indianapolis, where he commuted daily. His slicked back hair, tendency to drink, and saccharine personality defeated his celebrity in attracting the opposite sex. In other words, Fireman Bill couldn't get laid in a whorehouse... which is exactly what his apartment looked like. The black walled entrance flickered with candlelight on a curtain of plastic colored beads that clicked into a red carpet den. A leopard mattress on black bricks, covered with soft sheep skins, doubled as a couch with large overstuffed fake fur pillows. Red light bulbs hid behind burlap blanketed windows so as never allow anything real (like sunlight) to disturb the mood. Bracketed on the rear wall, next to the green beanbag chair, was a black wooden ladder. Its red carpet rungs led up through a hole in the ceiling to a wooden loft bedroom, complete with built-in Zenith 'Circle of Sound' speakers. No matter what time of day you entered the apartment it became night. And no female could resist the impulse to lie back on the leopard couch and open her legs. For the next four years, this would be my second home off-campus.

White Plains High School had prepared me well for college, having already covered most of the Freshman courses. Also, my practice of outlining everything in blue-lined notebooks for test taking meant simply picturing a section of my chicken scratch and regurgitating it. The mental Polaroid's would fade shortly after exams, but who wanted to remember any of that shit anyway?

A week after finals, on an otherwise normal *"Monday, Monday,"* Bailey went berserk. Out of a twilight nap his face raged, fists dragging me to the floor. Thank God Masowski was walking by in time to catch him in mid air. Grades had been posted, and although Bailey had passed, my perfect 4.0 was the proverbial 'last straw' for his overworked psyche. Flinching to avoid distorted hands, I made eye contact with bloodshot hate for the first time. A frightening flailing glimpse into the future... he did warn me....

A week later, I moved into the BAK House as a second semester (half class) pledge. The fraternity system, like the armed services, was based on forced humility and bonds built by adversity. In musicians' terms, "You've got to suffer to sing the blues." My fellow half-class sufferers included a friend from McNutt named Phil Roth, who decided to pledge with me; Nelson 'Handman' Phernot, a sleight of hand expert and card player from New Orleans; Hugh Lesser, later referred to as 'Useless' because that's what he was; Calvin 'Megaphone' Mercer, a Cincinnati native who talked through his nose; and Matthew Roseman, later referred to as 'The Rose.' And a colorful ensemble we were.

The BAK house was a large, modern looking split level home on the outskirts of Fraternity Row. The basement level, which was accessible from a parking area in the backyard, housed the main dining room, kitchen and storage rooms, and 'The Cage,' living quarters reserved for brothers who exhibited animalistic tendencies. On the main floor, the front door opened into a large foyer, next to a TV room that was 'off limits' to pledges, and leading to a substantial living room, complete with comfortable chairs, couches and a working fireplace. It was also 'off limits,' except when entertaining guests. The remainder of the house provided sleeping accommodations, bathroom and shower facilities. Each semi-private room on the main floor contained bunk beds shared by the brothers, while on the top floor, the pledges slept in a large dormitory lined with triple bunks. That floor also housed the trophy room which was also 'off limits.'

The Cage was ruled by 'The World,' a seven foot blond athlete who refused both a football and basketball scholarship to accept one for tennis, because he hated team sports. The World, was so named because you never knew where in the world he was, even when he was standing right there in front of you. The first time I knocked on his black painted door (done so in honor of the Rolling Stones' latest hit record), the room inside was pitch dark, windows covered by blankets, and the bunk bed ripped open and laid end to end. It smelled like death. Whoever he was, he didn't like to wash. "Fee fi fo fum, who the fuck is letting in the sun!" This guy was doing Alice Cooper ten years before his time. A scruffy blonde face dropped down from the ceiling. "Why are you interrupting my beauty sleep?" it crackled. When I replied that sleep wasn't gonna help, he broke out laughing and switched on the light. The room was littered with tennis paraphernalia, half-eaten pizza, dirty sweat socks and condoms blown into balloons. Here was a guy I could relate to.

When I got around to asking The World to be my Fraternity Father, he was touched. Actually this guy was more than a little 'touched.' We would do terrific father & son things together. Like when I told him I played high school ice hockey and he tore the telephone out of the wall, broke off the plastic receivers to use as pucks, and we practiced slap shots with brooms in the hallway. Unfortunately, it was the end of The World sometime after my second 'line up,' when he lost his temper at a tennis match, threw his racquet over the fence, and accidentally picked off one of the opposing cheerleaders.

'Line-ups' were hazing sessions when pledges were forced to take part in various degrading activities and given 'demerits' if they performed badly. Five demerits would result in a 'blackball,' which meant expulsion from the house and consequently from the fraternity system, since no other house wanted a 'blackballed' reject. Our first line-up was the 'Duck Walk,' squatting in single file around the dining room, with each pledge spitting into a cup, to the dulcet strains of *"Mellow Yellow"* (and the throbbing strains in our calves and knees and thighs). This was to continue until one of us was willing to drink from the 'Cup of Brotherhood' (the one we'd been spitting in). When it became painfully clear that none of us felt that 'brotherly,' the final solution was musical chairs. The loser would drink. By now the cramps in our legs made it difficult to move, let alone get up and run for a chair, and the Donovan song was as sickening as the sight of the mucous (which had been covertly replaced with raw egg whites). 'The Deacon,' so named for his religious affinity to torture, took great pleasure in slowly sliming the contents from the original paper cup to an official BAK House beer mug as the band played on. In the split second of silence that followed, Megaphone pulled a muscle and doubled over. With the choice of forcing him to drink anyway or starting again, we opted for another round, but pleaded for a song change. They changed it... by increasing the volume. Even the speakers couldn't take it anymore and began breaking up. Now it was *"Mellow Yellow"* on Steroids. When the noise stopped, The Rose was left standing. We all had to give him credit. He did get the heavy glass lip to his own... before vomiting into the sacred mug.

The next line-up was 'Ice Baseball.' After a week of studying the addresses and majors of the brothers, Ice Baseball was sort of a 'pop quiz.' Four blocks of ice were set up on the floor of the dinning room in the form of a baseball diamond, with a brother on the pitcher's mound in the center. Each pledge would take a turn 'at bat,' which meant sitting butt-naked on home plate. If you named the correct home town and major of the pitcher, you could move to first base and the next batter came up as the pitcher changed. Once around the bases you could put your pants back on. Three strikes and you had to stay and bat again with a new pitcher. You couldn't go to first until you got a correct 'hit' and, of course, got your frozen ass (and balls) free from the block of ice you were sitting on. Occasionally a pail of water was necessary. This game combined two of my least favorite things.... freezing cold and ice water.

The most memorable line-up though, was 'The Brick Toss.' The winter had not quite defrosted when we were marched up to the roof and ordered to stand along the edge. There in front of each of us was a limestone brick with a considerable length of string attached, which we were told to tie firmly to our manhood. Now this was no easy task considering the temperature. Not only were our fingers numb, but I never claimed to be especially well endowed, and the cold gave me very little to work with. When we all failed the first 'test pull,' the brothers were laughing so hard we thought for sure the lights would go on in the Alpha Pi sorority house across the street to catch us and our frozen red Popsicles. Luckily, only the stars continued to peak as we paired off to tie up each other, with a warning that failure this time would mean demerits to the knotsman.

Kneeling up close and personal to another guy's privates made me more than a little uncomfortable. Nowhere near as uncomfortable, however, as when Useless tied my dick so tight it was almost re-circumcised. And the worst was yet to come....

The Deacon gathered up the twine and proceeded to cut all BUT ONE string. Hand in hand, we watched helplessly, told that if anyone let go it would mean immediate demerits, as The Deacon proceeded to drop one of the bricks over the edge. A ball of twine unraveled into the darkness for an agonizing instant before the brick thumped to the grass below. 'Holy shit! Which of us was still tied to a brick and what if the string was too short?' The brothers began taking bets on who's schlong was gonna get stretched as The Deacon tossed another brick. Suddenly it wasn't cold anymore and sweat beaded on my forehead. With Megaphone on one side and Useless on the other we held white-knuckled as the next two bricks thumped to the ground. Now there were only two bricks left and there was a 50/50 chance that one of them was connected to one of us... The blood was pumping in both my heads, with the big one thinking "What the fuck am I doing here?" answered with, "If the other guys can take it, so can I," followed instantly by every mothers' words, "If your friends jump off a bridge does that mean you have to do it too?" We all stood on the bridge and listened with a simultaneous gasp as the second to last brick hit the ground. Then, unbelievably, The Deacon lost his mind, grabbed the final brick and threw it.... not just tossing it, the fucker actually threw it!... demerits or no we all dropped hands and grabbed the line in front of our cocks, holding on for dear life, waiting for the gigantic lunge we knew one of us was about to experience... and the final string kept going... and the brick kept flying... and we held fast, teeth clenched... and nothing happened. The uncut string was unattached. The brothers all yelled "Borass!" in unison, which was BAK slang for "Gotcha!" And lights went on in the Alpha Pi house across the street.

Now it's only fair to point out that turn around was fair play in the BAK house, and for every line-up, the brothers could expect retaliation from the pledge class. A few nights after our Duck Walk, for example, we built a brick wall on the front porch. The next morning the brothers were confronted with a barricade of cement and cinder blocks when they opened the doors to leave for class. It took weeks to even the score for Ice Baseball. Working in teams, Phil and I, Megaphone and Useless, Handman and The Rose, quietly snuck into every room, beginning precisely at 4:00 AM the night before Spring Break, to remove one shoe from every pair and to deposit them in the living room. The next morning when the brothers awoke, no one had a matching pair of shoes or sneakers to leave with. In the living room stood a sculpted pile with no less than 300 foot coverings of every make and size, along with a note suggesting they "Walk a mile in our shoes." Apparently the brothers failed to appreciate the irony or art, but used colorful language as they dug through the pile in an effort to find at least one matching shoe in time to catch a flight home... we took all of The Deacon's shoes... but misplaced them.

Payback for The Brick Toss would have to be something special. The answer came in a 'bull session' when Megaphone won a bet with The Rose that cows could walk up stairs but not down. First, we'd need a truck large enough to hold a cow, and second, an occasion that left the house deserted... like an inter-fraternity football game, when the pledge class was often left behind to clean up. Finding a cow to 'borrow' would be no problem, this was not New York City. As it turned out, the first difficulty came in convincing a relatively small cow, in broad daylight, to climb into our U-haul. As cars flew by on the Interstate, with a rope around her head, Phil and I pulled while Megaphone, Handman and Useless brought up the rear. It's amazing that no one stopped. But then again, this was Indiana, where all kinds of strange things were done with farm animals.

A little behind schedule, we pulled the U-haul up to the back door of the frat house and easily coaxed our hostage out. However, when her hooves hit the waxed linoleum hallway she looked like coach Whitebottom on ice skates. Slipping and sliding half way down The Cage corridor, Bessie flopped over on her side and slid ten feet in wide-eyed bewilderment. This was gonna be more difficult than we planned. Useless began petting her like dog and whispering in her ear. He was probably falling in love. Here was a female that couldn't run away from him and she wasn't even drunk, just slightly incapacitated. Amazingly, whatever he said worked; beaming with pride as his bovine beauty regained her balance and stood there staring at us. We next discovered that, although cows can in fact walk up stairs, they don't like it! The entire process turned out to be a little messier and more time consuming than we expected. By the time we reached the trophy room on the second floor, it would only be a matter of minutes before the brothers returned. The Rose had prepared a banquet of corn and molasses, spiked with a heavy dose of Ex-lax for our guest. Useless waved an affectionate goodbye as we darted down the soiled stairwell and across the street to the Alhpa Pi house to call the farmer and tell him where to retrieve his cow. You can probably imagine the rest... suffice it to say that cows absolutely can't walk down stairs and Ex-lax works on both of their stomachs just like it does on one of ours.

Pledging could have been a lot rougher on us, but as it turned out, Phil Roth's full name was actually Phillip Rothschild the Fourth, of the famous (and wealthy) New England family. That coupled with my celebrity made us a pledge class the BAK House couldn't afford to lose. Even though it was completely against the rules for a pledge to also live off-campus, my semi-residence at Fireman Bill's seduction pad was overlooked, along with my rebellious long hair. In fact, legends of my sexual escapades (often much more colorful than anything I could possibly have attempted) only contributed to my value as a BAK House pledge. Just being seen with Charlotte Hamilton for example, was a coup. She wouldn't even talk to anyone else. In fact, she barely talked to me unless it was after an hour of conversational foreplay. Sex was completely out of the question. But nobody would have guessed, especially when we danced.

Diana Mendenhill (from Freshman Camp), on the other hand, really didn't want her sorority sisters to know how much she loved to fuck.

You could tell what year a girl was in by her level of promiscuity. Freshmen were virgins, saving themselves for 'Mr. Right.' Sophomores got curious and began to experiment. Juniors actually started to like it. And Seniors were fucking their brains out. Diana was an advanced Junior. Everything about her was feline. She even purred when stroked. Diana loved to cuddle and stretch and lick and be touched. Her excitement would gradually build, rubbing against my legs until she desperately pawed me inside to climax after which she needed a quiet period before attempting the climb again. But she loved climbing.

This was the time of 'The Pill,' when the worst outcome of continuous unprotected sex for a man was curable with a shot of penicillin. I hate shots (another reason for not doing drugs) which kept me in denial for days of itching after a night with twin sisters from town. Self examination on the toilet in the cold tile fraternity bathroom revealed hundreds of microscopic parasites eating into my scrotum. I knew this was VD and if not treated immediately, my dick was gonna fall off and I'd go crazy like Al Capone. Searching in vain for a male nurse at the I.U. Health Center, there was eventually no alternative but to tell the girl behind the desk the purpose of my visit. I could sense the disgust under her matter-of-fact manner as she handed me a questionnaire asking the names and addresses of my sex partners for the last month. She was even more annoyed when I needed another sheet. The image of a long needle with yellow fluid being plunged into my balls preceded me into the antiseptic examining room. With my luck it would be a lady doctor. Could all of that sex have been worth this pain and humiliation.... silly question. I couldn't understand why the doctor laughed when I showed him my corroding cock and then tore up the questionnaire. As it turns out crabs don't kill you.

With each successive sex partner came enlightenment...and it kept cumming... the revelation that every girl is sexually unique. Some are more physical or athletic, others more sensual and fluid. This means seduction requires anything from animal roughness to soft gentle touch... or a combination and/or variation anywhere along this continuum, depending upon time and place and mood and how fuckin' horny she is. Men basically have two erogenous zones, and both of them are their heads. Women's are unlimited and varied. A girl's breasts, for example, can range from completely non-responsive to immediate orgasm. And that can change....or not. The nape of the neck or her ear is usually a good place to try, but sometimes all you get is wax in your mouth. Oral sex can stimulate or scare...depending upon what you do and how you do it. It's also important to understand that a man's cock by any other name is still his cock. But a cunt is both a clitoris and a vagina, each with its own identity and its own orgasm. Now we get to the 'Big O'....When a man cums, he shoots his wad and that's it. A woman, on the other hand (or in the other hand or with the other hand) can have a thousand different types of orgasms. Anything from a quiet little wetness to a screaming uncontrollable internal combustion. What's more, she can often do one on top of another.... Now that's entertainment!

The fact that I stay hard for hours, without getting soft between climaxes, is probably a function of my ego. But the power to make girls completely lose it is intoxicating. After constant stimulation, some would actually get scared when their bodies took off without them. Reactions ranged from crying, to fleeing, to holding on for dear life. I love to find those little places that even she doesn't know exist. Or teasing her with my cock, gently moving the tip in and out just enough to barely open her lips... back and forth until every inch of her is begging me to plunge in. Even if her breasts aren't especially sensitive, there's something about flicking her nipple with my tongue while doing the same thing inside that awakens instincts and smells and senses. Lovemaking is a dance and only really works when both dancers are in rhythm (and listening to the same music). Leadership can alternate, but each new move requires initiative. Here's where the Yin and Yang come in to play. It's been my experience that women are turned on by power, but 'power' relative to their own self image. If based on intelligence, a man's brilliance does it. If she works out and lives a physically demanding lifestyle, she wants muscles. The stronger she feels her partner is, in relation to her, the more it turns her on. And if she ever loses that respect... there goes the sex.

Although bellbottoms and mini-skirts were 'in,' unkempt anti-materialistic appearance was more a statement of disrespect for political 'correctness.' That lack of respect in government also resulted in its loss of power and control. In the spring of 1966, 350 long-haired students seized the administration offices at the nearby University of Chicago, protesting the college's co-operation with the draft while a crowd of more than 8,000 'intellectuals' voiced their opposition to an "un-winnable war" in Washington. One of those 'intellectuals' was Harrison 'Hairy' Greene, a grad student in political science at I.U. At first there was only a small group of us 'long hairs' that would gather at Hairy's apartment to discuss changing the world, along with my right to be part of the racist fraternity system that symbolized the old order. I argued that a group of guys living together was just a commune with a formal selection process but agreed that if based on race or religion it needed correction.

One of the more heated evenings at Hairy's home came the night before Secretary of State Dean Rusk was to speak on campus. The Students For a Democratic Society obtained stolen federal documents that proved casualties in Vietnam were no less than ten times what the government claimed, but the university refused any member of the anti-war movement the right to question Rusk following his address. Should we then even allow him to speak? Does a government official disseminating lies enjoy the constitutional right of free speech when no dissension is permitted? What level of dissension would be appropriate? By morning we were completely split. Although personally against it, I understood as my compatriots were dragged kicking and screaming from the auditorium. The majority of the audience cheered and the six o'clock news made it a riot.... the power of the press.

There were very few of us 'hippies' at that time, but every bit as much a national fraternity as the brotherhood of Beta Alpha Kappa. Wearing our political point of view on our sleeves, we became a subculture that communicated through underground newspapers cloaked in psychedelic cartoons populated by pig police. For our parents, the only male figure with long hair was Tarzan The Ape Man, and even he was clean-shaven. We spoke a language 'the straights' couldn't understand and could travel anywhere in the country by simply sticking out a thumb and waiting for a 'brother' to come along. Hitch-hiking was the preferred mode of transportation to neighboring 'peace rallies' in Wisconsin and Ohio where sleeping bags lined floors with empty refrigerators as the direct result of 'Reefer Madness.' Timothy Leary was arrested for smoking pot in his bedroom and Mao's 'Cultural Revolution' was launched in China as the 'all for one' mentality of Camp Thunderbird found its way into the consciousness of those of us that felt the nation had lost both its conscience and its way.

Simon & Garfunkel's *"Sounds of Silence"* could be heard over the stomping of Nancy Sinatra's patent leather *"Boots"* for a short time before *"The Ballad Of The Green Berets"* went to number one and Ronald Reagan won the Republican nomination for Governor of California. *"Mother's Little Helpers"* were exposed in *"Valley Of The Dolls"* while on TV, *"Batman"* and *"The Monkees"* laughed at *"Virginia Woolf"* and anything else that touched reality. We identified with *"The Man Of LaMancha,"* while *"A Man And A Woman"* proved that Europeans had a much better grasp on the meaning of sex than Raquel Welch (who each of us wanted to grasp differently). During the fifties, each Fall the country would wait for a special issue of *Playboy Magazine* that included pictures .... but not the ones you would expect. These were carefully kept under wraps and then all exposed at the same time, each model competing with the other for attention, to capture the imagination, and set a style trend for the coming year.... of the NEW CARS about to be introduced. In the sixties we waited with the same anticipation for each new Beatles album. In December of 1965, *"Rubber Soul"* opened our heads to new instruments and harmonies and sounds we had never experienced before in popular music. In the spring of '66, *"Revolver"* clicked into the growing sense of alienation taking place around us.

Meanwhile, despite my musical success, a small internal voice was convinced that there was always someone in the audience thinking, 'If he only had proper training.' (Amazing how we create our own insecurities) Actually one reason for my attending Indiana was its terrific music school, with a voice department that often managed to place students in the Metropolitan Opera Company. Unfortunately, a prevailing methodology involved something called a 'head voice' that strived to resonate the sound through your sinuses by singing "your weeny...your waynee...your weeny....your waynee" and other such exercises. I didn't know much, but at least I knew what my weeny was for, and it wasn't about singing. Attending recitals of the various voice instructors, I listened for one who didn't sound like he was playing with himself and arranged for private lessons. This resulted in paying a 'professional' to tell me that what I was doing was correct in the first place.

Those early trumpet lessons with Mr. Benedetti had me breathing from my diaphragm, which turned out to be the secret behind 'proper use of the voice.' When you expand your stomach to take a breath, it makes more room for your lungs to fill with air. Controlling the outflow of air with your stomach muscles, or diaphragm, is called 'breath control.' The more control you have over the air flowing through your vocal chords, like the reed of a wind instrument or mouthpiece of a trumpet, the more control you have over the sound being produced. Then of course genetics has something to do with the size and shape of your vocal chords, which is why some people can't sing for shit no matter how they breathe. There's a big difference though, between performing for the stage and singing on a microphone. Like film as opposed to theatre, the electronic medium is more intimate and introspective. But it took learning how to make big round sounds to realize how much I hated using the voice that way. To this day I find opera annoying.

Learning can also include deciding what to forget. As the only student taking jazz improv for the voice, the instructor, Dave Baker, had me sitting in the horn section making noises. It was great fun until my turn to solo. Staring at the sheet music, drawing from my years of trumpet lessons and musical theory, what resulted were notes but not music. "Don't think," he said. "Don't read. Forget about the notes and the key and all that formal shit..... just listen, and feel, and sing." So I discarded all those years of training and sang. It was the most important musical lesson of my life.

My jazz trio, made up of friends from improv class, was soon touring other colleges in the area, while at the same time I was finger picking folk guitar at The Kiva, the student union coffee house. This coupled with my fraternity pledging, anti-war and civil rights activities, and fucking, made getting to class a real drag. College would have been great if not for classes and studying.

Miss Murray, my second semester English Lit instructor, liked my poetry and was intrigued with the idea that perhaps I could arrange for a world famous poet from Greenwich Village to address the I.U. Poetry Society for a small stipend. She had no idea who Allen Ginsberg was. The modest auditorium filled with an assortment of proper ladies from town, English literature students, and a few fellow conspirators who had actually read some of Ginsberg's poetry. Allen walked into the room with electric hair sticking out, except where it clung to his ruffled red flannel shirt. Holding hands with an anemic male companion, Ginsberg swished to the podium and took center stage while most homosexuals were still in the closet. The entire spectacle caught the dumbfounded ladies of the I.U. Poetry Society with no established roles of etiquette. So they sat like a school of fish with round mouths sucking wind. Covering the hole in her face with an open palm, Miss Murray's eyes furtively darted about the room. When Ginsberg then leaned over and kissed his boyfriend, that did it...half the fish fled. A few, however, were so traumatized they couldn't move. Miss Murray swallowed her hand. As Allen proceeded with a graphic ode to masturbation, the sight of her actually sucking in her entire wrist was every bit as sexual as the images he painted aloud. This would be the last reading of the I.U. Poetry Society after which Miss Murray went on 'sabbatical.'

Originally, I wasn't even supposed to be in her class. At the start of second semester all the required English courses beginning after 10:00 AM were filled, so I changed my major to Philosophy and took Logic and Ethics. As it turned out, Logic was really algebra, taking normal English statements, reducing them to symbols to be calculated and then translated back to English. I was fucked. What's more, the teacher would answer a question by reading back the formula s-l-o-w-e-r, as if this was making everything clear. I was double fucked. Forced to compromise my principals, I changed major back to English and replaced Logic with Miss Murray's English Literature class. So actually, if Logic had really been philosophy and not math, I might have been a philosopher today; Allen Ginsberg would never have visited Indiana University; and Miss Murray would still have her job. Funny how little things can change the course of history.

Another historic event was marked by a bet with Handman over a new place in town that he said was actually selling 19 cent hamburgers and 15 cent fries. The first McDonalds in Bloomington was a miracle of modern technology. The shiny red plastic building sat dwarfed by two enormous yellow arches apparently constructed for the sole purpose of presenting a movie theater billboard that boldly proclaimed "Over 1 million sold!" This was obviously to reassure us that the food was safe. In fact, the thin crisp fries were even better than the greasy clunkers at the local diner. What's more, the whole assembly line concept... driving in, placing an order, and driving out 5 minutes later with a burger and fries... no waiting for a table, no waitress to tip, no smelly vinyl tablecloths and all for super-cheap, was as revolutionary as the times. Each week, as another million was added to the sign, I also learned an important lesson in capitalism. Instead of going out of business trying to compete, the local diner raised the cost of its burgers 50 cents and was selling more than ever. Go figure…

Back at the frat house was another practical lesson in economics, where Spitter had a rented car up on blocks, rear wheels spinning in reverse, with each pledge taking turns at the gas pedal, running the odometer backwards. Spitter was a short stocky New York gangster type, who couldn't speak without spraying the immediate vicinity. The mileage charge on a recent round trip to Jersey would have blown his beer budget and Spitter, of all people, could not afford dehydration. By the second day, the new Pontiac Skylark was wining and spewing blue exhaust, straining from the abuse. So were we. The Rose had thrown up again (we were thinking of changing his nickname) and at one point Megaphone actually passed out from the fumes. The only one not affected was Useless, who seemed to thrive on carbon-monoxide. Spitter somehow assumed that he'd get a refund for returning the car with less mileage than when it left. I vowed never to buy a used car from a rental company. Of course it was no longer clear where to buy a car since clean-cut Ralph Nader published *"Unsafe At Any Speed"* and scared the shit out of The Establishment more than any of us long-haired freaks. The President of General Motors was actually forced to apologize before a congressional committee for investigating Nader's 'private life' in an attempt to discredit him. Funny how today congress does what they used to make people apologize for.

In April and May, carloads of high school seniors began showing up for dinner on weekends as the frat house began trolling for next year's pledge class. Each wide-eyed hopeful was sized up by the brothers and judged, with special attention to 'legacies,' relatives of alumni. At the same time, preparations were underway for 'Hell Week,' when the main pledge class would be promoted into the brotherhood (or killed). Rumors of Hell Weeks past circulated the dorm at night like horror stories around a campfire, with actual pictures of former pledges that disappeared and were never heard from again. When it finally came, those of us in the half-class had to move out and were forbidden to return to the house until it was over. Considering the line-ups we had already experienced, we could only imagine the unspeakable acts being perpetrated in our absence.

Living the entire week with Bill Krane was not easy. If I changed the angle of a matchbox on the counter, Bill would unconsciously move it back to its original position. Every pillow had its place. Even the dishes had to be re-stacked in their original order. But it was his place and I couldn't afford to lose it. Despite his anal retentive nature, Bill was actually a good guy, who loved music and poetry, and could sing in a controlled falsetto that at times sounded amazingly like Johnny Mathis. In fact one night when Mathis was actually performing at the Auditorium, we convinced a house full of townies that we could arrange for the star to sing outside their window, if they promised not to come out and embarrass him. Our only other request was that they get naked for us. Within the first three notes of *"Misty,"* bras and panties came flying out the window and all five girls were screaming up and down. As Krane finished the line *"I'm as helpless as a kitten up a tree"* it was too much for three of them, and suddenly it was a foot race to my '63 Falcon parked around the corner. Here it was 2 o'clock in the morning and we were being chased down the streets of Bloomington by screeching naked girls.(Now this was the true meaning of college.) When porch lights began to pop on the three little piggies realized what they were doing, turned on their heels and squealed all the way home. That fleeting view of little pink tushies jiggling back into the darkness was a fitting image to close my Freshman year at I.U.

XII. (1966-67)
(Age 20, Sophomore year)

It so happened that Jed Longfeather's cousin, Thomas King, was the Indian Lore instructor at the local Westchester YMCA Day Camp, which meant I had a summer job. Two weeks before camp started, the annual gathering of the Iroquois Nation took place in the Catskill Mountains of New York. The 'people of the longhouse' were a league of six nations; the Cayuga, Mohawk, Oneida, Onondaga, Seneca, and Tuscarora; whose democratic form of government influenced us considerably more than their morality and reverence for the land. It was three days and nights of 'toe-heels' and the 'rabbit dance;' studies in beadwork and leather; tests of strength, speed, archery and the javelin; and tape recorded tribal songs that would later be transcribed phonetically for our campers. Sitting around the 'Dream Drum' at night, to the taste of rabbit and Indian Fry Bread (a variation on the Italian zeppoli or the American donut), were tall tales of warriors and spirits. Meanwhile, at a gathering in Detroit, the radical black-separatist Stokely Carmichael, was advising Negroes not to make the same mistake as the American Indian by ironically suggesting they establish reservations again to separate themselves from the White Man.

In another tribal ritual, Burnout and Jocko brought me to the pounding drums of a barge docked on the coast of Long Island, where musical warriors did battle on a wooden stage to the pungent odor of 3.2 beer. The beams shuddered beneath the thundering feet of brightly colored teenagers jumping around like a 'bunch of wild Indians.' In the months that I had been away, Felix's band had developed a faithful following and tonight it was rumored that manager Sid Bernstein was in the audience. Clad in bellbottoms and long hair, the noise level doubled when The Young Rascals hit the stage and turned up their Fender amplifiers to cut through the war cries of the crowd. The music was infectious and happy, in contrast to the times, and it was easy to get lost in the revelry. Within months, The Young Rascals' *"Good Lovin'"* would be on the charts along with The Beach Boys, The Association, The Mama's & The Papa's, The Beatles, and The Troggs. The exuberant music was more an antidote than a reflection of the country's mental state.

Despite harsh dissent, the Supreme Court overturned the conviction of rapist Ernesto Miranda, because he hadn't been informed of his rights. In the largest political ad ever published, 6,400 signed an appeal against the Vietnam War, after which LBJ stepped up bombing raids over Hanoi. When non-violent James Meredith tried to march for civil rights in Mississippi, he was shot in the back. And violence spread like a disease across the face of the news. With *"In Cold Blood"* sitting at the top of the best seller list, a former alter boy and Eagle Scout perched atop a 27-story tower at the University of Texas and spent a day killing people. Then ex-convict Richard Speck murdered eight student nurses in Chicago where, a few weeks later 4,000 National Guardsmen were called in to deal with shootings between police and Negro snipers. At the same time gangs of blacks, whites and Puerto Ricans rumbled in the streets of East New York, and in Cleveland, a young Negro mother was killed by police, triggering a series of riots. Political comedian Lenny Bruce took one final look at all this shit and over-dosed.

It seems that capitalism is the most successful and powerful economic system on earth because it 'capitalizes' on our competitive self-instincts. When coupled with a democratic form of government that allows the freedom to openly display our stupidity and hate anyone who doesn't respect it, the results can be disconcerting. As this internal combustion of American society erratically drove itself off the dirt roads of Mississippi into the jungles of Southeast Asia and through the fire-wall of Watts, it scared the crap out of everyone along the road, wondering who would get run over next. France pulled out of NATO, Britain went isolationist, and Mao's Cultural Revolution made perfect sense. The simple morality of communism: 'From each according to his abilities, to each according to his needs' sounds a lot like 'All for one, and one for all.' And all of this sounds great except for one thing....it doesn't fuckin' work because people are basically selfish. Look what happened to Camp Thunderbird.

The innocent sponges Indian-wrestling through the grass of the YMCA Day Camp, were a welcome relief. Each cabin was an Indian tribe (before they became 'Native American') and each camper competed for 'coup,' individual feathers indicating achievement. These were proudly displayed on 'coup sticks' that the little warriors carried, like Plains Indians of the past. The camp activities were all in preparation for the season ending Final Powwow. Every home run or swimming promotion or special act of kindness was rewarded with a feather. At the crafts shop a complete coup stick became a headdress to be adorned with beadwork and accompanied by leggings and lanyards, all to be worn on the 'big night.' Sunny days at the Indian Lore cabin would find laughing circles of 'duck duck goose' and mini-warriors avidly practicing 'heels,' like spinning tops bouncing on the lawn. On rainy days, the paneled wall of 'false face masks,' would inspire little mouths of wonderment, fantasizing on the spirits that visited dreams and created them. These were the clean slate years when everything was being written for the first time on their blackboards and it was fun to be the one holding the chalk.

At night I found work as an opening act for 'food money' in The Village, where folk music had been co-opted by the anti-war movement. Although there were a few surf shops along with the coffee houses and clubs on the strip, they now had peace signs on the walls, co-existing with African dens displaying dashikis and a sprinkling of 'head shops' selling rolling paper and water pipes. The drug culture was only just seeping in and you could still find posters of Jan & Dean and Bob Dylan with short hair, but the writing was on the walls. Richie Havens sang about *"Handsome Johnny"* marching off to war, while Phil Ochs proclaimed *"I Ain't A Marchin' Anymore."* Then U.S. planes napalmed a battalion of our own troops in South Vietnam and twenty American GI's died in agony, while at the same time 45,000 fans screamed over The Beatles, performing on center stage at Shea Stadium.

On the day of the final Powwow, the air bristled with anticipation as members of the Iroquois nation set up the 'Dream Drum.' A tanned deerskin was moistened and stretched over the mouth of a massive metal bowl, then secured with rawhide straps and belts on a circle of poles driven deep into the ground. Long wooden sticks, cushioned on the ends with cloth and cotton and covered with suede leather would beat out the rhythms that had been passed down by generations; Rhythms and words that our campers knew by heart (just like the fans at Shea Stadium). As darkness approached and parents began to stream in, the barbecue pit was ignited. After an authentic paper-plate dinner of charcoal broiled hamburgers and hot dogs, corn on the cob and baked beans, and closing with Indian Fry Bread covered with powdered sugar, the ceremonies were ready to begin.

The night flickered in the lamplight of kerosene torches as the elders began beating the rhythm of the round dance, and a hundred little Indian princesses, clad in their own hand-made cloths and beadwork, entered the circle of motion. Next came the littlest warriors, holding their coup sticks and concentrating on their toe-heels before the older teens somersaulted out in syncopated circles and the Dream Drum picked up the pace. With the entire camp chanting "Hoka Hey Ya Heya" in unison, little faces glowed with pride as members of the Iroquois Nation joined them in the center of the field with flaming batons thrown crackling into the sky. There was something simple and primal and honest and human taking place here, almost touching the child in me that once saw the world in black and white.

Things weren't right at the BAK house when I returned that September. At a special assembly The Deacon spoke. It was hard to believe that this was the same guy we were all joking with only a few months ago. Both his hands and voice trembled when he tried to explain how sorry he was, but lost the words before leaving the room sobbing. The house Prior (President), took over the podium. He started saying something about the real meaning of 'brotherhood' and 'fraternity' before we finally found out what was going on. It seemed that Spitter had fixed The Deacon up with his sister that summer and the Deacon really fell for her. She wasn't on the pill… then it got worse… attempting to get rid of her unwanted pregnancy illegally…she died on the abortion table.

At that moment, the front door slammed open and Spitter blasted into the room. Now supporting a full beard with a bottle of beer spilling from his left hand, he was obviously drunk and disoriented. "DEACON!" he yelled, in a gut wrenching voice. "I'm gonna rip out your stomach like you did to my sister! An eye for an eye, a life for a life! Where's the Deacon you fuckin' assholes?!" When the Prior tried to convince him The Deacon wasn't around, Spitter would have none of it. Banging into the wall, the brown bottle shattered as he tottered down the corridor kicking open the doors and shouting for The Deacon to come out and "face him like a man." We held our collective breath (like the Brick Toss night on the roof) wondering which door The Deacon was hiding behind and what would happen when Spitter found him. Useless wet his pants when Megaphone inadvertently announced "He's gone completely fuckin' crazy!" Luckily, this was out of Spitter's earshot. Thank God the Deacon was no where to be found.

Right then and there I decided this would be a good time to move back in with Fireman Bill. The brothers, however, made it clear that any such desertion would show a definite lack of commitment (and balls). Two new freshmen who chose a dorm retreat over being murdered in their beds by a madman were blackballed. At lunch the next afternoon, with The Deacon secretly hiding in a storage room, Spitter showed up again. This time a rented car squealed down the backyard driveway and up on to the grass. In the same alcohol soaked army fatigues, Spitter was a rabid dog, drool foaming into the sticky hair on his face. With wild eyes darting about the room in jerky head movements he barked, "Deacon! You can run but you can't hide! And this time it'll be your guts spilling out!" Spit was shooting from his mouth. "You son-of-a-bitch, I'm comin' for ya!" Then he grabbed Handman, who was unlucky enough to be sitting there, and with a knife to his throat, demanded "Where is he you little wise-ass weasel?" In a display of bravery I never would have expected, three of the brothers simultaneously jumped him, wrestling to the floor. As the knife skidded across the buffed linoleum, Spitter pulled himself free and vowed "You're dead! You're all dead! I'll kill every one of you motherfuckers if you don't give him up! You hear me Deacon? You're DEAD!" Then he got back in his car, spun the tires in the grass and floored it. This wasn't television, this was real shit happening. An emergency meeting of the entire fraternity was called for that evening.

Now this meeting turned out to be the stupidest thing I'd ever seen. Some of these idiots were actually speaking about the "meaning of fraternity" and "standing by our brother." They recounted how hard Spitter had worked to make it to college, pleading that turning him in would "destroy his future." Destroy HIS future! What planet were these guys from? Here we had a lunatic loose trying to kill people and they wanted to protect his resume. Pledges were usually not allowed at fraternity meetings but this time we were even allowed to speak. And we spoke with one voice... "CALL THE FUCKIN' COPS!" The debate became irrelevant when a police car pulled into the backyard driveway.

As two policemen approached the back door, the Prior made it clear that no one was to say anything until we voted. Following a brief encounter outside, he yielded the floor to one of the officers. "It seems we've had a minor problem in town." The cop began. "Nothing serious. No one was hurt. A sporting goods store was broken into and we found this wallet at the scene." We knew whose wallet without asking. "What was taken?" Megaphone called out. "That's the strange thing." He continued. "Even though there was more than $500 in the cash register, it wasn't touched. All we can ascertain to be missing at this time are a hand-gun, a rifle and a couple hundred rounds of ammunition." That did it... the place went berserk, yelling over the Prior's gavel, as it banged on the dinning room table. This was democracy at work, everyone with an equal voice... all at the same time. For a second there, we almost had a military coup, when the cop's hand instinctively went to his gun.

As the voting died down, the consensus was clear and the cops were apprised of our predicament. They then advised us of our rights, which included: The right to be scared shitless; The right to turn out all the lights in the house so as not to present easy targets; The right to place lookouts on the roof; The right to prey that they'd catch Spitter (or kill him) before he killed one of us. Other than that, they couldn't offer much assistance. The two men explained that they didn't have the manpower to post officers full time but that they would be patrolling regularly. Meanwhile it was suggested that we set up watches in shifts and to call them directly should Spitter appear.

As the red flashing patrol car backed up the driveway, every other light in the house was switched off and the meeting reconvened in the living room, by candlelight. The Deacon's face took on a ghostly hue as he cried in thanks. We were touched...(but secretly considered that we should have cut off his dick last semester when we had the chance). Meanwhile it was decided that the pledge class would take the first watch. The brothers would relieve us from midnight to 2:00 AM. Then we'd be awaken for the early morning shift. If there was a serious emergency, the fire alarm would sound, and we would all head for the living room. We paired off, avoiding windows along the way. Phil and I, assigned to the back door of The Cage, kidded each other about sneaking back to McNutt. After a while sounds we would ordinarily have taken for granted were amplified by the stillness. Here we were in college to avoid being shot in Vietnam, only to be crouching in the darkness, for fear of being picked off by a sniper in the woods of the Beta Alpha Kappa fraternity house. Meanwhile thousands of crickets were out there rubbing their legs together, pulsing in unison. How did they do that?

In the upstairs dorm that night Useless broke the tension by belching the entire alphabet (another of his special talents). It must have been about 1:30 in the morning when what sounded like firecrackers followed by the alarm set thirty bare feet racing downstairs through the corridor to the living room. Curled up in front of the TV room was the blood soaked body of The Deacon. Two attendants leaned over him with red splattered white coats, while Spitter was screaming somewhere downstairs. We barreled into the living room toppling sofas and tables as barricades. I remember moving from behind a soft cushioned chair to the giant oak table, thinking it better protection from bullets. The once distant cursing was growing louder on the other side of the wooden living room doors, which offered no protection since they opened out into the foyer where The Deacons body lay. I could picture Spitter spewing saliva, dripping down the brown cinderblock walls; with a gun in one hand and a bottle of beer in the other, bloodshot eyes staring at the doors, ready to open fire and finish what he'd begun. Over the incessant blare of the fire alarm, I cringed as the doors flew open, expecting to hear the crack of gunfire and see the table splinter above my head. There was a solid moment of complete panic that froze in time before all the lights went on simultaneously and the alarm was replaced with a rousing cheer of "BORASS!" There in the doorway stood a clean-shaven Spitter, with his smiling arms around The Deacon, the two police officers, the health workers, and the entire cast of the brotherhood laughing in unison… Like the crickets of the night.

The next evening was the Annual BAK House Murder Dance, where the brothers and their dates masqueraded as famous killers from the past. A band called The Mobsters was booked, dressed in black shirts and white ties. The house was appropriately decked out in gory posters and catsup-blood, designed to be as offensive as possible. My favorite was the "Wall Of Shame" which included 8x10 glossies of BAK House Murderers of the past. There in the center, in a blood red frame, was Spitter, clutching his trusty bottle of Budweiser, snarling into the camera. Even though my head knew it had all been a joke, my stomach still jumped when he walked into the room. I was about to get another shock, when Charlotte Hamilton arrived. Tossing back her long hair as she pranced through the door, Charlotte was clad in a short black dress, red boots, with a red scarf flowing carelessly across her nearly see-through top. Apparently my harping about 'living life to the fullest' had an unexpected cumulative effect. When she marched over and kissed me with an open mouth there was alcohol on her breath. Could this be Charlotte's evil twin? We didn't stay at the party long.

Borrowing one of the brother's rooms, this would not be lovemaking but compulsion. For a year I had visions of Charlotte naked. Her forbidden green eyes now laced with passion (and alcohol), glanced up as she pulled down her panties. Every pore tingled when she came forward and cradled my head in her hands, guiding my face to the thin wisps of pubic hair and the taste of her wetness. Instinctively I knew that this was completely out of character for her, but Giggy came all over the bed. Then twice again inside her when she mounted me. First she was Janie Weissberger, desperately seeking something lost in the darkness, then Jed's silhouette on a midnight ride, one hand whipping the air while clutching her own breast with the other, yelling "Fuck Me! Fuck Me Harder!" There were thin blue veins barely noticeable near the surface of her breast as she leaned forward to force her nipple into my mouth. Her eyes were lasers as she grabbed my cock to violently shove it back inside, jumping and slapping my chest. Each successive orgasm became more ferocious until finally she was flailing wildly and screaming. I pulled out and held her with both arms. "Don't Stop! I Want More!" she begged in my ear as I held on and felt her legs clamp around my waist. The pulsating pleading gradually diminished to a whisper. Then, for a terrible instant, everything ceased. Her arms fell limply to the mattress, legs still wrapped around me. I prayed she wasn't dead and held on hoping for some sign. The answer came with a rumbling belch as breathtaking, green-eyed Charlotte Hamilton threw up all over the bed, then turned to the wall and began to cry. I curled up behind her cupping her breasts with my hands.

The Mobsters were heavily into *"Hold On, I'm Comin' "* as Charlotte stumbled down the hallway, leaning on my shoulder, past the giant bloody posters of vampires and dead bodies, the smell of vomit and alcohol in her hair. As she continued to whisper "I'm sorry" in my ear, my conscience was apologizing to her. The autumn air had a fresh crisp cleansing effect as I cradled her in the front seat of my car, repeating that she'd done nothing wrong. But the images of that evening would remain as vivid as the scar on Charlie Post's hand. Sitting there under the street light, with the broken statue rocking in my arms, I felt even more ashamed as the night's chill made her nipples hard again, along with my cock. Men are pigs.

Unable to find an English class to fit my schedule, I changed my major to psychology. The first day of P101, better known as 'rat lab,' the instructor laughingly advised us not to wear good clothes for the next class, since we'd be getting our 'experimental subjects,' and they could sometimes be 'messy.' "That's easy," I suggested to the snobbish brunette sitting next to me, "I just won't wear any clothes at all." The professor off-handedly suggested, "I dare you," soliciting the appropriate class response before returning to his lesson. He obviously didn't know who he was dealing with.

It was raining the following Thursday morning. Coats were hung directly to the left of the blackboard, in front of the room. Arriving purposefully late, the entire class was seated as I stepped out of my rain boots and stood there... barefoot. The giggling then erupted when I stripped off my raincoat, displaying nothing but my favorite Groucho Marx under-pants, complete with a cigar strategically centered in the appropriate location. The professor looked my name up on the seating chart and commented, "You've definitely taught me an important lesson, sir. I must be very careful what I suggest to impressionable undergraduates in the future... Quite frankly, I didn't think you'd do it."

Undergraduate psychology majors were required to 'volunteer' as subjects for graduate student experiments. After class that day, I was 'volunteered' for an experiment. Sitting in a dark room in my Groucho Marx underwear, wires were attached to my forehead, arms, and chest "to measure various responses." With an open palm strapped down to a table, fingers straddling a triangular wood block, the lights went out and a series of colored shapes were displayed on a movie screen. This seemed easy enough until a giant wooden hammer came flying out of the darkness, smashing squarely on to the wedge between my fingers. Then just as quickly, it disappeared.

Well, that definitely got a response! A speaker in the corner calmly directed me to continue watching the screen. After a series of such encounters, I began to identify a pattern of images that coincided with the hammer drop, and the experiment was over. The results however, were fascinating. The monitoring of my skin response, breathing, heartbeat, etc., indicated that my body began to recognize the pattern of images and reacted, well before my conscious mind made the connection. The anomaly in my particular case however, was my breathing pattern. For some unknown reason, occasionally I would just stop breathing.

Breath control and the ability to sustain a note, longer than most people believed humanly possible, was just one of the tools in my arsenal on stage. The trick was knowing when and how to use it. On weekends performing at The Kiva, the first task was to break the invisible wall between artist and audience with casual conversation. Not 'performing' but simply talking. The opening song was vitally important. It had to establish an identity and at the same time draw in the audience. That usually meant something familiar, but done uniquely, showcasing my voice, but not giving it all away. Back then, for example, I'd open with my own version of *"They Call The Wind Mariah,"* or perhaps The Zombies' hit *"She's Not There."* If that first number went well it was clear sailing, but a screwed up sound system or a broken string at that juncture, would make the rest of the evening an uphill climb. Once rolling, songs like *"Summer In The City"* from The Lovin' Spoonful or Dylan's *"Don't Think Twice, It's Alright"* would fit nicely before attempting the anti-nuclear hymn, *"Just A Little Rain."* Next, some comic relief, with Country Joe & The Fish's *"I Feel Like I'm Fixin' To Die Rag."* From there out, I didn't like to babble between songs, moving from *"St James Infirmary Bay Blues"* to *"96 Tears"* from Question Mark & The Mysterians, into *"Wild Thing"* by The Troggs, breaking these up with dynamics, humor, or holding that unbelievable note. Finally, the closing number was as important as the opening. Not the dessert, that would be the encore, but the final course. Inspired by Richie Havens, I spent months perfecting the technique of alternately strumming and slapping the guitar in syncopated rhythm.

Increasing in speed with the train-ride of the song, soon the entire room was shaking as *"John Henry"* took his final blows, then 'laid down his hammer and he died'…It worked every time.

In contrast, performing with the jazz trio behind me was as unstructured as the music itself. Not required to sit in front of a microphone with a guitar in place, the freedom to move about the stage mimicked the notes dancing around the chords. No set was ever the same, especially with the input of three other musicians. Ironically, the cost of that creative liberation was the loss of individual freedom. It's never the music that breaks up a group, but conflicting egos, moods, and girlfriends…the very spices that make the music cook. It took a while to find Andy Panquin on keyboards, Tony Smith on bass, and Jimmy Goldstein on drums, but this combination definitely made one hellava musical soufflé.

Jimmy was about 6 inches taller than a midget, and overcompensated by refusing assistance with his extensive drum kit, like an ant balancing boxes three times his body size on to the stage. He also had what drummers refer to as 'complete independence,' the uncanny ability to play a different rhythm with each hand and foot…simultaneously. All accompanied by a perpetual smile. Tony was a tall thin Negro, still coming to terms with becoming 'black.' Although he rarely spoke, usually in concise measured sentences, he was considerably more vocal when slapping his stand-up bass. Andy was a nerd before nerds were cool. His clothes never fit (or matched), and his large black-rimmed glasses would often work their way to the tip of his nose as he played, precariously balanced until pushed back by an unconscious index finger that momentarily rebounded off the keyboard. There might have been better solo players around, but none who listened and reacted as intently as Andy, always finding the right color or inflection. Over the next three years we performed at colleges throughout the Midwest. Never making any money, but boy did we make music.

Tony's older sister Jasmine, was a political activist who came to rehearsals in authentic African garb, even though she was from

Detroit. It was all part of the 'Black Power' movement using words and symbols as tools of self-awareness. Negro leaders felt the word 'colored' implied a derivation of 'white,' something less pure. If we could call ourselves 'white' they would call themselves 'black.' If we could proudly display our European roots, they would do the same with their African heritage. The phrase "I'm black and I'm proud!" was coined as a self-fulfilling prophecy, when in fact, for the majority of Negroes in the United States, neither was true…yet. Words also began to lose their innocence. The term 'boy' suddenly came to symbolize the master-slave relationship. While Amos & Andy became Uncle Tom's, Bobby Seale and Huey Newton knew all too well the subliminal imagery of their 'Black Panther' movement. Not just the visual words but also the impact of dark angry faces in military black berets, urban guerillas that we were training to kill 'gooks' in Vietnam, staring back behind ghetto bars.

There were still only a relatively small vocal minority of us 'long hairs' demonstrating against the war when Hanoi insisted the US end bombing before peace talks could begin. With war expenses at $2 billion per month, LBJ flew over for a photo-op to tell the troops; "You know what you are fighting against: a vicious and illegal aggression across this little nation's frontier." (It was 'aggression' when they did it, and 'liberation' when we did.) The 'Silent Majority' either didn't care or didn't believe a report from Saigon that 40% of our aid was going to corruption or that we were bombing and killing innocent civilians. And Ronald Reagan was elected Governor of California.

For me there was now a more immediate threat… Hell Week! We knew it was coming, we just didn't know when. On a quiet Tuesday night while studying to the soothing Bossa Nova rhythms of *Sergio Mendez and Brazil 66* every light in the house suddenly went off… For the rest of the week we would answer the phone:

> "The time has come for this week of hell, many are sick and none are well, for we are the lowly pawns of the kings and bishops of Beta Alpha Kappa, who forever hold us in

constant checkmate. You are a king or queen calling for my master to speak, please let me know for whom I should seek?"

And so it began. After an initial hour of indiscriminant yelling, hazing, and aerobics, we faced our first Hell Week line-up, which involved toasted marshmallows... in our armpits... and jumping jacks. Luckily I had very little hair in that particular location... of course none of us did by the time it was over. We were then honored to receive new clothing accessories, "Burt" and "Beckie." Burt was a scratchy burlap sack that would serve as an undershirt and Beckie, a slab of raw liver stuffed in our jockey shorts. Neither was to be removed for the next three days on campus. As an added attraction, another string was tied to our dicks with a sign that read "Pull Me!" These new additions to our wardrobe were 'educational tools.' Beckie's smell and staining suggested empathy for a women's monthly 'friend.' Burt would teach us the meaning of irritation.

A pledge's mission was to 'duck walk' around the rules without breaking them (a life-lesson worth learning). Wednesday morning Sociology was spent at the laundry-mat, continually running Burt through the washer and dryer and a gallon of fabric softener before stopping at Bill's pad to boil Beckie, which made her much easier to live with. Instructed to report to the house for 'special duty' when not in class or the library, for me meant a full day at the library (a unique experience in my college career). We were also to return for dinner that night wearing a rubber ball around our necks. A six-pack of Jacks included the smallest soft rubber balls we could find (another life-lesson... it's not always good to have big balls). A wise move, since we then couldn't duck walk past a brother without reciting: "Oh most noble sir, please pull my chain and allow this humble turd to pass." After the ball bounced off our chest, it was: "Thank you sir. Please may I have another."

The brothers went out of their way to prepare a special meal for us that evening. This stuff made Mexican food look good. (Which to me always looks like it's already been eaten. Hell, they even use words like 'refried,' which doesn't exactly connote 'fresh' or 'burrito,' conjuring up images of ground baby-back donkey meat.) Anyway, in our case it was a concoction of catsup, mustard, Tabasco sauce, mashed potatoes, liver pate, Limburger cheese and raw eggs (Hell Week uses lots of eggs). The aroma was delightful. All accompanied by a fresh glass of cold water, complete with a live goldfish for each. One whiff and we all knew what to expect from The Rose. Useless, on the other hand, took on that same expression he wore when seducing the cow, went for a giant soup-spoon of gruel, swallowed the goldfish in one gulp, and proudly proclaimed, "Thank you sir. Please may I have another!" Then, right on cue, The Rose lost his lunch and his name. From that meal on, The Rose would instead forever be known as "The Retch."

When not taking part in line-ups, we became personal slaves to the brothers, cleaning everything from the walls to their shoes. The trick was to avoid being seen, either by hiding or taking on a job that would keep you behind closed doors, then dragging it out as long as possible (future union worker training). Handman actually hid in the clothes dryer downstairs, but that backfired when they found him and turned it on. Line-ups were an ongoing series of creative programs involving food and exercise. That night we were covered in Karo syrup, rolled in corn flakes, and served in milk. The whole class was given demerits though, when we tried hugging some of the brothers.

Like most things in life, the reality of Hell Week could never live up to the nightmare we anticipated. And so it went until the last night, which we knew would be more than just a pain in the ass. Over the fireplace hung the sacred paddle to be wielded by 'Shybo,' the BAK House version of Masowski, for the Final Swat. That afternoon we could hear him practicing his swing on a professional punching bag behind closed doors. This would be a night to remember. As darkness fell we were blindfolded and tied to chairs in the dining room, with metal pails on our heads while some sort of aboriginal music throbbed in the background. After a day of calisthenics and fasting, with raw eggs now drying on our skin, the room began to swirl. The brothers thoughtfully came to our aid by sporadically banging on the pails with various kitchen utensils and whispering in our ears that perhaps we should quit before it was too late. This went on for an eternity, soon accompanied by the pungent odor of vomit, donated by The Retch.

It was hard to ignore the wailing, hypnotic music (but at least it wasn't Donovan), and the mental image of the sacred paddle swishing through the air. Waiting was the hardest part as, one at a time, we were taken upstairs. I thought about Charlotte, and the cow, and the brick toss, and the giant hammer that once flew out of the darkness, until finally it was my turn to face the music. Since The World was no longer in residence, the Prior was assigned as my guide. Still blindfolded, I could hear the brothers raising hell in the den when we sidestepped into the TV room for some last minute advice. With a reassuring hand on my shoulder he explained that by now the guys were pretty drunk and it would be best to keep them laughing. "Don't let them get serious, especially Shybo. When he asks how many swats you want, instead of the customary, 'Oh most noble sir, one for each of the founding fathers, please,'" He suggested I "come up with something creative to make Shybo laugh. Also, if he misses, fall forward anyway and make believe it was a direct hit." Then, in a last minute inspiration, the Prior shoved a telephone book in my pants. When I protested, he assured me it was too dark in the room to be noticed and besides, he was "afraid of the legal ramifications" if I were seriously hurt. With that comforting thought, we headed for the living room.

When the wooden doors parted I felt like Daniel entering the lion's den, and with a few steps, having just seen *"A Man for All Seasons,"* jumped through history to the court of Henry VIII, and Thomas Moore facing his final destiny. I could picture Shybo's rippling muscles, his giant forearm, and the blood dribbling down the paddle from his previous victims. Jostled to the front of the room, the inebriated crowd was bubbling. Then with all the pomp and ceremony of a proper execution, the prescribed question was pronounced: "How many swats do you wish to receive? "Oh most noble sir," I began. Then paused for an internal debate... "As many swats as zits on your ass." The brothers couldn't believe their ears... "What! What did he say?" Instead of having the desired effect, the mob was incensed. "You disrespectful maggot!" Shybo bellowed in rhyme, "How dare you mock our history and tradition? You're gonna pay for what you just did... assume the position!" 'Assume the position' meant bend over, hold your balls, and kiss your ass goodbye. Then someone yelled, "Wait, wait, what's that in his pants!" As Shybo pulled out the phonebook, all hell broke loose. "You fuckin' cheat! Kill him! Kill the bastard! You're Blackballed! You're Outta Here!" It was a nightmare. Everything that could possibly go wrong did. The Prior rushed to my defense, explaining that it was his idea. That he was only looking out for the welfare of the fraternity. But the brothers were furious. Take down his pants. Make him take it naked! They screamed. Then it became a chant... 'Make him take it naked! Make him take it naked!' The mood had swung from boisterous to blood-thirsty and it was all my fault. The chant continued as I bent over again, with my pants around my ankles and held on for dear life. Then the chant stopped and the whole room counted in unison..."One....Two......Three!" There was a whoosh of air .. and nothing...he missed... he fuckin' missed.... I fell forward anyway, just like the Prior instructed, and hoped I had gotten away with it.... "BORASS!" There was no Final Swat. Pledging at the BAK House began with a borass, the BAK House Murder, and ended with one, the Final Swat.

It was then my turn to watch Handman and Useless handle the ordeal. Joining Phil, Megaphone and The Retch who had already gone, we were now part of the ensemble. Brawling on cue as the doors opened, Handman looked like he had been through the downstairs dryer again. His clothes in disarray and crooked blindfold half covering his nose, helplessly stumbling toward the front of the room, where Shybo waved the Sacred Paddle like a baton, conducting the cacophony.(God, it felt good to be on the other side.) Shybo silently pointed to the top of the phonebook peering out over the rim of his gray sweatpants as Handman leaned over without being told. "Stand up and face the brothers," Shybo barked, "No one told you to bend over yet!" Handman jerked to attention and the phonebook dropped into his pants almost taking them with it. With fists clenched on his waistband, sweat now soaking his blindfold, Handman struggled to maintain. Shybo then continued the script, "How many swats do you wish to receive?" A barely audible voice answered, "Oh most noble sir," we all waited to hear what he would say, "one for each of the founding fathers, please." At which point the room erupted, "What... eight swats... no one has ever taken the full eight swats!" Now it was Shybo's turn, "You pussy! Didn't your Fraternity Father tell you to come up with something original?" Handman just stood there dazed. "OK, you asked for it...In keeping with our history and tradition, now you're gonna pay...assume the position." Knowing he made the wrong choice, Handman struggled to bend over with one hand, still clutching his sweatpants with the other. "Both hands on the floor," Shybo demanded. And sure enough, as soon as Handman let go, the weight of the phonebook did its job. We all cheered in mock disbelief as the phonebook and Handman's white legs were laid bare simultaneously. Believing he had blown it, Handman crumbled to the floor when the chant rang out... "Make him take it naked!" Thrilled with the reprieve, he immediate 'dropped trou' and hit doggy position again. Then the whoosh of air, the fake fall, and Handman was officially a brother.

Next came Useless. This was the one everyone was waiting for. Unlike the rest of us, when the doors opened Useless burst in with both arms raised in peace signs and a giant shit-eating grin on his face. The brothers went ballistic! "You think this is a joke you asshole," I could hear Spike yelling, while The Deacon ran up and screamed into his face, "You'll never make it out of here alive! And if you do, your ass will hurt the rest of your worthless life!" Rather than immediately leading him to the front, Useless became a human pinball, bouncing around the room, ringing with cheers each time he lost his balance and hit the floor. But like an inflatable punching bag, he'd keep popping back up for more. We were all screaming at the top of our lungs by the time he reached Shybo, who lifted him like a rag-doll and shook the smile from his face. "Enough!" Shybo yelled and the noise level dipped, "Now comes the moment of truth... How many swats do you wish to receive?" The room fell silent. "Oh most noble sir," Useless began, with the faintest touch of a smirk. Then in full voice, "as many swats as the inches of your dick!" "Hard or soft," I yelled before the whole room joined in according to script. Then, in an angry voice that sounded chillingly real Shybo roared, "I'll show you how big my dick is you little asshole, bend over...In keeping with our history and tradition, now you're gonna pay...assume the position." As it turned out, Useless had secured the telephone book with masking tape, which didn't show until Shybo pulled down his pants. Then the proceedings took an unexpected turn. This time as the brothers began yelling "It's Over... He's blackballed," they actually led Useless out of the room in startled disbelief. Those of us that had spent the last two semesters pledging with him couldn't believe they were really throwing him out. Imagine our relief when the doors re-opened to the chant "Make him take it naked..." and Useless streaked back into the room, stark naked holding his balls as he assumed the position. "One...Two... Three" and Shybo even connected a bit before Useless theatrically flew through the air and sprawled out like he was dead. Everyone yelled "He missed, he missed, hit again, harder, harder!" Then they actually set him up again, before the final whoosh.

Darkness allows subconscious demons to lurk just beyond our sight, tweaking our other senses and imagination. This coupled with the black robes and candlelight all added solemnity to the final induction ceremony. In single file, we came forward to receive our fraternity pins, and allow a piece of paper, holding the secret words that were never to be revealed, to burn in our palms. Then the real fun began... the paddle exchange. Months earlier we had ordered foot-long, glazed wooden paddles, each with the fraternity emblem imprinted on one side, and the nickname of a pledge-brother on the other. The living room was cleared of furniture and re-lit for the spectacle. Each exchange required four participants: One bent over to receive the swat of his paddle, while another paddle was held just above his butt to protect the spine, one held below the ass to protect his heritage, and the presenter, with plenty of running room to 'wield the wood' before giving it up. The trick was wrist action, a flick of the wrist at the instant of impact for the ultimate whack. You could hear the crisp whipping sound of a welt being raised when it was done right. It's ironic that we did more damage to each other that night than any hell-week hazing and, based on residual bruising, no pledge would ever guess that the Final Swap was really a borass.

My first official function as a full brother was dinner with the DG's. As the debutantes of Delta Gamma sorority were led into the living room by the new pledge-class, there I stood like a Marine, having just survived the hell of boot-camp, with a medal fraternity pin proudly displayed on the lapel of a very sporty blue madras jacket. With names like Crystal, Buffy and Barbie, the dolls' fake eyelashes fluttered in, proud of their diversity in that some actually wore scandalous miniskirts as opposed to the more traditional formalwear. With proper giggles and blushes, they watched Handman perform card tricks and tried not to pull away from Useless when he got 'up close and personal.' Among them was Pricilla Wainwright, the snobbish brunette from my 'rat lab' class and AnnaLisa Harnswelder, the hairspray blonde captain of I.U.'s Cheerleading Squad (who probably shaved and powdered her cunt every night). Only the brightest whitest smiles made it through the Delta Gamma selection process. But in this time of 'civil rights' it was imperative they demonstrate their willingness to mix with the underclass, and we were about to prove just how under-class we could be.

We knew their sorority house usually served dinner at about 7:30, so purposefully set our invitation for 8:00, then made a point of serving drinks, but nothing to eat. By the time I got up to perform, some of the girls were having trouble crossing their legs. Pricilla sat swaying in front of me, licking her lips, with her miniskirt opening to display bright red panties as AnnaLisa loudly slurred, "So when-r-we gonna-eat already?" Megaphone repeated the line to the delight of the audience while I tried to finish my song. Ordinarily I would have then led Pricilla to a room and fucked her brains out, but tonight I didn't want to miss dinner. Half the sisters were trying desperately to maintain their composure while the other half were having trouble navigating the stairs. This was turning out better than we had expected.

The dining room tables were decked out in red tablecloths with white napkins, flickering in romantic candlelight. We could smell the tomato sauce and garlic simmering in the kitchen as steaming plates of spaghetti were placed in the center of each table. Then came the garlic-bread, and finally the sauce. But there was something missing, someone had forgotten the utensils. At which point Shybo emerged from the kitchen, his giant white apron smeared with tomato sauce, and the rehearsed announcement that all the silver-wear was stuck in the dishwasher, and could not be retrieved. Then, to the absolute horror of our stunned, starving, and somewhat inebriated guests, the brothers began grabbing the spaghetti with their bare hands, slapping it into their plates, pouring on sauce and sucking it down. If you think this sounds disgusting, it looked even worse. Our fingers and faces were dripping with sauce and strands of spaghetti, smeared away with swabs of garlic bread. Useless rubbed his face in his plate making gurgling sounds, then sat up and inhaled, whipping worms of pasta up his nose, splattering everywhere, including the face of the startled little blonde squealing in the seat next to him. Incensed, AnnaLisa lifted the bowl of sauce from the center of the table and dumped it on his head. And the rest was history…It must have looked like a mass murder in progress to passers-by as the sisters of Delta Gamma ran stumbling from the house, dressed to the nines, drenched in tomato blood. Following that night, Delta Gamma enacted a resolution, permanently banning any member of the sorority from ever entering the Beta Alpha Kappa fraternity, for any reason, on threat of national excommunication; Another example of democracy at work.

A liberal arts degree required proficiency in a second language. Unfortunately, having been forced to study Spanish in high school only succeeded in convincing me that I was linguistically challenged. Play a three-minute song once and I could sing it right back, but give me three lines of Spanish dialogue to memorize and it was all Greek to me. Luckily the Spanish instructor needed my help to get laid as much as I needed his to pass. At the same time Biology 101 required hours of extracurricular examination of the breasts of my graduate-student lab instructor, who blushed when I slid my finger in and out of a frog (mm...smelled like tuna). Learning to manipulate the system was integral to the college experience. Whether it was invisible ink cheat-sheets, the extensive test file of stolen past exams in the Frat house library, or creative 'improvisation.' Like the morning Useless wasn't ready for his Home Economics final, and wrote "There Will Be No Exam Today" on the blackboard before class, forcing the professor to reschedule when half the class didn't show.

After signing any number of Jasmine's petitions for increased African studies, the right to establish their own bookstore on campus, and more black faculty members, I was honored with an official invitation from the Black Activist Student Committee (BASC) to join them in attendance at the annual Indiana University Board of Trustees meeting. Held in a large amphitheater type classroom, the Trustees were seated center-stage around an oval wooden table. The President of the University, Elvis Stahr, Jr., (no kidding... that was really his name) presided in strict Parliamentary Procedure as the revered Chancellor, Herman Wells, looked on from the front row. Also near the front of the room sat Lancaster 'Lanc' Washington, the leader of BASC, with an obvious pile of petitions. An Assistant Professor in the Political Science Department, like Hairy Greene who was also in attendance with petitions of his own, Lanc was a bit more colorful. A former basketball player, at 6'5" his oversized brown and red dashiki, dark glasses and black beret, were hard to ignore. But ignore him they did. For more than two hours of minutes, old business, budgets, and rezoning parking permits, the room dissipated. The administration was obviously making this a test of endurance... if they only knew...

It was 10:00 o'clock when they finally started 'new business' and I would have booked two hours earlier if not for Jasmine's bare foot teasing my leg. Strange, she'd never come on to me before.

Meanwhile, 'The Chair' managed to 'recognize' everyone in the room except Lanc and Hairy, until an unassuming little man 'yielded The Floor' to Lanc. This ploy succeeded for no more than three minutes when a 'point of order' was called and the meeting adjourned due to the 'lateness of the hour.' This was OK with me since all I wanted to do was go home and fuck Jasmine. Boy, was I in for a surprise.

There were two main entrances and a fire escape behind the podium. Half the room was oblivious as Lanc arose like an African peacock and the exits were covertly manned by black militants, in fitted army fatigues, with rifles stiffly held across their chests. "Alright, you had your meeting," he proclaimed, "Now we gonna have mine!" At which point the armed guards slammed their rifle buts on the floor in precise unison. And The Floor stopped moving. Jasmine glanced back over her shoulder as she headed for the front. The shock was palpable. Historically a bastion of theoretical dissent, the university system was unprepared for massive civil disobedience, let alone an armed military takeover.

The Board's first impulse was to circle their wagons around Herman Wells as they hurled accusations in awkward restraint (for fear of being shot). The anger turned to 'how dare you' as two Trustees started toward an exit and three militants marched down to meet them eye to eye...(Guess who blinked?) Next came the legal threats and recriminations. Lanc just listened as the room got warmer and the minutes clocked on until he finally asked, "Are you gonna talk to me or just keep yellin' why we shouldn't be doin' what's already been done?" But the one-sided conversation continued until body language gradually changed. As shirt buttons opened and ties came loose, shouting became arguing and arguing, discussion. 'The Chair' turned into a person and 'The Floor' became pockets of people pitching and catching pieces of conversation. Words collided in mid air concerning the need for faculty evaluations, grading models and the purpose of education, literacy and culturally biased testing, the role of minorities in a democratic society and the responsibility of leadership. And stares became looks, then sight... to insight... to vision.

I soon found myself in a chair right next to Elvis (who I still referred to as 'President Stahr'), his navy-blue suit-jacket draped over the back of his chair, rolled up pinstriped shirt and 'ring around the collar.' It felt like another of those NCCJ sensitivity classes, as the players began to peer past preconceived prejudices and procedures. Then just as the game was going into extra innings, a thunderstorm of sirens and searchlights stopped the action. We were surrounded by the National Guard.

Word of our detention had leaked out and a portable radio reported the play-by-play. Apparently the local police and National Guard were fighting over jurisdiction. The yokels were ready to storm the place with tear gas and bayonets (white sheets optional), while the Feds were a little more reticent, aware of the national implications. For the first time that evening I was actually scared. Earlier the guns surrounding us had been disconcerting, but really only props. Now the sweating hands cocking them in wide-eyed stage fright signaled a radical role reversal. With red flashing megaphones feeding back through the radio, we searched for a way out without being shot or arrested. Along with the recent bonding, the room was now also united against a greater stupidity. Chancellor Wells volunteered to speak to the authorities on our behalf, but his continued presence was worth more as a deterrent. In the end, it would be Hairy Greene and President Stahr who would leave together to plead our case (in part because they were both white). But first we needed to decide exactly what our case would be...and fast.

As it turned out, Lanc had taken the precaution of not arming his guards, (which explained why they now looked so fuckin' scared). Ironically it also gave us the ammunition to argue that there had, in fact, been no 'armed takeover,' as mistakenly reported on the radio. *But what were the rifle-toting militants doing there?* They were acting as a deterrent, since Lanc had been receiving death threats. *So why were the Chancellor, the President, and all the Trustees still there?* It was an informal meeting convened at the 'invitation' of 'motivated student leaders.' (Which also meant there could be no reprisals later.) The art of diplomacy is converting lies into half-truths. Then you just tell whichever halves fit the occasion.

You could hear grumbling in the background when President Stahr aired a statement, removing the excuse to show the world what 'law & order' meant in Indiana. Our emissaries returned like conquering heroes. Hairy, a bit worse for wear having initially been tackled and beaten, but the bonds of adversity were in place. For the rest of that night and morning the dialogue continued. By the following day a joint resolution was signed sanctioning the Student Government's petition to allow us to grade our teachers, granting professors the option of offering courses on a pass/fail basis, and establishing a new 'Black Studies' department at Indiana University. Not bad for one night's work.

A Student Liaison Committee was also established, to act as a clearinghouse for the various campus political groups and to make recommendations to the University Administration. I became an 'Advisor On Race Relations,' to act as a 'universal translator.' Within days I enlisted the assistance of the local YMCA in forming a multi-racial 'Race Relations Advisory Group' under their auspices (and budget). Meanwhile the I.U. Student Organization had mimeograph machines running everywhere, printing ballots to be handed out with final exams, asking students to grade their professors on teaching skills, ability to cover the required material, and the overall value of their course. We were actually affecting our world and the rush was exhilarating!

And the world was changing. After sending Raquel Welch on a *"Fantastic Voyage,"* Walt Disney died, a month before the astronauts Grissom, White and Chaffee were burned alive on the launching pad at the newly re-named Cape Kennedy. The other Elvis married Priscilla in Vegas as Egypt's Nasser concluded a surprise alliance with Jordan's King Hussein, and lined up with Syria, Iraq, Kuwait, Algeria, and the Palestine Liberation

Organization to pull a *"Bambi Meets Godzilla"* on little Israel. When they tried it, Israel turned around like Clay vs Liston and beat the shit out of them. Meanwhile, Muhammad Ali was stripped of his title for refusing to fight for Uncle Sam. In China fingers and noses were being chopped off prisoners in their Cultural Revolution when Jane Mansfield was decapitated in a car accident. The Beatles signaled the dawn of what was to become the 'drug culture' with the release of *"Sgt. Pepper's Lonely Hearts Club Band,"* and 'head shops' began popping up selling Zig Zag rolling paper and water pipes. The smell of marijuana was as common as tobacco, when the FCC forced radio and TV stations to air health warnings with their cigarette commercials. We watched it all through the *"Purple Haze"* of Jimi Hendrix' guitar, the *"Pieces"* of Janis Joplin's *"Heart,"* hypnotized by Ravi Shankar's sitar, as a sea of tie-dyed t-shirts and flowers converged on Monterey Pop, converting the peace sign from a political statement to a fashion trend. And suddenly every high school senior had long hair.

XIII. (1967-68)
(Age 21, Junior Year)

My drummer, Jimmy Goldstein, had a standing gig each summer with the Sid Wayne Orchestra, at The Pines Resort in South Fallsburg, New York. The 'Borscht Belt' resorts of The Catskills were the last bastion of Burlesque and Vaudeville, where animal acts and jugglers, trapeze artists and comics, magicians and hypnotists, tap dancers and crooners; who showcased on "*The Ed Sullivan Show*," still found a relatively live audience. (Some more 'live' than others, conditioned on what percentage knew Moses personally.) Families booked in by the weekend, the week, the month, or the season, depending upon their pocketbooks. The wealthiest stayed at either Grossingers or The Concord, where headliners included Tony Bennett, Steve & Eydie, Joey Bishop, Buddy Hackett, etc. Next came the second tier hotels like The Raleigh, The Pines, The Browns, The Nevele, with headliners like Totie Fields, Hines, Hines & Dad (Gregory Hines, his father & brother), Joey Adams or Mr. Jiggs (the performing chimp). For the budget minded, there was the Homowack, Tamarack Lodge, or The President, with headliners like Hobo The Clown or Dingo The Dancing Dog. Then came the bungalow colonies, which were basically glorified trailer-camps, that could only afford local strippers and stars like me.

With Jimmy's help, my summer job resume landed a position at The Pines as Youth Director for about ten dollars a week and tips, room and board, and anything else I could do to generate income. This meant I was also a tennis partner and skating instructor by day, and sang in the bar or gave dance (or other less public) lessons at night. The main building was '60's modern,' turquoise and gold, and looked like the fins of a Dodge with large picture windows and valet parking. The gold-carpeted reception area was furnished with red velour sofas and a fake gold leaf Italian fountain. Double glass doors led into the main dining hall with massive round tables and assigned seating, based on length of stay. The season guests were placed by the windows and served first. Weekend visitors sat along the back wall. Kids were segregated to be seen but not dealt with. That was my job, which in compensation allowed me to dine with the guests while most of the staff ate leftovers in a linoleum room below the kitchen.

Housing for the waiters and general staff were dormitories with bunk-beds and screen doors. However, one of the perks of 'management' was a semi-private room in the 'old building,' once part of the original hotel before its renovation. I shared the two single beds and a wash-basin with Norman Axelrod, the Athletic Director. Norm was a strange contradiction; tall, dark handsome, and athletic, yet shy and insecure. From the outset we agreed that if either had a girl in the room, we'd place a rubber band on the doorknob. Poor Norman didn't get to sleep in his own bed very often. Another life's lesson… when it comes to getting laid, attitude beats looks and muscles every time.

Adjacent to the reception area was a large green-carpeted Card-Room, with birch-wood tables and red Naugahyde chairs, where the husbands spent most of their time when they weren't on the golf course. Below the Card-Room was an ice rink where I charged $15 per hour for private lessons ($10 of which went to the resort). The main building and Card-Room formed an 'L' around the shuffleboard and volleyball area and Olympic size pool, complete with triple high dive and surrounded by cabanas. From the large picture windows along the rear of the Card-Room husbands could wave to their wives down at the pool…or not.

Past the dining room and down the hall to the rear of the main building was the Night Lounge with a good-sized dance-floor, sound system and bar, preceding the brass and red leather doors that opened into the Main Show Room. The acoustically designed Main Room was built in three tiers leading down to an orchestra pit fronting the fully equipped raised hardwood stage and massive turquoise curtain, trimmed in gold. With dark wood paneled walls and maroon carpet, small red lights imbedded in the floor were complemented by red glass candleholders on the tables and recessed lighting in the ceiling. The top tier of seating was round-tops, but long thin tables lined the next two levels, perpendicular to the stage. Each stocked with wooden knockers for banging approval on the tabletops. (God forbid a woman should break a nail or a man strain his card-hand by clapping like a normal person... besides, the knockers made more noise.) Stage lighting included three massive follow spots that actually smoked when they heated-up and a full array of colors and effects on-stage. Sound was controlled by a mixing console in a glass-enclosed booth at the rear, which also serviced the lounge on the other side. When the houselights dimmed and the curtain parted, it was night school for me.

Shows opened with the 'big band sound' of the Sid Wayne Orchestra, followed by a 'family act,' before the kids were excused. But even the spinning plates of the jugglers or spangled trapeze lady somersaulting without a net, right there in front of our eyes, had an immediacy lost through the looking glass of TV. And then there was the sound of the knockers, like a plague of attacking woodpeckers, in place of canned laughter and applause. This was live theater! A 'warm-up act' usually preceded the headliner. (Comics with a Jewish accent were allowed a one-joke home-field advantage.) Attitude, ability, and technique were the keys. Like getting laid, attitude was paramount and the 'theory of trying too hard' persisted on stage, just like in life. Audiences turned on insecurity or turned-on to self-confidence, like a light switch. But all the confidence in the world couldn't compensate for lousy material or a lack of talent and techniques varied with each performer. Comics like Dick Shawn or Professor Irwin Corey, used the entire stage and body language to force a laugh, while others quietly drew the audience in, like Senor Wences, sitting on a stool, talking to his hand. Sergio Franchi's dramatic gestures accompanied his big voice, while Eartha Kitt stared at the audience with cat-eyes and gracefully prowled the stage. Timing and props were tools of the trade, like the spaces between punch lines that Alan King delivered to his cigar, or Scoey Mitchell's rapid-fire cigarette pointing between puffs. And for me, the revelation that the microphone, the stand, even the electrical chord, could be used, touched, held, squeezed, whipped, or placed on the floor for dramatic effect.

In the Night Lounge, after the main show, my apprenticeship continued, with Jimmy and a couple of guys from the band, performing *"What Kind Of Fool Am I"* or *"The Shadow Of Your Smile,"* a ginger ale in hand. I discovered the subliminal presence of a quality microphone as opposed to the harsh feel and feedback of cheaper models. Leaving the mike on the stand and adjusting it while speaking, gave me something to do with my hands and a place to go when I removed it. Returning it was the cue to open my collar and tie, while continually making eye contact with the listeners, even when blinded by the follow spot. Some performers actually stared over the heads of the audience, so as not to embarrass anyone (or perhaps piss-off a jealous husband). I chose to live dangerously, making eye contact with older women sitting alone or in groups, but never at a table with a man. Flirting with giggling teenagers up past their bedtime was usually safe enough (I looked much older in my suit and ginger ale), as was a passing glance to a single guy at the bar, since 'gay' still only meant 'happy.' But there were complications.

On those late-night weekends, Norman was already sound asleep in our room and hotel guests usually had roommates which meant, once again, even working in the middle of a fuckin' hotel, I had no place to get laid! Occasionally, there'd be an unoccupied room, but that involved making the bed afterwards and hoping incoming guests didn't notice the fresh cum stains on their sheets. This could also get housekeeping fired, so they tended to be a bit overprotective. What's more, staff was strictly forbidden from 'fraternizing' (from the word 'fraternity') with the guests, on threat of immediate 'termination.' This word took on a special meaning when considering that a number of the guests were directly related to Meyer Lansky. Like the cigar chewing 'shmata'(clothing) salesman, who caught his prune-faced wife pinching my ass, and later led me aside under his armpit. "You wanna 'shtoop'(screw) my wife, that's OK. Just stay away from my girlfriend," as he pointed with pride to a bleach-blonde bimbo doing her nails, "and your little pecker will stay attached... 'vishtase' (understand?)" Upon which he shoved a five-dollar bill in my palm, pushing me back toward the table where *"Mrs. Robinson"* fluttered her eye-bags, "Go, have a good time." So maybe eye contact wasn't such a good idea.

Conspicuous consumption was the cornerstone for catering to the clientele that arrived in the summer's heat draped in diamonds and furs and 'svitzing'(sweating) like you wouldn't believe. Like the 'shmata guy,' half the men were 60+, with secret 20 year-old girlfriends, and what looked like 80 year-old wives, making it hard to figure who was attached where. Families split on arrival, with the kids 10 to 13 reporting to me. Teenagers were on their own, and the little ones were handled by Jerri Cohen, a loud, hook-nosed hard-body from Queens, who didn't take shit from anybody (and was 'fair game' if I was brave enough to take a shot at her). The kids were often prima-donnas that believed if they couldn't hit a home-run they could always buy one and found the word 'tip' more powerful than 'please.' Used as leverage by their offspring, the once private 'thank you' had evolved into a public display of fake generosity for their parents to impress each other. That is when they weren't overdressing and bragging about never paying retail. So here I was, kowtowing to the very 'pigs' I had been demonstrating against, with my long hair greased back, singing *"The Impossible Dream."* The contradictions of life sometimes get lost in the moments of living.

The Catskill Mountains blocked the TV smoke signals of race riots burning Newark, New York, Detroit, Toledo, Grand Rapids, and Los Angeles that summer, while patrons of The Pines complained about their overcooked brisket and I was busy studying stage presence and trying to get laid without losing my dick. At first blush, I thought the safest partner would be Jerri, even if she was a little loud. As it turned out, she also harbored a deep-seated sexual guilt with a strange compulsion to say "No! Stop!" when she meant "Yes! Go!" This was especially disconcerting in the heat of passion, when she'd grab my ass and force me inside while literally screaming "Stop! Don't! It's Wrong!" On our second night together, poor Norman splintered the door off its hinges to rescue her, only to find Jerri leaping up and down on my cock, yelling "Stop! You Asshole! You're Raping Me!" He froze in mid hurdle, like a cartoon character caught in an X-rated movie, while Jerri continued to fuck my brains out until the hallway filled with gawkers and she suddenly screeched off to cover herself. Ever the performer, I laid back and asked for other female volunteers from the audience, while our hero Norman turned to a pillar of salt.

It's a fact of nature that the male will often risk death to get laid. Veronica Handelman, a sultry tan Ali McGraw look-alike, really belonged at Grossingers with her real-estate husband. Occasionally I'd catch the fleeting hint of recognition from her, hidden behind his trademark white-linen suit, but for weeks she remained a fantasy. Then, one smoke-filled night in the Lounge, after Totie Fields had done a terrific show in the Main Room, I blew the place away performing Peggy Lee's *"Fever"* and Sam Handelman invited me to join their table, with Totie, her manager, and Mrs. Handelman. There I sat with one of the wealthiest men in New York, a major star, and her manager all interested in me and my career, trying to control Giggy. Avoiding eye contact with Veronica, it began to sink in that this could be one of the most important nights of my life when Totie's manager gave me his business card.

The next afternoon, Mrs. Handelman made her usual pool entrance to the sucking-in of stomachs and the sucking-up of pool boys. As muscles flexed and high-divers jackknifed, Veronica stretched out on her chaise lounge acting oblivious to the attention. With the Lifeguards watching my kids, this was usually the time-slot to earn extra money. It took every ounce of self-control, not to drop everything when she lifted her torso in my direction and waved. Simply waving back as if it meant nothing, meant everything. A woman who usually gets what she wants, always wants what she can't have, and now Mrs. Handelman began to want me.

Instead of joining her, I plugged in the record player to organize the *"Hokey Pokey."* We humans have this weird fascination with synchronization. Whether it's a marching band, The Rockettes, or 'The Wave,' we like to watch or join a bunch of people doing the same exact thing at the same time. The *"Hokey Pokey"* especially appealed to kids and grandmas since you had to be either juvenile or senile to do it:

> *"You put your right foot in; You put your right foot out; You put your right foot in, and you shake it all about; You do the Hokey Pokey and you turn yourself around; That's what it's all about."*

It was always good for at least ten dollars in tips from the old ladies. So here I was, putting my foot in it, when Veronica began to apply suntan oil, and suddenly more than my foot was sticking out. This did not go un-noticed by her or old 'prune face' (Mrs. Shmata) in the front row, who began shaking her 'hokey pokeys' to beat the band. One look at everything flapping on *"Mrs. Robinson"* was enough to solve the problem until Veronica sat up straddling her chaise and with her legs wide open, carefully dripped oil between her breasts. Poor Giggy was becoming a bi-polar manic depressive. As much as I hate cold water, as soon as the record ended, it was into the pool for a swim.

Some of my kids came over to sit while I dried off and watched Veronica tease a banana daiquiri with her tongue. With no idea how we'd ever consummate the game (especially in light of the omnipresent white suit clearly visible in the Card Room window), I laid on my stomach to hold that thought, occasionally glancing over to play eye-tag, while joking with the kids. Then she did the unthinkable… Mrs. Handelman actually got up and began walking toward me. It was the mountain coming to Mohammad (with twin-peaks glistening in the sunlight). I couldn't believe she had the stones… and she didn't. She simply walked right by, accidentally dropping one of her towels as she passed and disappeared around the corner. Her scent was still on the white terrycloth as I reached over to place it on a table, and there concealed in the folds was a private cabana key and a napkin with three cryptic words scrawled in pink lipstick, "This Time Tomorrow." The clock over the shower-room door read 2:30.

Scheduled to perform at a nearby bungalow colony that night, Jimmy and I were forced to troll for local musicians desperate enough to accept $25 each for the night. We uncovered a toothy limp-wristed Fender bass player and an old colored keyboardist named Horsetail Williams, who purported to have toured with Billy Eckstine. It was downhill from there when the Beth Shalom Bungalows turned out to be orthodox 'Hasidik' Jews, direct descendants of a religious sect from a small town somewhere in Lithuania. All the men were cloned in identical long black suits with full beards and curls dangling in front of their ears that almost looked attached to their traditional squat black top hats. The women, in long-sleeved dresses and heavy black shoes, hid their hair under a wide assortment of bad wigs. (Of course, there was nothing here any stranger than worshipping the wooden replica of a half naked dead body nailed on the wall with thorns stuck in its head.) The 'Tzaddik' (Head Rabbi) led us past what looked like Appalachian shacks to a patchwork screened dining hall with a plywood floor. The sound system was an old tube amplifier in a gray metal box wired to a bare speaker, perched on a wooden side table. A large 1940's RCA radio microphone hung by its chord on a rusty stand in front of an upright Steinway, with only a few half-slices of ivory left on the keys. And it was about to get worse...

On these bungalow gigs we usually worked off a 'Fake Book,' an underground compilation of pirated lead sheets and lyrics. Now, 20 minutes before show time my two latest band members confessed that they couldn't read music. What I began to feel wasn't exactly stage-freight... it was more like panic. Trying to gracefully bow out, I suggested to the rabbi that perhaps they really wanted a Klezmer band. "No, no," he insisted, "Our young people are very excited for tonight." It wasn't clear which ones were the 'young people' (since even some of the woman had beards) or exactly what we could play that wouldn't be offensive (or if we could play at all).

As the residents began to stream in, the men and women moved to opposite sides of the room. Apparently a married man was not allowed to touch, or even brush up against a woman other than his wife. So, for safety sake, the sexes sat separately. After a brief introduction from the Tzaddik, I opened with *"Climb Every Mountain."* It turned into a variation on Masada (The legendary summit in Israel where Jews sacrificed themselves to the surrounding Romans.) Horsetail got it confused with *"Gonna Build A Mountain"* and the tooth fairy, who didn't know either song, simply let his fingers do the walking… somewhere else. The heavy microphone was hard to control with one hand and kept cutting out as blank stares suggested, 'If this is modern music, we'd rather be in Siberia.'

In an attempt at resurrection, I cued Jimmy to hit the brushes for a practiced dance routine. Then a revelation… how about dance lessons? Starting with a Cha Cha, but afraid to touch any of the women, as Horsetail began to pick out *"Cherry Pink And Apple Blossom White,"* I picked out a man from the sidelines and suddenly my bass player got with the program…now we were cookin'. With the bewildered look of a lamb being led to slaughter, my poor kosher guinea pig stared at his feet as if they belonged to someone else and froze. Standing directly in front of him, and holding both his hands, I chanted "One, Two, One Two Three… One, Two, One Two Three," exaggerating my steps with an encouraging smile, while both of us prayed for the same miracle. If this didn't work I was dead meat.

It wasn't a big miracle, but it was enough, when the biblical scholar began banging the beats out loud with his black Buster Brown shoes, to the utter delight of the community. Back and forth we traveled until, like teaching a child to ride a bike, we dropped hands and he was on his own. The family cheered. Next, as a prelude to the waltz, I started the whole place chanting "Uum Pa Pa" in unison and allowed the sacrificial lamb to return to his flock. Beneath their jackets all of the men wore something called 'Tzitzies,' embroidered shawls with fringes that were completely incongruous to their somber dress. With Horsetail playing the *"Lara's Theme From Doctor Zhivago,"* and the steady "Uum Pa Pa" of the audience, my next lesson found me embracing a heavy-set bearded man, swirling about the room, with his ear curls and Tzitzies waving as we brought the entire throng to their feet. Now with everyone standing, it was time for *"The Twist."* So with the men on one side and the women on the other, I picked up the microphone with both hands and folded back the chord to keep it from shorting. Doing my best Chubby Checker, the room shook with 18th Century European Jews in black suits and top hats and sweating wigs *"Twisting The Night Away."* As the chord began to come away from the mike, I sliced it off with a utility knife and tossed the microphone to the audience. The response was joyous. After seeing all the men dancing with each other, my new bass player was considering conversion, when the Tzaddik congratulated us on the "Best show we ever had," but deducted $25 for "damages."

At breakfast the Handelmans socialized at their normal window table, with Veronica just out of eye contact, obstructed by the white suits of waiters, busboys, and her husband. The question was, would I take a chance on blowing everything just to sleep with the most beautiful woman in the world?... silly question. Off to The Raleigh with my kids for a baseball game, the problem was time. If the game went into extra innings, I could miss my opening. By making sure that every kid got to play, we lost big time, also assuring that no one wanted to stay around any longer than necessary. It was just before 2:00 PM when we made it back to the pool at The Pines. Neither Veronica nor Sam's white suit were anywhere in sight, which made it easier to slip into their poolside cabana un-noticed. Once inside, reality set in. What the fuck was I thinking? What if someone saw me fumbling with the key and reported it? What if they came down for a swim together? What would I say when they opened the door? How would I explain the key? The cabana itself was just four walls on a cement floor, a cot, a chair and vanity table, and in their case, a private shower. That was it. And for the next twenty minutes there were kids splashing, people talking, chairs folding, glasses clinking, and no way out other than the way I came in.

Still really a boy playing at adulthood, I had only fantasized about older women. Veronica Handelman was the embodiment of that fantasy and when the door handle turned and she slipped into the room, I was back in the attic with daddy's *Playboys*. Clad in a yellow silk robe to contrast the tan, her simple "Hi" was poignant. While I sat tongue-tied at the vanity table, she casually walked in, dropped her purse, and stepped up on to the cot to peer out the ventilation window near the ceiling, checking for Sam's white suit in the Card Room window. From my vantage point below it was explicitly clear she had nothing on underneath. Like a ballerina perched on one leg with the other open just enough, she held her position, pretending to strain for a better view. My dick was doing the same. Coquettishly glancing down over her shoulder, she flirted with my crotch before making eye contact again. "Your bathing suit looks a little tight," she joked. "Yeah, I've been meaning to do something about that," I answered as she turned, allowing her robe to open in front. An erotic tan line emphasizing the forbidden places where not even the sun was privy, highlighted a perfectly manicured triangle of black pubic hair. Maintaining eye contact, her fingers slipped gracefully down to ever so gently touch the lips in the center of the small mound between her thighs. Taut nipples still hid behind the yellow silk until she leaned forward and I came in my bathing suit, forming a wet spot, pulsating as Veronica whispered, "Perhaps I can let it out for you." The elegant arch of her breasts danced in the air as she leaned back, continuing to touch herself before stepping down off the cot and crouching in front of my open legs. Her nipple brushed my knee as her free hand reached into my trunks, cold at first, but quickly warming up and down. Both of her hands now wet, she threw back her hair and closed her eyes, quietly purring in synchronized motion. Her nipples began to get harder and more erect along with me. Wetting my fingers to tickle her tips, she stifled a squeal, then quietly moaned as my palms messaged her breasts. Suddenly her eyes opened for an instant of ecstasy before ripping down my suit with both hands and forcing me to cum in her mouth. Her head continued to bob in my lap in exquisite warmth. Between her lips and her hand and her mouth and her tongue, I completely understood how a male preying mantis could allow itself to be eaten alive. The silk robe fell to the floor as we moved to the cot and she lay back with her legs wide open. Gently opening the petals and toying with her stem, barely able to see over the mound of pubic hair, her undulating increased with muffled whimpers. Alternating between my finger and tongue in a continual steady rhythm, she began bucking like a bronco, clenching the side if the cot with one hand and the back of my head with the other. When the series of orgasms climaxed, I reached up and grabbed her breasts, squeezing her nipples hard, prolonging the moment. Now I was in control, pinning her legs back with my arms and plunging inside, feeling her soaking the mattress beneath us.

It was almost 5:30 PM when Mrs. Handelman made one of her regular checks at the window and Sam's suit was gone. Having taken a shower earlier (but unavoidably detained), this time Veronica grabbed a bathing suit from the wall, threw on her robe, and stopped at the door just long enough to flash me, before darting off to apologize to her husband for falling asleep in the cabana. I could have been fired for neglecting my kids, but it would definitely have been worth it. As it happened, no one even noticed.

That night Vanilla Fudge was playing locally and a bunch of us went to get our heads blown off. As summer radio opened with Billy Joe McAllister throwing *"Something Stupid"* off a bridge and the Young Rascals *"Groovin',"* groups like Vanilla Fudge, The Turtles and the Doors began pushing the pop envelope and decibel level. Earplugs were unheard of when amplifiers began to hit the pain threshold for the first time and scared the shit out of me afterwards, as mouths moved muffled for at least an hour. Meanwhile, back at my room, sitting up on the night table next to the bed, was a letter from Sam Handelman. With his company letterhead in the corner and my full name typed out, it was clearly not from Veronica. It took a while to get up the courage to finger it open, unfold the single sheet of paper inside, and a second reading before the words completely registered. Tomorrow night Totie Fields was coming to The Browns, and afterwards her manager was bringing an agent from William Morris to catch my show… not what I expected!

At breakfast amidst the finger pointing, Sam waved me over to confirm the message. Veronica commented that I had, "the attitude, ability, and technique to blow them away," precariously parroting from our private conversations. (God, I wanted to fuck her again!) Casually thanking her, and then focusing on Sam, I didn't hear a word he said. In the Main Room that night, Henny Youngman had them in stitches with one liners delivered to a violin he never played, after which the Night Lounge filled to capacity for my big shot. Half way through the second number the dignitaries arrived, declining a front table for one in the rear. (Probably for an easy escape if I stunk.) This was the culmination of a journey that started with *"Kisses Sweeter Than Wine"* at the Fourth Grade Dance, and by the third encore, with the room in an uproar and my sweat-drenched white shirt glistening in the spotlight, everyone knew I was destined to be a star.

A week later found me in the glass corner office of a skyscraper in Manhattan, with a contract to wonderland. There was one major catch... it meant leaving college, thus losing my student exemption and eligible for the draft. A guarantee of placement in the National Guard sounded reasonable but had its complications. Next was the music... Did I really want to be a Las Vegas lounge act? Sure it would have been great in the 50's but... And what's more this was only an Agency and Management Contract, not a record deal. On the other hand, it was a major step in that direction. Then there was my commitment to Mom and Dad to 'at least get a college degree,' and the money they had already invested. There was no immediate answer to that one, other than they loved me and would probably support whatever decision I made... eventually. But there was also college itself, the lifestyle, and my place in that world. Would I sell out my principles for a career in show business? Probably... In the end, it came down to self-confidence. 'If these guys believed in me now,' I reasoned, 'they should be there when I graduate.' It just made more sense to finish college first. Or maybe it wasn't self-confidence at all, but a fear of failure (or success). It was the most difficult decision I'd ever made. And one I would second-guess the rest of my life.

The country had aged dramatically that summer, with Rip Van Winkle locks waving across a campus that only a few months earlier was fitfully sleeping in conservative bliss. Now every long-haired freshman chanted slogans like "Make Love Not War" and "Down With The Pigs!" throwing two fingers instead of one at the body bags coming home from Vietnam. Negroes, 'blackened' by the summer's race riots, read *"The Confessions Of Nat Turner"* and heard Stokely Carmichael and H. Rap Brown of the Student Non-violent Coordinating Committee now advocating 'armed revolution,' as Thurgood Marshall was appointed to the Supreme Court in an attempt at appeasement. George Lincoln Rockwell, leader of the American Nazi Party, was gunned down by his former assistant just before the Beast of Buchenwald, hung herself in a German prison. And Brian Epstein, the man who discovered The Beatles, OD'd on sleeping pills playing *"Lucy In The Sky With Diamonds."* Violent images of atrocities coated the airwaves and seeped into our daily diet accompanied by a heavy dose of drugs.

Against this backdrop, the BAK House Murder took on a surreal 'theater of the absurd.' We refused to let Useless play The Murderer, fearing he'd identify too closely with the part and perhaps never come out of it, making him The Victim instead (also a better fit since we all wanted to kill him at one time or another). The leading role went to Handman, whose 'poker face' and sleight-of-hand talents made him the natural selection. But this year, instead of panicking, pockets of pledges just locked in rooms, they did so much dope they didn't give a shit. Lineups were also a problem, since half of them couldn't remember their own names, let alone those of the brothers. During Ice Baseball we'd sit a pledge on a block of ice and he'd just look up and say, "Hey man, this is cool shit," not realizing his ass was frozen until two days later.

Drugs had basically two purposes, to enhance the senses or numb them, depending upon type and quantity. Marijuana (Grass) was the entry level euphoric that varied in potency depending upon how many stems and seeds (and fillers like oregano) were mixed with the leaves, followed by the more concentrated Hashish (Hash), which required a pipe of some sort to smoke. 'Uppers' like caffeine or methyl-amphetamines (Speed) were used to accelerate the metabolism while 'downers' like Quaaludes (Ludes), did the opposite. Hallucinogenics ranged from nature's peyote and psilocybin to chemical variations on Lysergic Acid (LSD). Like during prohibition, everything was illegal or restricted and readily available.

Fireman Bill's pad became our private opium den, music and massage parlor, complete with a Doberman guard-dog named Oppy, who especially liked Hash in his Alpo. Nobody, including The Pigs, would come near the place without an invitation (and prior warning). Still a control freak and hesitant to take anything mind-altering, second-hand smoke nevertheless had me on a perpetual 'contact high,' alternating between giggling and eating everything in the refrigerator. Jam sessions were a regular activity along with varying degrees of group sex and therapy. But occasionally there were problems...

For the most part I kept my fraternity life separate from The Pad, living two simultaneous lifestyles. Allowing a few of the brothers a glimpse behind the beaded curtain one night, turned out to be a mistake I would never make again. At first it was fun watching the counter-culture virgins explore wonderland to the sound of a bubbling water pipe and Ravi Shankar on the Circle of Sound. Megaphone cackled as Handman dripped saliva on a sizzling light bulb and Shybo blissfully floated in the corner like a massive Buddha. But when an extra tab of acid kicked in on Shybo, he began to freak. At first staring at his hand as if he'd never seen it before, when his expression changed from bewilderment to fear, so did mine. "The green blood... the green blood is trying to kill me!" he bellowed, bumping to his feet and staring in disbelief at his right hand, desperately holding it back with his left. "It's flowing...it's flowing inside... I have to move in the opposite direction ... I know what I have to do." And he began spinning, slowly at first, then faster, repeating, "I know what I have to do," still clutching his own hand and knocking over everything around him. The nearby green lavaliere lamp shattered on the floor with splashes of color seeping into the rug as everyone ducked for cover and Shybo lost his balance, crashing into the pole lamp in the corner. With light bulbs popping, he looked like a beached whale in a panic attack, flailing at demons only he could see. "There's spiders in the walls," he cried, now staring into the wallpaper, "They're after the green blood.... Don't let them eat my hand...don't let them eat my hand" and he punched a hole in the wall, slicing the top of his wrist as it withdrew. Everyone that wasn't trapped upstairs was out the front door, naked or not, and Oppy went berserk, straining at his chain, white teeth snapping and howling at the refugees huddled beneath the yellow door lamp. Strangely inside, the site of his own blood had a calming effect on Shybo, now hunched over in the corner, licking his hand and sobbing, "It's red again. Thank God, it's red again. See?" And he turned to display his bleeding fist. Knowing he could re-erupt with the slightest provocation, we carried on a soothing nonsensical conversation until his sentences began to connect and it was safe to let the shivering expatriates back inside. Even though it was clearly the drugs, I could never look at Shybo with the same eyes again, reaffirming my fear of artificial intelligence.

Registration was a resounding success that semester, with green covered Student Faculty Evaluation booklets everywhere. It was so cool to look up a course and check out the professor's rating before signing up. Now a sociology major, half the required classes after 10:00 AM were taught by rejects, so I enrolled in Life Drawing, Photography, Political Science (kind of an oxymoron) and Social Psychology from both the sociology and psychology departments, figuring I could cross-collateralize the workload.

Life Drawing was a trip. It required sitting and staring at naked girls for two hours of college credit, giving new meaning to 'liberal arts.' (Unfortunately I wasn't allowed to practice photography at the same time.) Actually nudity, without the mystery, the 'forbidden factor,' and the allure of the chase, is not sexy. It was those first few minutes of class, when the robed model walked in. Anticipating the size and shape of her nipples, the extent of her pubic hair or the color, the firmness of her body or the amount of space between her thighs (and of course, what she'd be like to fuck!). Once she disrobed and sat there like a lox (smoked salmon), it was the ultimate anti-climax. Soon I'd find myself concentrating on a shape or a line, the play of light or the texture of the charcoal, forgetting completely that the figure I was trying to capture was a live naked girl. That was until her break, when the art object stood up and woke Giggy. With her vagina right there in touching distance, a little eye contact was all it took to remind me why I was there in the first place.

Conforming in my non-conformity, while everyone was 'toking on weed,' looking for natural ingredients on soup cans and going 'vegetarian,' I made a deal with the local pizzeria to sing at the manager's 'private parties' for leftover pies each night, the more meat the better. (Pizza is probably my favorite food group. With three basic ingredients: tomato sauce, dough and cheese, the variations and toppings are then endless and taste different everywhere.) Down the street from the pizzeria, Jasmine was helping put the finishing touches on The Black Market Bookstore And African Emporium. Inter-racial dating was a rarity, so it was *"Guess Who's Coming To Dinner"* when we'd come back to the pizzeria together for a slice. Males saw a slave-master and his concubine, females, a social climbing bitch and a sucker. No one saw two people (including us). For me it was the kick of controversy, coupled with a heavy dose of sexual curiosity, and for Jasmine, a statement of defiance. It took a while to discover that under her attitude was a just frightened little girl trying to 'get over.'

On a cold but sunny afternoon, dabbing paint around The Black Market sign from a wooden ladder, I paid no attention to the dark blue Chevy slowing down on Kirkwood Avenue. When the window shattered below me, gunshots hit the shingles to the snapping of what sounded like cap pistols. Pieces of wood flinched on the porch where I fell. Diving headfirst for cover, smack into the red brick wall of the adjacent building, the second window blew out from the inside in a delayed reaction with a shutter of glass and flames. As the car pulled away through the billowing black smoke were the familiar eyes of hate still fresh in my memory book behind the nose-picking finger of Bailey Links. Luckily, Jasmine and another worker inside escaped through the back door before the explosion and miraculously no one was killed. But for some reason both the police and fire department seemed to be off duty that afternoon as the green and red paint bubbled and crackled, licked by the flames that enveloped the wood-framed building for half-an-hour before the first sirens sounded. Dating back to the days of Wyatt Earp, there's been a thin line between law-breakers and its enforcers. Making reports to jackal-smiling officers only re-enforced the Nazi images of another precinct room. At the time of the 'incident' it seemed, Bailey had been playing cards at McNutt with 'friends' (some of whom were now in uniform taking our statements).

The enormity of what just happened really didn't sink in until the next day, standing in front of the charred remains, like the Camp Thunderbird Totem Pole, and the sardonic smoldering sign now as black as its name. There was no musical soundtrack to make it feel momentous, or special effects or camera angles or enhanced sound. It just happened, like a car crash. But the sight of the gutted wood carcass was frightening and infuriating. And, along with the cuts and bruises of the morning after, were bristles on the back of my neck from a close brush with death. This wasn't a fraternity prank or a 'coming of age' escapade but a sobering reality check. I began to shuttle between the Student Government offices and BASC as The Black Market became a flashpoint for the civil rights movement on campus. Soon there were green and red cans everywhere, collecting money for its re-construction along with massive 'peace rallies' on the lawn in front of the Student Union, merging with the anti-war movement, to form a united front against hate, stupidity and deceit.

Ironically, one target became 'The Greeks,' and secret discriminatory clauses hidden in some of the national bi-laws. Appearing like a street-beggar at a bankers convention, to the blue blazer Inter-fraternity Council I was a radical, and to the campus radicals, a collaborator (the ultimate non-conformist). As poker-faced local chapters denied the existence of such clauses, my 'ace in the hole' was the Race Relations Advisory Group of the YMCA and direct access to the University Administration through the Student Liaison Committee. With a hand of irrefutable hard evidence compiled by a network of 'Y' informants, I didn't think it would be a big deal for the offending chapters to simply disavow themselves from any such language. Not realizing that this was a direct attack on the national fraternities, the truth became a 'wild card' when their lawyers sat in.

First they denied the authenticity of the documents (even though we all knew they were real) while at the same time threatening to prosecute whoever supplied them. The YMCA was named as a potential defendant, for "suborning and encouraging the illegal actions of person or persons under its jurisdiction for the procurement of private and confidential materials in breach of both written and implied contractual obligations." Meanwhile both BASC and the Student Government were served with injunctions barring us from making public any of the "unauthenticated documentation" in our possession on threat of prosecution for "libel with malicious intent." In other words, they denied the existence of the evidence while threatening to sue if we showed it to anybody and prosecute whoever gave it to us if we tried to prove it was authentic. I just couldn't believe the university would knuckle under to this type of intimidation, but was about to get a practical lesson in 'political science.'

It seemed that some of the university's most substantial alumni were members of the fraternities and sororities under attack, which meant any action by the Administration could cost the school millions in grants and donations, not to mention legal fees. No one returned my calls. Meanwhile the YMCA regretted that, "due to a temporary shortage of funds and available space," they could no longer house us, which was in "no way to imply a lack of commitment to the Group or its goals." The kicker came when we arrived to find that in boxing up our supplies, many of the files had been inadvertently 'misplaced,' including the original evidence…But obstacles can be opportunities in disguise… Since we had no way of knowing where the evidence had gone, I could not be blamed when green and red flyers began to appear all over campus reprinting the most flagrant clauses, identifying each by fraternal organization, backed by a photo of the smoldering Black Market over the drawing of a Klansman. Now, relocated in Hairy's living room, the telephone began ringing. We really didn't need the phone though, we could hear the yelling all the way from the Administration Building.

After weeks of huffing and puffing, a compromise was reached in the form of a waiver to be signed by all on-campus housing, neither confirming nor denying the existence of any alleged discriminatory language or practices but agreeing to delete any such provisions that might exist and to renounce any such behavior in the future. Three fraternities refused to sign. One eventually came around, another was thrown off campus (all five members), and the third forced to divest itself from its national and change its name.

At the BAK House we went a step further, co-sponsoring the first inter-racial fraternity-sorority dance with black, Alpha Kappa Alpha, all proceeds to be donated to The Black Market Reconstruction Fund. To perform that night, the sorority suggested a group from Gary rumored to have just signed with Motown. The YMCA gym filled to capacity when a black family, starting in their teens down to a little guy not more than eleven years old, took the floor with their father running the sound system. The Jacksons blew us all away. Especially little Michael, who sang like an angel while spinning in provocative routines that had every girl in the place, black and white, fantasizing about taking him home with other than motherly intent. (But everything has its cost, including fame and a childhood denied.) One disturbing note was Charlotte, apparently drunk again. When I tried to catch her she just spun away slurring that she "never had a father and didn't need one now," eventually stumbling out of the room on the arm of a football player and his friends, one of which was Masowski, now on the varsity squad. A new dance trend was also launched that night, when a group of blacks raised a fist in rhythm, chanting what sounded like an ode to the popular Roadrunner cartoon, "Ah Beep Beep...Ah Beep Beep." The gimmick caught on, and soon kids all over campus were dancing with one fist in the air mimicking Roadrunner. This was especially amusing to the members of BASC who knew that what those first few blacks were really chanting were the initials 'B.P.'... for 'Black Power!'

Inspired by The Jacksons and dwelling on my decision to put off William Morris, it was clear I needed some 'rock-n-roll in my soul.' Also, 'bread' was tight and the jazz group just wasn't makin' it. A rock band playing fraternity dances could probably pay for a fridge full of late night munchies, not to mention fix my car which, blind-sided by a tree, was now held together with rope and masking tape. Even though it was 'un-cool' to dwell on material things, driving around with no windows in November was fuckin' cold! But where would I find the time, or musicians willing to learn the latest hits? The answer came while watching *"Star Trek"* with some high school kids at the Student Union and realizing they had afternoons and weekends free and knew every song on the radio. An ad in the Bloomington paper, "Auditioning high school seniors for a band to play college frat houses for BIG BUCKS!!!" resulted in weeks of bad hair, uncovering a cancer cluster of the 'musically challenged.' I was convinced it was a conspiracy, a practical joke, or Thalidomide in the water supply that resulted in so many tone-deaf musicians in the same geographic location. Then a group came in called The Boomerangs who proceeded to nail a cover version of *"The Letter"* by the Box Tops, complete with their own sound system and Leslie Speakers attached to a Farfiza organ. My trek to "boldly go where no man had gone before," was mercifully over. The deal was, they would practice on their own all week, and I'd sit in whenever possible to lay in the lead vocals. My main responsibility was lining up gigs. It also took a while to agree on a new name. We settled on The Sot-weed Factory, in deference to the recently revised John Barth novel.

While The Sot-weed Factory practiced *"Light My Fire,"* draft cards were burned in front of churches and federal offices in Chicago, Philadelphia, Boston, Cincinnati, Portland, Oregon, and Oakland,

California, where Joan Baez was among those arrested for 'disturbing the peace.'(Not an editorial comment on her voice.) It was *"A Happening"* when more than 50,000 marchers arrived at the Lincoln Memorial suggesting *"All You Need Is Love"* as they moved across the Memorial Bridge to the Pentagon, where hundreds were beaten and arrested by helmeted soldiers and federal marshals. The sidewalk was splattered with blood as a Roman Catholic priest did the same to Selective Service files in Baltimore urging, "move with us from dissent to resistance." Although Aaron Neville pleaded *"Tell It Like It Is,"* Vice President Humphrey assured the nation that we were "winning the war in Vietnam." (And if we believed that, he had a bloody bridge to sell in Washington.) With thousands pleading for a change of heart, Dr. Christiaan Barnard actually pulled one off in South Africa while Allen Ginsberg was arrested with famed pediatrician Dr. Spock (not to be confused with *"Star Trek's"* Mr. Spock), trying to close down an armed forces induction center in New York City (politics and strange bedfellows). And even though it was acceptable to display Che Guevara's bullet-riddled body and heads being blown off in Vietnam on the nightly news, the nation was appalled at the graphic violence in *"Bonnie & Clyde."*

In both my Social Psychology courses we learned how to convert common sense into technical jargon like 'cognitive dissonance,' which basically says we're not comfortable when the truth doesn't jibe with our beliefs. To compensate we either rationalize or ignore what doesn't fit. The country was definitely experiencing some serious cognitive dissonance. But the education system itself was symptomatic of a larger problem. The sociologist believed society caused individuals to act contrary to their beliefs while the psychologist insisted it was individual behavior causing society to malfunction, each discounting the other's perspective. As a practical matter, it meant every paper I wrote had to justify the professor's viewpoint or it was 'wrong.'(So much for cross-collateralizing the workload.)

With the next semester came another reality check...I didn't have enough credits in any one department to major in anything and graduate as a senior. Both Sociology and Psychology required Statistics, which I'd never pass, and neither acknowledged any Art or Philosophy courses. Although my English credits were recognized by Social Sciences, it wasn't reciprocal. That left Political Science, which accepted almost everything, but there I only had three credits. That meant nothing but Poli-Sci for the rest of my college career, including summer school, to graduate. FUCK!! I should have signed with William Morris! Arranging that Hairy be assigned as my 'faculty advisor' we devised a solution… With a new Race Relations bill passing through the British Parliament, who better to go over and report on it than the administration's Advisor On Race Relations? In Hairy's opinion a summer's study and paper could easily warrant nine credit hours from the Political Science department. But this would require approvals and the only way to deal with the bureaucracy was to circumvent it. President Stahr was a little surprised to find me on his doorstep. When I explained that without his OK he might have me around for an extra year, he was happy to comply. (It's always good to know The President.)

Meanwhile, back at the frat house, my living quarters were relegated to The Cage with no freshman allowed, since the last two who shared my room flunked out. Despite the drugs and depleted membership, line-ups and practical jokes still kept us on our toes, especially when the pledges poured manure in the halls one night and pulled the fire alarm. In retaliation, my favorite line-up was the 'Sex Test.' The pledges were gathered downstairs and told there was a hooker up in the Trophy Room waiting to fuck and grade each of them on their ability. Any pledge who failed to 'perform' would be blackballed (in every sense of the word). One at a time, accompanied to the pitch-black third floor, each was told to feel his way to the Trophy Room and knock. A sexy female voice beckoned from within, requesting he remove his clothes before entering. As the door opened in the darkness he could hear her moaning, asking if he was naked and ready. Then came the flashbulbs and lights for the brothers and a room full of sorority sisters to applaud. The pictures would be enlarged for display at the upcoming Toga Party (and The Sot-weed Factory's maiden performance).

The Toga Party was an ideal first gig, with everyone draped in bed sheets, kegs of beer and a giant wooden vat in the center of the floor, filled with grape Jell-O to be trampled by barefoot dancers, nobody really cared about the music as long as it was loud. University rules required that an approved 'house mother' be present for all such occasions to lend "an air of civility" to the proceedings. But the authorities were unaware that our loveable Mrs. Moorehead had a secret affinity for the bottle that rendered her unconscious when accompanied by an aspirin or two. In fact that night, an hour after dozing off in the TV room, a few inebriated brothers managed to surreptitiously remove her support hose during *"Rowan And Martin's Laugh In,"* inserting a dab of Readi-Whip between her thighs while Arte Johnson keeled over on the screen. Downstairs the simulated Greek orgy got pretty authentic, making me a hero in the incredulous eyes of my band of high school virgins. They'd heard stories about fraternity dances but couldn't believe the vision of drunken coeds disrobing to the strains of *"Louie Louie,"* or the disgusting sight of Useless emerging from his bedroom, face and robe covered with blood from his plastered paramour's monthly period. The soggy floor sloshed with beer and Jell-O and whipped cream as we pounded out *"Sunshine Of Your Love"* to the throbbing bodies sweating with fists in the air chanting "Ah…Beep! Beep!" And The Sot-weed Factory's inauguration was a resounding success.

This was more than could be said for President Johnson. Gearing up for the next election, he barely won the New Hampshire primary over 'peace candidate' Eugene McCarthy while Senator Robert Kennedy officially threw his anti-war helmet into the ring. January's Tet Offensive by the Viet Cong had severely shaken the nation's confidence, especially watching General Westmoreland flatly deny the scenes of civilians and soldiers hysterically fleeing Saigon on the screen behind him. Under other circumstances it might have been laughable, except for the fact that we now had more than a half a million Americans over there ordered to die defending the honor of political prostitution. It got personal when LBJ abolished graduate school draft deferments and Hairy received an official letter that opened with the word, "Greetings." The night before his induction physical he did all the drugs in the medicine cabinet while we painted every inch of his body (including private parts) in DayGlow peace slogans. His clothes stapled with press clippings documenting years of anti-war protests, poor Hairy was so stoned that morning he couldn't figure out how to open the induction center thumb-latch door. For a moment he just wavered like a brightly colored pinwheel, press clippings and long hair flapping in the wind, until another pigeon herded him inside. Greene was eventually granted 'Conscientious Objector'(CO) status and required to provide two years of community service in lieu of the military, which meant I still had a 'faculty advisor.' But the real victory came the night before April Fools Day when President Johnson shocked the nation announcing, "I shall not seek and I will not accept the nomination of my party as your president." This meant that, provided the democratic party not shoot itself in the foot, there was a good chance either McCarthy or Kennedy could be our next president and we'd finally get out of Vietnam.

Our elation was short lived. Five days later the Rev. Dr. Martin Luther King Jr. was gunned-down and the country exploded. In Chicago, 5,000 federal troops were dispatched to quell the sniping gunfire, street fighting and raging fires. Five died in Baltimore where Governor Spiro Agnew ordered 6,000 National Guardsmen in to arrest over 500 looters. A white graduate student was pulled from his car and stabbed to death while attempting to drive through a black area of Cincinnati, and entire sections of the nation's capital went up in flames. But these were just cracks in the surface from ripping off a scab of complacency that had only just begun to heal over the JFK amputation. The real damage was deep within the nation's soul as we lost another limb to a cancerous genetic human defect; A reminder that beneath the bandages and restraints of civilization, we're just animals that tend to kill our own. Within a week, the Civil Rights Act of 1968 was signed into law in an attempt to cauterize the wound. But as a practical matter, hate and distrust continued to ooze in black and white and would fester for years to come.

Perhaps it's just the irony of existence that we need disease, famine, and warfare to survive as a species, killing our peacemakers while glorifying killers as a mechanism of population control. On an episode of *"Star Trek"* we sent a robot out into the universe to wipe out 'infestations' only to have it turn around and come after us. Are we not in fact an amazingly adaptable virus, destroying our host planet as we nest and multiply? And what happens when we finish fouling the water and the air and the atmosphere and the earth? Will we mutate and adapt, or in the words of *"Tobacco Road,"* "blow it and start all over again."…Unanswerable questions to be relegated to God… instinct… and Giggy.

A month after King's assassination, Robert Kennedy won his first presidential primary in Indiana and the U.S. and North Vietnamese opened peace talks in Paris, where the student protest movement had sparked a kindred flame. By the end of May, France was on the brink of civil war as both students and workers rebelled against 'the capitalist establishment,' virtually shutting down the country. To our north, Pierre Trudeau and his Liberal Party took control of Canada while ripples of radical idealism even surfaced in the 'Prague Spring' of Czechoslovakia. More blacks were wearing 'Afros' now, separating themselves from whites, as *"Hair"* moved from an off-Broadway Greenwich Village theater to the heart of the 'Great White Way.'

Skinny-dipping at the quarries was a well-worn Bloomington tradition. Deserted limestone excavations, often hundreds of feet deep, would fill with dark blue water and serve as a repository for over-used cars, driven off the cliffs by teenage townies and college students that liked to get naked and jump in afterwards. Afraid that Giggy would raise his ugly head, I was hesitant, but encouraged by Life Drawing the previous semester to try and 'become one with nature.' As it turned out, a bunch of people sitting around 'au natural' made it glaringly obvious why there was so much money in the clothing business. And dangling freely in the water with childhood memories of snapping turtles and snakes convinced me that this 'back to nature' shit was not my thing.

Returning to The Pad that afternoon, the sight of Charlotte waiting in stiletto heels and a push-up bra was a shock on many levels (giving new meaning to the concept of extremism). She'd apparently been pacing for hours, just out of Oppy's snarling range. And there was something different about her. Gone was the self-destructive air, replaced by the slightest hint of Chanel #5 and a sense of purpose. Bill was away for the weekend and once alone inside, her controlled passion was both surprising and titillating as she stepped out of her dress but remained in the heels, unsnapping but not removing her bra before ascending the red carpeted ladder to the loft, then allowing the bra to flutter back down through the hole in the ceiling. As my head popped up through the opening, Charlotte lay naked on the bed, an index finger encircling her rigged nipple, tongue wetting her lips while those sensuous green eyes peered through her tousled jet-black hair. God, she was breathtaking!

We made love for hours, laced with threads of conversation and laughter. In the throws of passion I'd occasionally flash on that night at the frat house, but this was a different girl now holding me, eyes sparkling with poise, intelligence, and wit. Along with other emotions was my own sense of pride in her makeover. But an unforeseen side effect would come to light in the morning. At one point the tin roof rattled with raindrops, a signal to let Oppy in for the night wagging his stump. Sharing the apartment with Oppy was like living with a Mafia hit-man, playful and loving with a propensity to kill on command (not exactly in the spirit of 'peace and love'). Back upstairs, lacking natural light, time was marked by periods of sex, sleep and occasional food breaks until, totally satiated, we snuggled in silence before Charlotte haltingly sat up to face me. Re-living our first encounters on the bus, the late night phone calls, the exhilaration in our dancing, my patience with her overindulgence and acting out, and the quiet stability I provided...we were both in tears when Charlotte asked me...to MARRY her!... Holy Shit!!

Caught completely off-guard, I had no idea what to do or say next. While I was having sex for the past fourteen hours, she had been 'making love.' To paraphrase the immortal words of *"Cool Hand Luke's"* Strother Martin, "What we had here was a failure to communicate!" At first all I could do was hold on, like a boxer winded by a low blow, stalling for time. But there was no way out of the ring without hurting her. Beginning by acknowledging my pride in the person she'd become, and that she was probably the most beautiful girl I had ever seen, "but with my lifestyle and aspirations, marriage and committing to one lover was something I would probably never do." Charlotte latched on as I tried to get up, insisting that it need not be a 'formal' marriage, that she could even share me with other girls (I must admit, that gave me pause to think). Sensing her desperation I laid back and waited. But each time I moved, she tightened her grip, insisting that she could "sew and cook, and support me in every way a man could ever want." Changing tactics, I turned toward her and sat up holding her hand. "Be realistic Charlotte," I contended, "You'd only come to resent me." "No! I swear that would never happen!" she pleaded, "Just give me half a chance? You know you love me… admit it! You said it yourself. You'll never find another girl as beautiful who will love you like I do." Now squeezing my hand, "Admit it! Admit it!" What could I say? I couldn't tell her I didn't love her, and I couldn't tell her I did. There was nothing for me but to reach the ladder …quick. Oppy stood at attention when I hit the floor, then cocked his head at the sound of Charlotte upstairs crying. Some 'Henry Higgins' I turned out to be.

That week, while packing for my summer in England, I couldn't shake the guilt and pain as Charlotte called everyday, waiting outside my classes, and sitting on my doorstep. Then just when I thought it couldn't get any worse… Robert Kennedy was smiling with two fingers in a 'victory sign' after winning the California primary (coincidently also the 'peace sign'). I'd even arranged to return in time for the Democratic Convention to support him. Moments later he lay bleeding on the cement floor with two bullets in his head. "Some men see things as they are and say why." He would say, "I dream things that never were and say, why not." Now those things would never be. At the funeral, Senator Edward

Kennedy choked back his tears, "My brother need not be idealized or enlarged in death beyond what he was in life. He should be remembered simply as a good and decent man, who saw wrong and tried to right it, saw suffering and tried to heal it, saw war and tried to stop it." …And then there were none… Riding to the airport for what should have been the beginning of a new adventure, felt more like running away.

XIV. (Summer - 1968)
(Expanding my world)

My first impression of England was that it was old. No glass skyscrapers or billboards, in fact very little advertising at all. Even London's famed Piccadilly Circus was tame by U.S. standards, with one large neon Coca-Cola sign, some theaters, and a statue from the 1800's, around which 'bobbies' directed traffic and patrolled with little sticks. I knew the country had been almost bombed out of existence during WWII, but it appeared to have been reconstructed with the original parts. Submerged from birth in an environment littered with loud commercialism and numb to the noise, now suddenly without it, I could feel the quiet. The only 'groovey' sight was a brightly colored theater poster for *"Yellow Submarine,"* where a street musician sat, one foot kicking a drum while the other flattened a squeeze box, playing guitar and singing the theme song, a harmonica protruding from around his neck. Flocks of 'birds'(girls) in the vicinity however, were distracting, with eyelashes longer than their micro-mini skirts cut off just below the cunt. After dropping a few coins in his cup, I spent the next two hours shooting legs with my photography class Pentax before heading into 'the tube' with my suitcase and guitar.

The tube was as antiseptic as it sounded, with not as much as a gum wrapper on the floor. The university had arranged a 'bed and breakfast' in Muswell Hill, a working class neighborhood about 25 miles north of London. Also unlike New York subways, tickets were purchased by destination and it took some doing to figure out the pence, pounds, and unfamiliar places. Actually the money made a lot more sense than ours in different colors and sizes relative to value, and with very few 'Yanks' yet bumming overseas, people were helpfully curious. The row of red brick and wood tenements, trimmed with chimneys and TV antennas, were a good twenty-minute walk from the Highgate station in a subdued British version of Brooklyn. The family putting me up (or putting up with me) maintained a strict breakfast timetable and firm "no pets or guests" policy. Otherwise, I was on my own. Breakfast consisted of either cornflakes or poached eggs on toast, and thick undercooked bacon lined with grizzle along the upper edge. They also served a sausage made with blood and fat, deceptively named 'Black Pudding.' English food was not one of its attractions. The popular 'Ploughman's Lunch' was a cheese and pickle sandwich served in bars with warm beer and dinners usually involved some form of meat, baked beans, and two overcooked vegetables. Of course there were also Indian restaurants where 'mild' meant only first-degree burns of the mouth and esophagus. My favorites were the Whimpy Bars for cheap hamburgers and 'chips,' thick fries served in newspaper with vinegar and salt.

'White and wimpy' was also my first impression of the typical British male (which meant more horny girls for me). The real 'characters' were the Scots and Irish who boozed, brawled and bellowed with the best of them, as I would come to learn first hand. Earl's Court was London's answer to Greenwich Village, lined with 'folk pubs' and imitation hippies. Arriving in my orange bell-bottoms, guitar in hand, I asked directions from a pair of legs dangling under a car. When the rest of the body came rolling out, a full-bearded Scotsman with a wrench in his hand looked up and appointed himself my 'manager.' Alastair was a burly, bubbling, loveable braggart, who invented my resume off the top of his head for Duncan, the owner of his favorite Irish pub with the unlikely name of La Fiesta. Within hours I had a trial gig at an Irish pub with a Spanish name and a Scottish manager who'd never heard me sing. (Now all I needed was a French whore.) Just to be safe that night, Alastair padded the house with friends and musicians. It wasn't exactly The Kiva, as beer mugs banged on the tables and soon half the crowd was up around the microphone singing *"Wild Thing"* in unison. As glasses fell off the bar along with some of the well-oiled patrons, Duncan was ringing the cash register in rhythm and laughing out loud. I was hired, three nights a week for the next two weeks with Alastair handling the finances. But the night was still young, or so I thought...

It wasn't even eleven o'clock when Alastair and his crew waved goodbye as they tottered down the wet alley behind the club and I headed off to catch the tube, guitar case and head spinning out to Earl's Court Road and smack into the *"Sounds Of Silence."* The street was completely deserted. Not a shop was open. Nothing moved but a blinking amber street signal and the rain. Even the tube station was closed. No one bothered to tell me that the trains stopped running at ten, after which the only public transportation were sporadic all-night buses that stopped someplace in British Idaho. While attempting to scale a chained fence into Hyde Park, a Bobbie appeared from the shadows to politely explain the 'no loitering' laws and 'escort' me to a bus-stop. Returning home in time to hear Black Pudding sizzling in the kitchen, I hung my soaking orange bell-bottoms out in the morning haze before blacking out.

The weather in London, ranked right up there with the food. If it wasn't raining, it was faking it, except occasionally when the clouds took on a yellowish hue and Brits flocked to Hyde Park to 'sun bathe.' The English economy reflected the weather. Firmly in the grip of the worldwide recession, with outdated factories prevented from modernization by a strongly unionized workforce, the pound had already been devalued the year before. Things were in fact so desperate that Prime Minister Harold Wilson had secretly authorized preparation of a plan to abandon sterling. If implemented, it could have meant frozen foreign assets, a ban on travel or cash leaving the country, and a possible collapse of the currency. Defense cutbacks led to withdrawal of troops from east of the Suez and a heated discussion on possibly relinquishing sovereignty of the Falkland Islands to Argentina, while students demonstrated against the U.S.-Vietnam policy in downtown London. Superimpose on this, a massive influx of Kenyan Asians thrown out by the African country when it won its independence, to compete in England for non-existent jobs and strain the welfare system. The result was a cloudburst of racial violence and political unrest.

An MP named Enoch Powell advocated 'sending them all back where they came from,' warning of race riots in "rivers of blood" as

Parliament wrestled with the Race Relations Act, counter balanced by a tough new immigration law. Unfortunately for me, news coverage was sparse, filtered through the BBC, with practically nothing topical printed in any of the public or private libraries I visited throughout London. With no 'official' copies of the proposed Race Relations Act available through any government agency, as it was still 'under discussion,' it soon became obvious that the only place to find the story would be in the black community. I then discovered there was no such thing. 'Coloureds' in England were primarily in three mutually exclusive groups: Indian, West Indian, and Pakistani, splintered by a history of religious and cultural animosity. There would never be a unified 'Black Power' movement in Britain, which in the end would be the theme of my paper, especially considering that the Race Relations Act had no provisions for policing its declarations. Wandering through the immigrant communities was not especially dangerous, in the absence of drugs and weapons, just depressing in its overpopulation and eventually led me to the Cultural Center For Indian Studies. There, in the rear of a red brick building, an unassuming silk-haired scholar spent his days translating a library of news clipping, articles, and legal documents as they related to his community. These included drafts of proposed legislation with detailed critiques, and would serve as my research center every day thereafter.

On the nights I performed, Duncan let me sleep in the bar after closing. That was until the night Molly O'Donnell came in with a group of friends. With flaming red hair, half the guys in the place were staring at her braless breasts swaying to *"Hey Jude,"* beer mugs in the air on the final round (the other half were blind drunk). Alastair had invited Molly and a carload of her friends down from the Hornsey Art School, coincidently located near my rooming house. Scrunged in the back seat of their Vauxhall, her legs spread across my knees, Molly slugged the brunette to my left when she inadvertently stuck her tongue in my ear. The kid on my right was passed out against the window while the couple in front was having trouble staying on the road as she kept falling in his lap. I probably should have been the 'designated driver' except for the fact that I didn't know where the fuck we were and couldn't get used to driving on the wrong side of the road anyway. The car smelled of cigarettes and beer as both Molly and the brunette began taking turns kissing me and sharing a Viceroy. When I explained the "no pets or guests" policy standing at my front door Molly lifted her sweater while the brunette lifted her skirt. Hell, I could always find another place to live.

With my mini bed frame leaned up against the wall and mattress on the floor, bordered with rolled up sweaters, underwear and dirty socks, the noises emanating from my cubical could not have been mistaken for sleep. Molly was vivacious and full-bodied, with ultra-white skin and a tendency to squeal, while Jill (the brunette) was languid and sensual, moaning up until the moment of climax when she'd inhale a whimper with her mouth wide open. Molly liked to be on top, with everything bouncing, occasionally grabbing her own breasts or anything she could get her hands on. Jill liked to recline, arching her back to meet me, fingering herself while pinching her small hard nipples with her fingertips. At first we were alternating when Jill reached across to slide her fingers in O'Donnell, who stared for a long moment of uncertainty until Jill introduced her tongue. The rest of the night gave new meaning to the phrase "One for all and all for one." We took turns sneaking to the bathroom and slept well through morning before slipping back down the stairs and out into the daylight, avoiding the confrontation I knew was yet to come.

But confrontation was in the air. The Hornsey Art School was more contemporary than its surroundings with cheesy wallboard construction, picture windows, and another administration at odds with its students. The strict dress code and ban on 'political activities,' inspired a group of dissenters to force their way in 'artistically clothed,' with anti-war posters and peace signs. Already clad for the occasion, it just seemed natural to join in. This was obviously not an American demonstration, as the protestors politely permitted a terse pronouncement by a school representative before demurring to "vacate the premises in good and orderly fashion."

During the afternoon it was like summer camp, telling tall stories of U.S. college takeovers to the finger painted novices with peace-placard coup sticks. Later that day tensions rose as the police arrived with dogs and BBC cameras in tow. The images of angelic British art students with flowers in their hair feeding apples and cheese sandwiches to the German Shepherds made international headlines and everyone went home proud of their day's work.

I got back to find my room locked and a note from the landlord. Seeing this as another opportunity instead of a problem, I packed off my research and extra clothes to finish the paper when I got home. Molly agreed to mail a series of post-dated letters I prepared to the University and I was off to see the world with jeans, camera, t-shirts, underwear and a bathing suit rolled up in a blanket on my back. Although the Eurail Pass was good for unlimited European travel, by joining the International Student Association, I could fly almost everywhere for the same price. Hairy had supplied me with an SDS booklet of cheap underground youth hostels and with the extra earnings from La Fiesta, I could sing for food money. Desperate to see the sun, my first stop would be by train to Copenhagen, with student flights to Rome, Barcelona, Paris, and back to London for my connection home.

With an extra day to kill before leaving, and everything packed away, I caught the tube to the first Wimbledon "open" to both amateurs and professionals. Gradually sardine-canning to the front of Center Court's "free standing zone," I marveled at the speed of Clark Grabner's serve and the freakish Popeye forearm of Rod Laver. This was the epitome of British sport, with everyone sitting in their proper place, the players in 'Wimbledon whites,' and silence in the stands, except for an occasional gasp and polite applause, where appropriate. Calls were never argued, not even by little American Billy Jean King. This was a country where playing by the rules was more important than winning and social status was established at birth, unalterable by wealth or power. On a human level, it meant you weren't judged by what you had, but who you were as a person, and what you did for a living wasn't as important as how well you did it. Despite my other misgivings about England, these were attitudes well worth holding on to.

After a farewell performance at La Fiesta and a final night with Molly, I slept a bit on the train to the coast to catch a new high-speed boat called the Seacat. Once underway the monstrous catamaran almost took flight, pontoons barely skimming along the top of the water as it sailed at what felt like 90 miles-an-hour. More sleep, a series of train connections and a ferry brought me in to Copenhagen by late afternoon, emerging from weeks of fog into the sunlight of a magical kingdom of blondes and health nuts. Everyone, at every age, was on a bicycle, barely leaving room for the pastel mini cars and electric trolleys trailing between the cycle lanes lining the streets. Water fountains bubbled next to sidewalk cafes, bakeries, fresh fish wagons and smorgasbord windows of delicacies on little round slices of black bread. My SDS booklet referenced a centrally located hostel for about $3 a night, with two rooms of bunk-beds (segregated by sex) and a central bathroom, partitioned down the middle. My bunkmate was a broad-smiling Nigerian with no English, but animated expressions that were eminently readable, especially when he saw my camera and made it clear not to leave it unattended. This ran counter to everything the student movement symbolized. Coveting material things was our parents' 'bag.' Longhairs never stole 'things,' we shared them. Catching my reaction, the manager explained in broken English that the problem wasn't my fellow travelers but drug addicts from town who sometimes slipped in unnoticed.

Denmark was an amazingly permissive society, probably because the king was secretly a queen. Sex shops openly displayed magazine covers of men in full bloom and naked women with their legs wide open, ignored by everyone except foreigners like me. Copenhagen sparkled at night with rivers and canals running through the city and Tivoli Gardens in the center on Hans Christian Andersen Boulevard, where I half expected Danny Kaye to pop out singing the *"Ugly Duckling"* song. Tivoli was an adult theme park without the rides. Floral arrangements lined paths to band shells ranging from rock, to polka, to chamber music, an outdoor 60's music mall, where the town gathered after work to socialize. There was even a small folk club to audition after a good night's sleep and a day in the sun.

The closest beach was a plain flat sandy area outside the city, sprinkled with sidewalk vendors providing ice cream and hotdogs covered with crispy deep-fried onions. On one of those philosophical nights at The Pad 'under the influence,' came the notion that life could be a perpetual dream and reality, a delusion. This was a plausible explanation for Merete. Every kid in America who ever opened Playboy fantasized about meeting the Playmate of The Month. Here I was on a beach in Denmark, finding Danes to be very 'private,' when a friendly voice broke the ice in English. Merete was a Canadian Playmate, who just finished shooting her spread, and was on vacation in Copenhagen visiting family. One look at her perfect air-brushed body in a brief black two-piece, with blonde movie-star looks smiling through designer sunglasses and I suddenly felt skinny in my bathing suit. She was apparently accustomed to guys overcompensating with stupid conversation while they held in their stomachs, and simply ignored it until I relaxed. By the end of the day there were five of us speaking English on a circle of towels in the sand, including two kids from South Africa and an Aussie named Ned, who I picked up at the hot dog stand. That night we all agreed to meet at a jazz club Merete recommended, to hear Yusef Lateef.

Back when I was at Gerdes Folk City in The Village, Lateef could be found at The Blue Note or The Village Gate with the likes of Donald Byrd or Cannonball Adderley. Shunning the 'jazz' label as too confining, he played every wind instrument you could imagine (and some you couldn't) often simultaneously, in a mixture that could best be described as 'World Music' before it had a name. Permissive Copenhagen appreciated his lack of boundaries. Trying to impress Merete, I made believe I knew him. Ned quietly sat back and smiled while I took over. Maybe they didn't have Playboy in Australia? But at the end of the night Merete left with him.

Before heading to the beach the next morning, I ventured down to the port to view the famous Little Mermaid, a small stupid bronze statue sitting on a rock (I guess I wasn't in a very good mood). Back at the beach, Merete was mercifully alone and happy to see me. We spent the day laughing, joking and not mentioning Ned. Unable to join me for dinner due to a 'family commitment,' we agreed to meet again the next day. You can't remake a first impression or change a girl's mind once you're 'just friends,' but with my flight to Rome two days away, it beat being poked in the eye with a pointed stick.

That night the folk club at Tivoli flatly refused me an audition, so I set up directly in front, opened my guitar case, threw in some coins and began to play. Nobody cared. Apparently in a society where anything goes, exhibitionists don't. My saving grace was a genuine love of music and when I stopped looking for attention and just played from the heart, people began to listen. (Somewhere along the way, I had forgotten the 'theory of trying too hard.') One such listener was a shy little blonde who sat off behind a tree and closed her eyes while I sang. When I started to pack up she quietly slipped away. 'Not so fast,' I thought to myself, following her pink jacket past the polka center and a statue peeing in the air, when suddenly the jacket disappeared. Rushing down the flowered path toward the main entrance, all I could do was guess on her direction, but the jacket was nowhere in sight. For the first time in a long time, I felt alone. Then, ever so quietly, a soft voice behind me whispered, "I liked your playing very much." I turned to Krista, standing there in her pink jacket, blushing as she stared down at her toes and almost kissed her right then and there.

A few of the smorgasbord places along Hans Christian Andersen Boulevard were open all night. We stopped for mini breads of smoked salmon and cheese, then walked along a canal toward her apartment. Apologizing for her nearly perfect English, (outside America I discovered most of the world was multilingual) she was also fluent in Swedish, German and French. A draftswoman by trade, her pale yellow apartment included a drawing table of precise mechanicals alongside the freehand sketch of a dancer that might have been a self-portrait. Contrary to her delicate demeanor was a quiet competence, assuming we were going to bed and casually undressing while we talked. But she crossed her arms and popped up to kill the lights when I pulled back the covers to look at her, then lit a candle on the night table. Reaching for the sheets again to cover up, I stopped her with a gentle kiss and followed the flickering light with my tongue, licking her nipples while fingertips lightly danced in her hair, then down the length of her body.

Krista slept as morning poured in. Her surprisingly full breasts, more blonde than white, sat up and smiled over the edge of the cotton sheets tucked around her. The evening had been a series of *"Dangling Conversations"* entwined in athletic eroticism. It was that wonderful beginning, unwrapping each other for the first time. She'd been a dancer, forced to fall back on her drawing by uncooperative knees. Unsure whether to accept the added responsibilities of a promotion, we debated living in the moment as opposed to my goal obsessed lifestyle and contentment verses happiness. A bundle of dualities, she was at once vulnerable and strong, simple and complex, private and passionate. I knew I should let her sleep, but couldn't resist her breast teasing me in the sunlight. It was past noon before we made it out of bed and Krista agreed to come with me to meet Merete.

After Merete's rejection, there was a sense of validation in arriving at the beach with Krista. But wilting in public, Krista clung to her blanket as we walked out on the sand. Another contradiction, a former dancer uncomfortable in the spotlight. Even on the weekend, it was easy to spot Merete, like a starlet surrounded by extras. When she stood up and waved gleefully at our approach, Krista smiled at the uninhibited gesture. The two of them were soon jabbering in English, but occasionally glancing over and laughing at me in Danish. Krista actually had a better figure, hidden under her heavy fabric bathing suit, and sensed my thoughts with a private smile. But Merete was stunning. While most of the sun-bathers made a point of keeping to themselves, by the end of the day, no less than four guys had joined us to 'practice' their English. These included a good-natured German mountain climber named Hans, who also took our number. Merete reveled in the attention while Krista chose instead to cuddle up with her head on my shoulder. Merete offered a sisterly smile of approval as we left her there entertaining the troops.

My flight to Rome was at 11:00 AM, which meant I'd have to leave Krista at least three hours before. When the moment of truth came, I watched the sunlight stream in through her yellow curtains, across her sleeping breasts to my ticket on the night table, fluttering in the morning breeze… turned over and went back to sleep. I was never leaving Copenhagen! It was probably 10:00 AM when Krista woke me in a panic. Feigning distress, I reached for my pants and fell off the bed. When she stifled a laugh, I popped up, slipped on the sheets and knocked over the night table, ending up with the ticket in my mouth. That did it… we spent the next two hours rolling around naked on the floor, giggling and fucking... If the university could only see how dedicated I was to my research!

When Krista went back to work the next day, sitting alone in her apartment, reality set in. Then Hans called, probably expecting her to answer. As I suspected, he had been with Merete until she left and was looking for another playmate. I offered myself as a substitute. After visiting Town Hall and the World Clock, we agreed that Danish girls were a much worthier attraction. Taking up a position in the center of town, we soon had two lovelies crossing their legs discussing rock 'n' roll and mountain climbing in broken English. When I left to pick up Krista, Hans had his arms around both of them, smiling like a cat about to eat a canary (or two).

Krista and I spent that night in each other's arms facing the truth. I had a year to go in college and my dreams and she really just wanted a family. It was more than timing, we were two completely compatible people who were totally incompatible (sounds like something Yogi Berra would say). It was cloudy that morning when she left for work, and I had trouble reading the train schedule, partially because of the tears but mostly because the damned thing was in Danish. Then Hans called again, and when I told him I was leaving, he suggested we go together and "stop in Innsbruck to teach me mountain climbing." Sounded like a plan. At the platform that night, he boarded to reserve a compartment while Krista and I held each other until the last minute. Faking a pratfall when I turned for the door, Krista forced a smile and stood there softly waving with her hand just below her chin as the train pulled away. I had trouble seeing her, partially because of the tears, but mostly because she was waving in Danish.

The train was basically empty, so we sequestered a compartment convenient to the bathroom and proceeded to unpack for dinner. My provisions for the week included a Swiss Army Knife, a loaf of bread, a large pink Scandinavian salami, mustard, and the requisite chocolate bar, all in a plastic bag. Hans, on the other hand, flipped over his elaborate back-pack to remove a personal little dining/writing table, napkins and real silverware, tins of food including various pates, caviar, and smoked herring, a collection of cheeses, two different breads, and an assortment of pastries and butter cookies. All to be washed down from his goatskin 'bota' of fine red wine. I had a heavy glass bottle of Evian water (plastic bottles weren't available yet). Although going to the same place, we were obviously coming from two different directions (or vice versa).

Hans was a little vague about his source of income, but probably would have been flying if not for me. With our feet up on the empty seats, he confessed envy at my ability to attract people but suggested that, if we wanted room to sleep, we keep to ourselves and pulled down the hallway shades. This was the 'milk-train' making all stops to Munich, where Hans needed some 'provisions' before heading on to Innsbruck. At one point during the night, intending to use the bathroom, I opened the door to the sight of people sleeping on top of each other in the corridor, apparently assuming ours was a private compartment. Feeling guilty, I thought we should at least allow the young mother with her baby and a frail looking old man to join us. That didn't exactly work out. Like opening a faucet, people poured in until we were all equally uncomfortable, including some Russian soldiers leaning on their rifles... a practical lesson in communism.

Munich was in the midst of constructing a new subway system in preparation for the upcoming '72 Olympics, with dirt piles, digging, and detours everywhere. Luckily Hans knew his way around, and despite the devastation, the streets were brimming with activity. Like London, much of the city destroyed during the war had been reconstructed in the image of its past, with no glass skyscrapers or commercialism, just large Bavarian buildings, punctuated with spiraling cathedrals on almost every block. Founded near a Benedictine Abbey and at one time the center of German Catholicism, 'Munchen' literally means "at the monks." The Marienplatz (center square), once the site of jousting tournaments and now filled with vendors and street performers, was bordered by the Gothic Neues Rathaus clock tower, with almost life-sized glockenspiel figures mechanically moving across its balcony as much of the populace did the same below. A few blocks from the square, Hans dragged me into a store with hunting and fishing gear in the window where suddenly I was being fitted for a pair of hiking boots I couldn't afford to buy or carry later. Hans insisted on paying, assuring me he could always find someone to use them, and that my sneakers just wouldn't hold up in the mountains...(but would I?)

The train to Innsbruck snaked through lush green pastures chugging across jagged rock formations and mountain passes used for generations to climb into the snow-capped Tyrolean attic. Like the train to Munich, it was unusually crowded and the Innsbruck waiting room clogged with teenage Russian soldiers, sitting on their backpacks, all part of some massive military exercise. But one step out of the station was like walking into an alpine picture-postcard. An 800-year-old city of chalets and castles encircled by serrated white-topped summer mountains poking up through the clouds, and probably the only place in the world where straight men actually walked around in lederhosen. Hans had booked us into a stucco chalet with a red cable roof, flower boxes of geraniums and embroidered curtains at the windows, antique furniture, and a bath and shower, not to mention our private wooden balcony overlooking the Inn River. This was definitely not a youth hostel. When I told him I couldn't even afford the towels, Hans just laughed and announced that this trip was on him. That night I tried wiener schnitzel for the first time (sliced and breaded deep fried veal), along with a green salad, string beans in a butter sauce with sliced almonds and fresh cut fries, followed by an ice-cream topped wedge of German chocolate cake... my first complete meal in Europe. Now I could tackle the mountains, but first I would sing for my supper...

Just up the street from our hotel was a cavernous basement tavern filled with red-checkered tablecloths and a wall of beer kegs, where predominantly male patrons congregated for the nightly shared experience of a community drunk. There were no microphones or performers but songs would start at a table and spread across the room or compete with another nearby, edged on by mustached men behind the full length wooden bar. Barmaids, trussed up in red vests forcing their breasts to overflow into white ruffled blouses, circulated about the room replacing pitchers of beer and baskets of pretzels, often spilled on the cement floor when the crowd came to its feet in a spontaneous wave. Hans waved to a friend as we joined a table of revelers who stared when I ordered a Coke, then laughed with understanding at the news that I was an American folksinger. "Play a Bob Dylan," one called out. Then another, "Yah, yah, you know *'Blowin Inda Winda'*?" Clearly an alien in a room of men in knee socks and suspenders who thought yodeling was normal, once again music proved the great equalizer as I reached the chorus for the first time and the whole room joined in phonetically. Now the center of attention, Hans basked in the shared spotlight, initiating *"Michael Row The Boat Ashore"* with a beer mug salute as an accordion player joined us from behind the bar. On the final "Hallelujah" the room broke into applause, capped by what looked like a fraternity drinking contest, accompanied by glasses banging on the tables (like the knockers at The Pines). "Now, we teach you some songs, yes?" the bartender announced. "Yah!" I answered, and the room erupted with another round.

By the end of the night Hans was literally under the table and I had been treated to every Germanic drinking song ever written. Wired on caffeine and sugar from a night of Coca-Colas, I was easily the last person standing in Innsbruck when the Tavern door closed behind us. Hans was feeling no pain, which was good because he kept falling on the cobblestones while assuring me he wasn't drunk. Eventually propping him up against a wall, I ran back to the hotel to deposit my guitar and returned to catch him peeing in someone's flowerbox while a rooster sounded an alarm someplace in the distance. Needless to say, we didn't do any mountain climbing that day.

When we finally did venture into The Alps, the jagged volcanic rocks made it clear why Hans replaced my sneakers with rugged leather boots. Each mountain route offered alternative pathways, some more physically demanding than others. The intermediate trails had me shimmying between crevices, with muscles not generally used in folk singing (or the *"Kama Sutra"*), so after the first hour it was the paths of least resistance for me. But what an amazing feeling of self-validation to reach the summit, balancing on a rock ledge jutting above the clouds, looking down on mountain tops and facing my own mortality, feeling that tingle in the pit of my stomach, fighting back the impulse to simply open my arms and fly. The brisk thin air was also dizzying, and it was reassuring to feel Hans' firm grasp on my shoulder, pulling me back from the edge. On our way down we stopped to rest along a grassy slope. Looking out over the tiny dots of people and livestock one could almost understand how Hitler conceived *"Mein Kampf"* growing up here. Hans had mixed feelings on the subject. While admitting that the German people would forever carry a sense of guilt for what they had done to the world, at the same time he was tired of apologizing for a generation he had nothing to do with.

It was dark by the time we made it back to the hotel. With cuts and bruises and muscles aching in places I didn't know I had, a hot shower only served to emphasize the damage. The last thing I remember about that night was closing my eyes for a few minutes. The next morning I awoke to find my body on strike, demanding less strenuous working conditions and refusing to move without gentle assurances that things would be different. Checkout was at noon. Repacking his knapsack, Hans laughed at my 'hangover' as I wobbled to the bathroom with a new appreciation for the aged. The train station was still filled with Russian troops as we said our goodbyes with false promises to 'stay in touch,' and Hans boarded the train back to Munich. Even though it was fun, a perceived difference in class had felt more like using than sharing each other's friendship. A little worse for the wear, I had nonetheless eaten well and still had most of my Scandinavian salami intact.

The train-ride through The Dolomites was spectacular, followed by an obvious change in climate, emerging in the warm Italian countryside, which quickly heated up as the un-air-conditioned train continued south. Soon sliding down the windows only served to circulate the summer's heat. As the bright pink salami took on a new pliable consistency and aroma, not un-noticed by the hitch-hiking flies, my poor gushy chocolate bar made the bottom of the plastic bag look like a disposable diaper. But by late afternoon with nothing else to eat, it tasted much better than it looked. Arriving in Florence at dusk, I found a hostel that was more like an inexpensive hotel with small private quarters and a central bathroom and shower. My room looked out on a typical narrow stone street lined with Vespas (personal motorcycles) that sputtered around the city, interrupted by an occasional Fiat or Alfa Romeo, barreling through and forcing pedestrians to flatten against the walls. It seemed that human behavior warmed up with the climate. The Scandinavians had been private and aloof. The Germans and Austrians were definitely more physical and outgoing, but the Italians hugged each other just to say hello and enjoyed arguing about everything with exaggerated hand and facial expressions. Later that night an attractive streetwalker in a paisley dress flirtatiously negotiated with a patron below my window before I fell asleep with a hard-on and a smile.

In the light of day Florence itself was a hand-carved work of art, with the simplest hallways adorned by frescos from centuries past. The city was teeming with young artists from all over the world, sketching and working on renovations to art that had been damaged by floods a few years earlier. Walking ancient streets with stone framed doorways designed when people were shorter, eventually led to structures like the Duomo cathedral, originally built in the 13th century and 'newly' renovated with pink, white and green marble in the late 1800's. The heart of the city was the Piazza della Signoria, where heretics were burned at the stake during the Inquisition in front of the fortress-like Palazzo Vecchio, guarded by a replica of Michelangelo's *'David'* on one side, where the original once stood, and Ammanati's *'Neptune'* on the other. The original *'David'* was moved to a museum where it now stands, with its dramatic oversized hands and conspicuously small penis, probably in deference to the male egos of Michelangelo's Medici sponsors, who might not have wanted a 'hard standard' against which to be judged by their wives and girlfriends. With very few Americans around, I drew a pretty good crowd performing at the foot of the *'David'* replica until broken up by police, who apparently felt I was detracting from the solemnity of the art (or simply had to prove the size of their dicks).

Initially overwhelmed by the 1,500 Lira thrown in my guitar case, it only converted to $2.40 (a lot less today). Next came my quest for authentic Italian Pizza, which turned out to be a 'fool's errand' since pizza was more an American passion and only served where they catered to tourists. Undaunted, I eventually found a place that lost something in the translation, interpreting 'sausage and pepperoni' to mean 'salami and green peppers.' (Apparently no one in Italy had ever heard of pepperoni.) But everybody in the restaurant seemed to have a relative in The States, and soon I was surrounded by stories and wallets full of pictures, encouraged by the excitable owner, occasionally adjusting his obvious hairpiece as he spoke of visiting Times Square and The Empire State Building someday. When a communist two tables away inserted something about our presence in Vietnam, the owner threw him out. Surprised at my own reaction, even though I agreed with the dissident, I didn't like hearing it from an 'outsider.' Realizing this was not a rock 'n' roll crowd, an appropriately emotional version of Gershwin's *"Summertime"* paid for my dinner.

After another day of simply walking around awestruck at man's ability to capture emotions in stone, my next stop was Rome, once the center of the universe. Hairy's book came in handy in locating a cheap hostel a few blocks from the Spanish Steps, a staircase at the site of the Spanish Embassy to the Vatican, and customary hangout for longhairs and street level drug dealers. Unlike everyplace else I had been in Europe, Rome was loud and filthy with indifference, bordering on disdain, for the crumbling artifacts of its past. (I understand things have since changed, but in the 60's the neglect was pervasive.) Vatican City, on the other hand, which is actually an independent country sitting in the center of Rome, was so clean they had a 'dress code.' A geographic version of *"The Odd Couple."*

Playing at the Spanish Steps for a destitute audience of fellow travelers only resulted in occasional coins from 'real tourists,' there to see us 'hippies' and throw alms at the animals. Some of my compatriots were so stoned they thought I was Bob Dylan in disguise and kept asking for my autograph (which I humbly gave in his name). By mid afternoon most of the shops were closed in deference to the summer's heat, which offered a good opportunity for sightseeing, minus the crowds. My first disappointment was the once magnificent Colosseum, eroding from the horns and screeching tires of incessant traffic closely circling the walls. Inside, the combat field had long-since collapsed revealing the skeletal underbelly of passages once used by gladiators and lions. Also, perhaps jaded by 'The House That Ruth Built,' the place just didn't look big enough for Ben Hur's chariot race and 50,000 spectators (unless they were midgets). As it got darker the cafes came back to life and painted ladies took to the streets, framed by flashing neon lights. Back at the hostel a pretty kindergarten teacher from California caught me at the front door and asked if I would accompany her for a bite to eat. I simply assumed Lenora had seen me playing that afternoon, or was taken by my animal magnetism, but as it turned out, I could have been anybody. She just needed a bodyguard.

With local women locked in chastity belts of Catholicism, foreign females were 'fair game' for demonstrations of Italian machismo.

Until that walk I had been oblivious to the harassment, as leering lotharios would literally pass by and pinch her, even in my presence, then wave it off with a wink and a smile. I could only imagine what it was like on her own. A recent USC grad, even though traveling on a budget, her manicured nails and tailored clothes suggested she wasn't exactly homeless, so I didn't feel guilty when she paid for dinner. Afterwards we decided to visit the Trevi Fountain, the inspiration for *"Three Coins In A Fountain"* and Anita Ekberg's memorable splash in *"La Dolce Vita."* Tucked away in a small piazza, the dramatic winged horses and mythical sea-creatures were barely visible, its wishing-well coins mixed with gum wrappers and bottle tops, another example of Roman disregard. Despite her hair pulled back in a conservative bun, Lenora's childlike eyes sparkled behind a protective veneer that kept us at arms length. Back at the hostel, she suggested we meet in the morning and perhaps visit The Vatican together.

The forbidden local girls were rarely seen, but often dark and stunning. On the other hand, they all seemed susceptible to a strange hereditary trait that turned their mothers into blimps. As Lenora came down the stairs with her dark hair and eyes, I couldn't help but wonder if she was part Italian. Despite her adventurous spirit, there was very little chemistry between us. This was new for me, since I never before met a pretty girl I didn't want to fuck. I couldn't put my finger on it (literally or figuratively), but usually my mind's eye could picture a girl climaxing. In Lenora's case, the closest I could get was a vision of her licking an ice-cream cone.

They were actually shooting a movie in the center of St. Peter's Square, which stretched out like a massive film set of the Holy Roman Empire, with St. Peter's Basilica surrounded by literally hundreds of towering columns and statues, protecting a courtyard of manicured stone the size of two football fields. Lenora crossed herself as we stood for the first few minutes and just stared. A guided tour (required inside) began with Michelangelo's pure white *'Pieta,'* carved when he was 20, then passing a bronze statue of St. Peter, its foot worn away by centuries of idol worship. At the Sistine

Chapel it was hard to conceive of anyone painting upside down on a scaffold for four years, especially with my muscles still sore from one day of climbing. Even muted with age, the ceiling remained a miraculous depiction of man's creation of God in his own image. After a day of gilded ceilings, the religious renderings of Raphael, Caravaggio, and da Vinci, and real estate representing un-calculable wealth, the thought of Catholics starving around the world seemed irreconcilable.

With very few unattached girls to chose from (none that spoke English) and Lenora uncomfortable traveling on her own, ours was a marriage of convenience. Although requiring three meals a day and avoiding any activity that might chip a nail, she did contribute cash to cover the added costs of comfort. This meant air-conditioned buses to visit the ancient Roman Forum and The Catacombs, both littered with cigarette wrappers and food containers. The last day before my flight to Barcelona was spent in the coin-laundry and once again playing on the Spanish Steps, fed up with culture and ready for some fun. It was also the first time Lenora had seen me perform. By early evening she was sitting much closer, the veneer gone along with the image of ice-cream cones. With a floor between us and unable to consummate the marriage in Rome, we would travel to Barcelona together.

The morning flight was definitely a case of 'you get what you pay for.' The vintage dual-engine crop duster vibrated down the runway and into the air with propellers loudly protesting the full load of twenty-eight passengers. It was a half-hour before Lenora loosened her grip as the stewardess offered a choice of Italian, French or Spanish newspapers with headlines about an Algerian plane hijacking. Our tray tables were down, holding plastic containers of 'mystery meat' and salad, when everything literally hit the ceiling and the plane dropped out of the sky. Momentarily weightless and restrained by the seat belt, I could see the flight attendant bang her head as the sea was suddenly visible beneath us. In that instant of panic, we all lost our breath and held on for dear life. Shaking out the cobwebs, the stewardess motioning with palms down for everyone to remain calm as the plane regained altitude. Removing a slice of lettuce from Lenora's hair, my comment that "Italians really knew how to toss a salad" got picked up in waves of nervous laughter while everyone clutched their hand rests and didn't let go until the wheels finally touched down in an exhale of applause.

My initial intention to complain was squelched by rifle toting police, who stared at my long hair with distain. (Franco's armed dictatorship was apparently not open to constructive criticism.) Waiting for Lenora's oversized suitcase, a heavy-set man standing next to us did an extravagant double take, with giant yellow teeth, waving his finger, "Ah, Meester 'tossed salad,' veddy, veddy goood!" Then laughing out loud, "The leetle planes, sometimes they no fly so goood, huh?" (A minor detail omitted at the International Student Association travel desk.) Arriving on Sunday was also not such a good idea since most of the city was closed, including the banks and public transportation. The 'share-a-ride' airport mini-bus took two hours to reach the first listing in Lenora's official "*Arthur Frommer's Budget Travel Guide*." After three years of Spanish, I knew I was an idiot when I couldn't understand a goddamned thing, unaware that in Barcelona they spoke an unintelligible Catalan dialect that only sounded like Spanish. And there were other problems; first, no hotel would rent to an un-married couple; and second, this was the last weekend in July, when Europe was closing down and heading to Spain for vacation… There wasn't a fuckin' room left!

After a series of hotel rejections, we started on the list of accredited youth hostels to no avail. As it got dark, Lenora began to shake with uncertainly. Putting my arms around her for the first time, her protective shell gave way to a torrent of tears. Embarrassed, she wiped her eyes and apologized as I touched my lips to her forehead and suggested she hold on so that I could have a turn. No matter what happened next, we needed something to eat. Places had begun to open for dinner, all happy to accept our American dollars. 'Tapas' were small plates used to sample from the salad bars, with tables of olives and peppers, fried calamari and shrimp, cold-cuts and bread rubbed with tomato, garlic and olive oil, always accompanied by a flask of red wine (the water wasn't safe). Re-energized after the extravagant $6 meal, it was time to switch over to Hairy's book of underground 'pensiones.'

As we gravitated into a poor residential area, even the first two 'unofficial' locations were filled. Skipping to the bottom of the list, with lead arms from lugging around Lenora's Samsonite suitcase, it took what little strength I had left to make it up the stairs to an unmarked door on the second floor of a unlikely looking apartment building, and what felt like our last chance for shelter. When a longhaired freak answered and smiled at the sight of my guitar, there was hope. Ushered in to a small foyer, he motioned for us to stay while knocking on the manager's door. Behind him were two darkened rooms with mattress pads lining the floors holding a commingled assortment of travelers. (Not exactly the kind of place Lenora was used to.) As 'the office' door opened, there stood 'La Senora' in a pink ruffled robe out of Central Casting as Lila Kedrova in *"Zorba The Greek."* The wall of her bedroom 'office' covered with pictures of relationships she instigated and overly proud of her intuition, our host immediately decided that Lenora and I did not belong together. Of course we didn't know what the fuck was going on when she separated us, placing Lenora next to a tall British art student in one room and me next to a Peruvian nymphomaniac in the other. The lady was truly gifted.

Shortly thereafter she emerged again from her 'office' with two large bottles of homemade wine, one for each room, as a 'thirst quencher' since the water wasn't fit to drink. The nightly event generated income for her, as everyone pitched in something, while also serving as a social lubricant. Soon mattress pads were pairing up as we all got to know each other better… much better. After a brief sing-a-long, Vicki, my Peruvian neighbor, made it abundantly clear that music was not the only universal language. La Senora beamed with pride and headed back to her 'office' as the rooms began to undulate with the harmony of international relations.

What a relief to wake up the next morning and discover that Vicki wasn't a leper. Worried about Lenora, I tiptoed into the adjoining room where she lay sleeping fully dressed in the arms of Reginald, the next couple for La Senora's wall. Returning to my corner, Vicki welcomed me back with open legs. About a third of the tenants were actually full-time residents. She worked at a lingerie shop downtown. The rest of us became an instant tour group, traveling together. Near the Old Port, I left the others to spend time with handmade guitars hanging in shops hidden away down narrow cobble streets, where pride was taken in generations of craftsmanship. I kept returning to one glorious, red faced, twelve-string guitar, that echoed through the small shop where it was made, with a price tag of about $85 I didn't have. In fact I was running out of food money. The streets of Barcelona were not conducive to performing, patrolled by heavily armed police, leery of anything that smelled of liberalism. But despite the military dictatorship, Barcelona bubbled with art, photography, poetry and music just under the surface, along with an affinity for anything American. A giant travel poster for the USA, was simply a collage of words: "Cowboy, Jeep, Supermarket, Jazz, Grand Canyon, Niagara Falls, Bar-B-Que, Hot Dog, Snack Bar, Broadway, A-OK." There were also two words they weren't allowed to print, that went unsaid… "Freedom" and "Democracy."

That night the noise of laughter and music led to a local café, where a line of instruments hung above the bar for anyone to use. The opposite wall was covered with drawings by the neighborhood kids behind small marble tabletops cluttered with bottles of beer and Coke, and green plastic watering cans of sangria. The patrons ranged from grandparents to businessmen still in their white shirts and ties, to students, all talking and singing at the same time. In the center of the action sat the local 'beauty queen' and her protective boyfriend, flexing his muscle shirt as she sang into a microphone amplified through a record player on the table in front of them. Welcomed like a long lost relative with my guitar, a white-haired violinist and heavy-set trumpet player moved over to make room at their table. Soon I had the whole place singing *"Guantanamera"* in unison, the only Spanish song I knew. *"A Rose In Spanish Harlem"* lost something in the translation, but *"Louie Louie"* worked great, unintelligible in any language. Once again able to eat and drink 'on the house,' I still wasn't making anything but friends and memories. When the beauty queen began flirting and her boyfriend took out a knife to clean his fingernails, it was obviously time to leave.

Back at the pensionė, Vicki suggested I work the wealthy beachfront at Sitges, just south along the coast, then proceeded to fuck my brains out saying 'hasta luego.' Unable to move the next morning, I stuffed myself with shellfish before catching the late afternoon train, arriving in the resort town just after dinner. There were no youth hostels in Sitges, with its manicured lawns, private estates, and pricey hotels, all fully booked. After hours of searching for a place to sleep, I eventually settled on a secluded plot of lush grass overlooking the ocean, under the stars, where the police wouldn't bother me... in a graveyard. I've often wondered why there aren't more graveyards. There have obviously been millions of more dead people than there are live ones. Why aren't there more graveyards than apartment houses? And another thing, how does the funeral industry continue to get over, charging exorbitant prices to shovel remains in fancy airtight non-degradable caskets, so that nothing gets recycled? Hell, why not use Styrofoam!... Needless to say, it was very quiet.

Waking at dawn to the sound of seagulls and the crashing surf, sitting on a gravestone and watching the town come to life had a certain irony about it. With my belongings stored in a coin locker, and stretched out in the sand, I melted into oblivion until a platoon of Aussie and American students hit the beach for some tackle football. Thrilled to hear English again, I volunteered for the U.S. cause. The rules were simple; when we got the ball it was American football, with blocking and forward passes; when they had the ball it was Australian rugby with laterals and drop kicks... a test of superiority. We set up in formation, with diagramed plays, everyone knowing his specific responsibility. They ran around like a bunch of wild aborigines. And in the end...it was no contest...they killed us!

I had almost forgotten what no-holds-barred fun felt like. Bruised and brimming with testosterone, now I needed some red meat. With a touch of homesickness as the guys headed back to Barcelona, I set out once again to sing for my supper.

"Sin Street"' (Carrer del pecat), was the main walking thoroughfare, lined with cafes and pubs, and the scent of suntan oil, wine and charcoal grills. Draped in my blanket, like Clint Eastwood's silent stranger in *"Fistful Of Dollars,"* complete with a short brimmed straw hat, I surveyed the terrain before opening my guitar case. Within minutes there was a crowd throwing money. When the restaurant owner behind me cleared a table stocked with drinks, it was *"A Happening."* A little Frenchman named Marc elected himself president of my fan club, passing the straw hat, demanding contributions. In that one day I made more than a week at La Fiesta, not to mention a steak dinner. But despite my instant celebrity, there still wasn't a vacancy in town. The night before I noticed what appeared to be an empty estate with a realty sign on the lawn. After a half-hour of uncertainty, looking for dogs or some sort of alarm system, I jumped the fence, following the bushes around the perimeter to a pool and patio in the rear. After the first hour, flinching at the slightest noise, I gradually relaxed into sleep on a chaise lounge under a blue and white striped canvas awning in the moonlight. Pushing my luck the next morning, I couldn't resist a quick dip before making my way back over the fence with my trusty guitar and desperado blanket draped over my shoulder.

Everyone on Sin Street seemed to know me when Marc appeared with $35 in pesetas and a promise of unlimited food and drink. Just up the street from my performance the day before, a generous pub owner was standing with a table and a smile. Marc also noted his roommates would be bringing some 'important people.' Later that afternoon as he assaulted the crowd for tips, his roommates arrived, Yvonne and Yvette, two French GoGo Dancers who cavorted nightly in cages above the main stage at the expansive and expensive Club Numero Uno (Number One). The nightclub owner himself, wearing a diamond pinky-ring and garish gold chain under his open-chest white ruffled shirt, and various hangers-on, all stood in typical French fashion... off by themselves. After my imitation of Oscar Brown Jr.'s *"Signifyin' Monkey,"* 'Mr. Cool' dropped $50 U.S. in my hat, with an offer to have his limo bring me to the club that night. Everyone laughed when I confessed homelessness, and Marc assured me there was plenty of room at his place. Marc's apartment turned out to be a two-bedroom, luxury condominium on the water, with sliding glass doors to a private Jacuzzi. One bedroom was his, the other shared by the girls, with a large living room, kitchen and an office/guest room for me. As the *"In Crowd"* sat around laughing in French, I made two significant discoveries: One, I was the only 'straight' one in the place; and two, there was no lock on the office/guest room door.

Club Numero Uno was a cross between a Vegas showroom and a New York dance hall, the floor packed with fashion plates flirting in flickering black lights to an over amplified cover band. On breaks, Yvonne and Yvette took to the neon cages as records played. It was 2:00 AM when the music stopped and a single microphone placed on stage for me to hunch over with my guitar so that neither was effective. The trendy audience mulled around in confusion before heading for the exits, as I slapped the guitar and sang over the feedback. After a few unsuccessful attempts at resurrection, I was ready for the graveyard again. Following Marc's reassurances on an otherwise deadly ride home, he retired with the limo driver. The girls, who occasionally glanced over, but otherwise ignored me, slipped into the Jacuzzi and closed the sliding glass doors. As steam-fogged flesh tones merged in the dark, I masturbated. In that moment after climaxing, with millions of sperm soaking a paper napkin in my hand, came the weird premonition that maybe someday, as a means of preserving our species, non-productive homosexuality might become the norm, and heterosexuals, outcasts. Perhaps even outlawed in favor of genetic control, giving new meaning to eventually becoming a 'dirty old man.'

It was mid-afternoon when the French crew gathered at a local restaurant famous for its 'paella,' a shared dish of yellow rice filled with shellfish, sausage, and spices. Arrogantly demanding a large separate table, when served drinks, they proceeded to throw their ice on the floor in disgust, berating the staff for treating them like 'ignorant tourists.' Unaware that the ice was from polluted local water, to me the group simply looked like obnoxious French aristocrats, while peasants in the kitchen were probably pissing in the paella. When the yellow rice arrived steaming at the table, I took one look, excused myself, and headed for the beach. Baking in the sun, the disappointment of the previous night slowly dissipated in the heat. Then suddenly my guitar case had a heart attack and with a loud shudder, fell over in the sand. Inside the temperature and stress had melted and snapped the bridge off the guitar. I hadn't thought to loosen the strings, which dangled helplessly attached to the fractured wooden piece. Guitar surgery meant returning to Barcelona.

Problems in gathering my things and the train schedule resulted in a late night arrival, only to find La Senora's apartment fully packed. But when Vicki reached up in the darkness and pulled me down on top of her, La Senora shook her fists smiling, "bien! bien! bien!"(good! good! good!), before waddling back to her room in triumph... another notch for her wall. Of course, I didn't get much sleep... everything has its price! After making arrangements to buy and ship the red twelve-string back to Fireman Bill's apartment, and a few nightly marathons with Vicki while waiting for my guitar, next came Paris, and some badly needed time alone.

Following the riots and strikes of May and fearing a communist takeover, DeGaulle had declared marshal law in France. Paris was in a state of suspended animation. With the U.S. stuck in Vietnam, the U.K. on the brink of economic ruin, and France politically paralyzed, NATO forces were powerless as Russian tanks rolled in to crush Czechoslovakia. The soldiers that had clogged the trains in Germany and Austria were now shooting Czech citizens throwing sticks and stones, desperately defending their brief flirtation with freedom. After hibernating for two days in the Louvre amidst life-size paintings glorifying the Napoleonic wars, my plane back to London completed the connection home as France overcompensated with an H-Bomb test in the Pacific. Arriving in Chicago only to find another armed camp, this one defending the 'Democratic' Convention against democracy.

XV. (1968-69)
(End of an Era)

Chicago looked like 'Czechago,' with barricades and helmeted riot police riding barbed wire-laced jeeps, like the Russians in Prague. MOBE (National Mobilization Committee To End The War In Vietnam) in conjunction with the SDS, organized but were refused permits to march as Mayor Daley formally opened the convention at the Amphitheatre. That night there were at least 1,000 of us in Lincoln Park with chairs, blankets and anything we could get our hands on, building a barricade to prevent the police from evicting us as the 11:00 PM curfew approached. When the first police car nosed through, we picked up stones to throw as canisters of tear gas began spinning in the grass. You don't really smell tear gas. It just feels like breathing acid as your eyes, and nose, and mouth and skin start to burn. Unable to see, with my eyelids twitching from the searing fumes, all I could do was aimlessly run from the bonsai cheers of the helmeted pigs, clubbing and grunting in my direction. Blindly fleeing in the dark, I tumbled into a row of shrubbery and lay there rubbing my eyes and swallowing air to the thumping of my pulse. Peering through the leaves with partial vision, kids were being pummeled on the ground, while others bravely fought back, kicking and punching until beaten unconscious by gangs of bloody night sticks. When a beam of light scoured the ground nearby, I crawled away on my stomach toward a stone partition that separated the park from the street. Flashing red lights on the other side convinced me it might be safer to climb a tree. Perched atop a massive oak was a bird's eye view of the violence, as hordes of white helmets rampaged through the nearby streets, sometimes actually pulling protesting residents from their porches and beating them into straggling 'meat wagons.' How could this be America? It felt like I left one country and came back to another.

It was 3:00 AM before I made it down along the perimeter of the park to an empty street, and eventually to a MOBE crash pad in Old Town packed with bandaged refugees. At first news coverage was sparse, until battered reporters began filing their stories. As Bobby Seale spoke in Lincoln Park that evening, I couldn't help but notice most blacks standing together as a group, not mixing like in the past. Many of us then headed south to Grant Park, in front of the Hilton, where television cameras would be watching. At curfew, even though Lincoln Park was again cleared with tear gas and clubs, Grant Park was allowed open all night for speeches by Julian Bond, Rennie Davis, Tom Hayden, and the songs of Mary Travers and Peter Yarrow. Sleeping on the ground, I awoke the next morning to find the band shell surrounded by police and National Guard as it filled to capacity for the day's antiwar rally and appearances by Dick Gregory, Allen Ginsberg, and Norman Mailer. Later that day, when news that the proposed peace plank for the Democratic platform was voted down at the Convention, a long-haired freak began to lower the American flag and was tackled and arrested before the crowd finished his initiative and raised a blood-splattered shirt in its place. Hundreds of officers charged, beating Rennie Davis unconscious as the entire park emptied into the streets to face clubs and Mace, chanting, "The whole world is watching!"

We'd seen blood soaked images of defenseless protestors and rioting police before, but this wasn't black and white… it was white on white… in the center of America's heartland. On TV that night, in his speech nominating George McGovern, Senator Ribicoff denounced the "Gestapo tactics on the streets of Chicago" as Mayor Daley cursed him from the floor and Hubert Humphrey won the party's nomination on the first ballot. A televised testament to political corruption, like watching a prizefight, all the time knowing 'the fix' was in. And we'd seen reporters caught up in a mêlée before, but never the entire mainstream press, intimidated and beaten as they pointed fingers in disbelief at the hijacking of the democratic process. This one event, more than any other, would change the media's coverage of government and its officials, no longer editing, but now focusing on misconduct and stupidity, epitomized by the repeated airing of Mayor Daley's defensive press conference misstatement: "The policeman isn't there to create disorder, the policeman is there to preserve disorder!"

And disorder was evident back on campus, where President Stahr had resigned in the face of an entire student body in long hair and tie-dyed shirts, spouting pop-culture phrases that had long since lost their meaning. The frat house was half empty, deemed 'un-cool' as undergraduates simply assumed college was the place to rebel against their parents by dressing like bums and attending peace rallies to get laid and smoke pot. Like atheists following religious rituals because they liked the wine. At our first house meeting, I suggested we shake things up and go coed, but the brothers had trouble concentrating since our only two half class pledges had stuffed Limburger cheese in the air ducts. (At least the spirit of borass was still alive.) That night they were blindfolded, stripped naked, and placed on a train to Terra Haute (famous for its whorehouses). Speaking of whores, Useless now had a 'girlfriend' named Janet Polasky, whose name was scrawled on more bathroom walls than the word 'fuck,' when her concerned roommate, Ingrid, an attractive Norwegian I wanted to date, called for a confidential favor. She asked if I would be willing to use my celebrity to boost Janet's self-image and try to do something to curb her self-destructive promiscuity.

Sitting in the dorm lobby, waiting for the elevator to blink down nine floors, I had no idea what to expect when an unassuming dirty-blonde in a beige skirt, with uneven short hair, haltingly introduced herself. Avoiding eye contact, Polasky said she'd seen me play at The Kiva and loved The Sot-Weed Factory, before asking if I wanted a quick blow-job or "something else." This wasn't sexual freedom, it was an emotional slavery I'd seen before... even her hair was the same color as Lillian's. Uneasy when I asked her to sit and talk for a few minutes, she fidgeted with a small silver cross around her neck. Too insecure to be defensive, Janet smiled sheepishly at the suggestion she was more attractive than I expected, and that it wasn't against the 'student protest dress code' to wear a little make-up now and then. Apparently most of her 'dates' didn't give a shit. She actually got excited when I asked if she would mind changing into something more colorful, realizing this was to be a 'real date.'

Proudly attached to my arm, Janet raised her head a bit higher with each greeting as we casually strolled through the Student Union, now in a flowered dress from Ingrid and a smile she'd almost lost. Grinning over an ice cream soda, "It feels like my birthday," she confessed, glancing about, half expecting someone to recognize her and spoil everything. Afraid that bringing her to The Pad would signal the wrong message, I led her instead to the comfortable leather chairs of the Alumni Library to talk. An only child at 12, when her mom died of cancer, she confided how holding her father at night for comfort became "something else." For the next four years she'd come home from school each day to cook and clean and service her father, until a social worker uncovered everything and she was placed in foster care. Having outgrown the "stupid dating stuff" of kids her own age, with both her foster parents working, she'd just lock herself in her room after school and masturbate. When she confided in her foster father, he began to come home early from work... and she'd leave her bedroom door unlocked. "Soon it was a game," she smirked, "sitting between them in the TV parlor with no panties. I'd open up so he could see me touch myself when she left the room, and then play innocent when she came back." Janet's body language had gone from stilted to seductive, twirling her hair with one finger while wetting her lips, opening and closing her legs, and pulling up the hem of her flowered dress as she spoke. This was gonna take more will power than I expected. When I called her on it, like snapping out of a trance, back came the insecure waif, suddenly clumsy in her chair. After a long pause, Janet cocked her head and softly asked, "Don't you want to fuck me?"

We talked about the awesome power of sex, often causing people to act against their conscience. But the idea there could be something more between a boy and a girl, was difficult for her. No male had ever done anything but use her, until she just accepted the role, and learned how to play it to the hilt. In Janet's reality, the concept of love and caring between two people was simply a fairy tale that never came true. Hiding her tears as she looked away, my first impulse was to hold her, but I reached across to take her hand instead. Then came the hardest questions of all, pulling her hand away and turning back in frustration, "Why are you doing this?" she demanded, "You don't even know me..." Suddenly standing, "What do you want from me? Why do you care how I live my life?" Caught off guard, trying to analyze my intentions and put them into words at the same time, I got up and put my arms around her waist, "It's hard to explain but... you see I've been blessed with all the advantages of life and somehow I guess... I feel like I should be doing something to deserve it... or pay for it... or justify it... or share it." Forcing my hands away she cried, "So what am I, some kind of charity case to take on so you can feel good?" This was obviously going the wrong way. All I could do was stop and let the silence reset while she stood facing the wall. After an inordinately long pause, I responded, "You know that's not what I meant." Still collecting my thoughts, "Life is a balance of good and evil, positive and negative... You know that Karma thing, getting back what you put out." Realizing my Freudian slip, "Well, maybe 'putting out' isn't such a good choice of words in this case." Janet turned with a fake punch while I tried to finish my thought, "And I guess I also believe the best way to change the world into the kind of place I want to live, is one person at a time..." Stopping to look into her eyes, "Do you understand?" She answered with a nod and leaned forward, resting her body against me.

After another hour of intimate conversation, walking back to her dorm, Janet asked why it was OK for me to fuck around but not her, "How come when a guy does it he's cool, but the girl is a slut?" "Obviously, part of it is that old 'double standard' from before the pill." I suggested (with sales that had gone from nine million in 1960 to 1.5 billion in '69). But now the answer was more complex. "I guess it comes down to self respect; If two people are fucking each other... no problem. But if one person is screwing the other... big problem. Like, it's one thing to go after a guy because you want to get laid. It's something else to let someone use you 'cause he wants to get off." As we approached her dorm, Janet began trying the door handles of the cars parked along the street. Finding an open latch, she stopped with a proposition, "OK, I'll tell you what... I'll stop having sex with everyone...except you... at least once a week." Before I could answer, she opened the car door, pulled me toward her, and fell backwards into the seat. With her hands holding me against her open crotch, all I could think was, 'What would Ingrid say?' "Wait a second...wait a second!" I pleaded. Grabbing my hand, she forced it down between her legs and held it against her soaking vagina while pulling at my pants. "No...No more talk," she growled. And I could smell her wetness and feel her whole body squirming and sucking me in. "OK, OK...But it's got to be our secret!?" Digging her fingernails into the back of my hand, forcing it inside while staring wildly at the ceiling she cried out, "I swear it! I swear it!... Now FUCK ME! FUCK ME!" (It wasn't clear whether this was mutual, or I was getting screwed?)

Like Homer returning from my odyssey overseas, Oppy snarled as I arrived at The Pad, until recognizing my scent and wagging his body in welcome. Inside, Bill was already playing the twelve-string for two freshmen coeds, giggling on the floor as they shared a joint. "Hey, look what I got in the mail!" he smiled as the plastic beads clicked behind me. When I asked if he'd heard anything from Charlotte, he said not lately, but there were "a slew of messages near the phone." With her old phone disconnected and no forwarding number, I tried information to no avail and spent the next half-hour tracking her down. Apparently she'd dropped out and was living off campus with Simon 'Black' Aimes. Black was a part-time student and full-time drug dealer, who always dressed in black and used his Negro heritage when it suited him. Driving out to his place, my smashed up Falcon had trouble making the hills, and I once again vowed to replace it, stalling in the driveway. Charlotte knew what I thought of Black, and so did he, bounding out with his giant fake smile, then hugging me in a Sammy Davis, Jr. gesture of 'peace & love.' Catching a brief glimpse of her at the window, when I started toward the door, Black intervened "Destitute" to advise me that, "Charlotte was not accepting visitors at this time." When I tried to get around him, he produced a gun, teasing his Afro with the barrel and suggesting I "return on a more auspicious occasion."

Searching for some answers in town, walking through the front door of the renovated Black Market felt like entering an enemy camp, as unfamiliar black faces either scowled or ignored me when I asked for Lanc or Jasmine. Finally the guy at the register called out to the back, "Hey Jasmine, some honkey out here to see you." Jasmine looked as if she'd just seen a ghost, not sure how to react in front of 'the brothers' when I opened my arms in greeting. Then, in a newly acquired accent, she flipped her palm in my direction saying, "Hey man, I ain't down wit dat integration shit no mo. You in da wrong place at da wrong time my friend." Now it was my turn to be surprised. At least she called me 'friend' instead of 'mo fo'(mother fucker). Where did she learn to talk like that? It was like "*Invasion Of The Body Snatchers.*" As my green Falcon rattled up to Lanc's apartment, two armed militants I recognized from the Trustees Takeover snapped to attention on his porch. Then Lanc came out in one of his more colorful dashikis and smiled as I came up the steps, "Hey my brother, we gots-to-getchu a better ride." At least this was still Lanc.

Sitting under a massive blow-up of Malcolm X pointing across the room to one of fingers pointing back from the railing of the Memphis motel where Martin Luther King was gunned down, Lanc apologized for Jasmine's behavior, but explained that it "probably 'ill be best if you not come 'round no more." From behind his desk sprawled with placards, papers, piles of envelopes and an African fertility statue, he continued, "Blacks in this country have to stop lookin' to 'whitey' for a handout, and start offerin' each other a hand up. We need to stand on our own feet, in our own shoes, that we make in our own factories, and pay for with our own money, and spend in our own communities. We need to learn our own history, and teach our children that black *is* beautiful... and, as much as I appreciate the goodness of your intentions and of your heart, my brother, we gotta do this ourselves."

Heading back to The Pad, still reeling from the day's events, a blue Chevrolet I had seen someplace before briefly followed and turned off. Bill left a note that he would be gone for the weekend, to feed

Oppy, and "PS: Welcome Back"... yeah, some welcome. After a leftover sausage and pepperoni pizza and some practice on my new guitar, I fell asleep, until the phone rang and a muffled voice suggested I go to the front door. Assuming it was a wrong number, I had just turned over when it rang again, "Take a look out your front door, you mother-fuckin' nigger lover!" And suddenly I remembered that blue Chevy and Bailey's face in the rear window. Scared, and not sure what to do next, the phone rang again with a barrage of obscenities. 'No sense calling the police,' I reasoned, 'they were probably in on it,' and dialed Lanc. "Hang on, my brother," he answered, "We'll be right there." Before he could say anything else the phone went dead... and then the explosion. With the front door completely blown away, through the smoke and debris, I could see the limp body of Oppy dangling from a noose with a cross of gasoline burning in the grass beneath him. Attached to his body was a note that read, "Nigger-Lover, Next Time It's Your Turn!"

In a matter of minutes, Lanc and a team of black commandos arrived with fire extinguishers and rifles. This time they were loaded. The police took a little longer to show up, more interested in harassing the militants than any sort of investigation. Lanc posted two guards at my door for the night and arranged to have Oppy taken away. But I couldn't lose the smoky image of his glazed-over eyes, tongue flopping from his head when they lowered him to the ground. I actually got a shovel that night and turned over the grass under the tree to obliterate any sign of the burning cross. The next morning a few handymen from the BAK house came by to help replace the door and later that afternoon, as the new door frame was being completed, another unexpected surprise... My two bodyguards from the previous night drove up in a shiny black & white 1954 Nash, complete with a chrome winged Venus on the hood and fitted round spare tire holder mounted on the trunk, and presented me with the keys and a note: "One of our elderly church sisters donated this car to the cause. Drive it safely and in good health with our blessings and thanks for your support and sacrifice... Sincerely, Lancaster Washington on behalf of the brothers and sisters of the Black

Activist Student Committee." Sort of a 'thank you note' and 'go away present' rolled into one.

Registered for 15 hours of Political Science, it was difficult, however, to touch base with Hairy concerning my summer paper as he juggled his teaching schedule and CO duties at the Bloomington Hospital. At the Olympics in Mexico, the entire world misread the glove-fisted black unity salutes of Tommy Smith and John Carlos as gestures of hate, and a gangly white guy named Dick Fosbury broke all the rules in typical 60's fashion, to win the high jump with his revolutionary 'Fosbury Flop.' Meanwhile I arranged for The Sot-Weed Factory to play at the first "Kick-off Party" of the Fall Semester, practicing the new Rascals' hit *"People Got To Be Free,"* and the psychedelic *"Born To Be Wild"* by Steppenwolf, while continuing my occasional Friday night solo gigs at The Kiva. Then the university broke precedent and offered me the stage for the Judges Intermission at the upcoming I.U. Sing Competition, an honor reserved in the past for the outstanding graduating senior from the Music School. By now the most recognized face on campus, rarely having to wait for a table, stand on line, or pay for anything, everyone was my 'best friend.' That fame, coupled with the new sexual liberation, meant I could fuck any girl I wanted (and some I didn't want) and say or do anything without being criticized or challenged. But like the *"Twilight Zone"* episode of a gambler who died and went to 'heaven,' where everything was rigged so he couldn't lose, it took a while to realize that it was in fact 'the other place.' Although intoxicating at first, with all the mirrors around me distorted, it became hard to put things in perspective, to know what or who was real.

Shortly after the marriage of the stylish Jackie Kennedy to a wrinkled Greek shipping toad, and in the wake of the Democratic Party's attempted suicide in Chicago, the perennial Republican loser and former high executioner in Joseph McCarthy's communist witch hunts of the 50's, Richard M. Nixon, was elected President. Back on campus, a lot of other horny losers were pissed, including Useless, when word spread that Polasky wasn't 'doing it' anymore. In fact, one night, while fulfilling my weekly obligation to Janet, Ingrid actually called to thank me. With Polasky's wet bush in my face, I had the balls to ask Ingrid for a date, before Janet's hand on the back of my head forced me to take a quick breath and hang up. Although Janet accepted our 'arrangement' as temporary, she demanded to be included. Convinced that Ingrid wouldn't go for a threesome the first time out, I needed a male stand-in to join us.

Despite his athletic good looks and extreme wealth, Phil Rothschild never dated, alone in his room each night, on the phone to Pam, his pre-arranged fiancé in Boston. It bothered the shit out of me that this really good guy, who loved to philosophize about life, was missing it all. Even though unsuccessful in coaxing him out before, this time he was curious to meet the girl behind the name he'd seen and heard so much about, and besides, we were 'just going to the movies.' Pulling up to the dorm in my Nash, even though Ingrid was supposedly my date, Janet jumped into the front seat. It was downhill from there… literally… when after stopping at a light on our way to see "*2001:A Space Odyssey*," the break pedal flattened under my foot and the wheels began to roll. Down the hill, a dirty green pickup sat oblivious to our approach. Dropping the automatic into low, and pulling on the emergency break slowed the descent, but only slightly. Leaning on the horn, and out our windows waving frantically, the pickup hauled ass just in time. Phil instinctively wrapped his arms around Ingrid, rolling to the floor as Janet braced against the dashboard. A Sunday driver casually backing out of a spot ahead, stared in disbelief as all he saw was an idiot, over anxious for a parking space, barely missing his front fender and bouncing off the brick wall in front of him. With the Nash built like a tank, the only damage was to the wall, but accidental bonding in the back seat was about to change the lives of three people dramatically.

Soon Phil was spending his days on campus with Ingrid and his nights on the phone with Pam, cursing me for his dilemma. As the Apollo 8 astronauts orbited the moon that Christmas Eve, Phil was back in Boston trying to decide which one he really loved. For my part, that Christmas was spent making love to some townies in front of the fireplace at the deserted BAK House, and later that night alone on the roof *"Counting My Blessings."* Surveying the lights of my campus domain, with outstretched arms, I began spinning in a reverie of faces, and places, and experiences of a lifetime I had already lived, and the wonder of what was yet to be... crying in happiness at the gift of being part of it all. But the manic elation was temporary.

Finishing my summer paper during that Christmas break, Hairy submitted it to the university for 9 hours of pass/fail credit. One final semester of nothing but Poli–Sci and I could graduate on time. Its leadership killed or imprisoned, the Civil Rights Movement was relegated to a 'Poor Peoples March,' and nobody gave a shit, as the hate and mistrust between black and white was internalized, like venereal disease, into the body of the nation. The Paris Peace Talks were now in full swing, and rhetoric from the right had moved from 'Victory In Vietnam' to 'Peace With Honor.' The war to end the war now conceded, its symbols evolved into a war to end all war. Peace rallies became 'Love-Ins,' no longer political protests as much as music festivals to spread the gospel of 'Love Thy Neighbor'(and to do it right out there on the lawn). 'Back to nature' was the call, and the fertilizer piled up, giving bloom to a new generation of 'Flower Power.'

Everything was losing meaning, as the people around me began to feel like remora (sucker fish that attach to sharks and feed off their leftovers). A constant cadre of naked girls competed for my attention and bed, the ones that didn't fit each night settled for Bill, interchangeable flowers in the parade. On a Sunday morning with my car in the shop, Duckbill, a pledge so named for his flat-tipped nose, came to The Pad to retrieve me for brunch and a required house meeting. When he pulled up in his cute little red MG, two of my flower girls danced out to his car stark naked, nipples freezing, and ran back in. His hands clenched on the steering wheel, mouth open, and eyes staring straight ahead, Duckbill had never seen a real naked girl before. When he finally turned to look at me as I got in the car, he saw a god. The meeting that afternoon was serious. Apparently, money had been disappearing and treated bills planted to uncover the thief, the telltale coating visible under black light. As one at a time, the brothers ran their hands under the light, the culprit was uncovered... innocent little Duckbill was a fucking thief.

That night another thief paid me a visit. It must have been 2:00 AM when Black appeared at The Pad, calling me "brother" and asking a "favor." He needed to leave some "things" overnight, and if I "would be so inclined as to transport them" out to his "domicile" the next morning, "Charlotte would be pleased to greet me." Before I could answer he was filling the foyer with obviously stolen goods and gone. In another place and time, I would have just called the cops, but based on recent experience, they would probably have arrested me. And more than anything, I wanted to see Charlotte. After picking up my car that morning, it was noon when I arrived at Black's, his stolen TV and stereo equipment covered with a blanket in the back seat. "I anticipated your eminent arrival this morning," he announced, words freezing in the January air. "Unavoidably detained," I answered, with the engine running and the car doors locked, as two of his lackeys came down to retrieve their booty. "Where's Charlotte?" I asked. "She is presently upstairs making herself presentable," he stalled, waiting to hear the doors unlock. "Why don't you endeavor to join us, while my associates relieve you of your burden, " beckoning with his hands. Climbing out the driver's side but re-locking the door, I headed up to the lion's den, his two goons shivering behind me, relying on my celebrity as protection and wishing Shybo was still around. Inside, the place reeked of burning incense and stale pot, the windows covered with flowered bed sheets. A massive Indian water pipe graced an elaborate wood-carved table in the center of the room, surrounded by a circular ottoman of large multi-color silk pillows. Against the back wall, a table was stacked with glassine packets of white powder and grass, accompanied by a revolver, which one of his henchmen immediately recovered as we entered the room. After an uneasy moment, Charlotte appeared at the top of the stairs like a ghost, hesitating for an instant before relying on the handrail to come down, reaching the floor as if it were an accomplishment. With crocodile teeth, Black wrapped his arm around her as Charlotte put on one of his smiles to tell me how "happy" she was to see me. He then sent her across the room for my car keys. Unsteady on her feet, her pupils dilated, with the chill of her fingers touching my hand, everything inside of me wanted to just grab her and run. But she couldn't run... she could barely walk.

Eyes watering from the cold, I drove back to the fraternity, haunted by what I had done to Charlotte and what I couldn't do now. 'How could she end up like this? Was it attempted suicide, retribution, or both?' Half hoping the brothers could help mount a rescue, I arrived to find the house surrounded by police. 'Now what? Was this about the stolen goods?' But before I could come up with a story, Handman and Megaphone were led out the front door in handcuffs. For months they had been signing up for the Columbia House Record Club under fictitious names, collecting literally hundreds of promotional albums, and then returning the invoices marked 'addressee unknown.' Meanwhile Phil had returned from Boston convinced his true love was Pam, ready to break it off with Ingrid until the moment he saw her again. Now both he and Ingrid refused to talk to me, especially after Ingrid found out I was fucking Janet. Nor would Useless, who hadn't got laid since I 'ruined' his 'girlfriend.' Janet, on the other hand, with her blonde hair now flowing down over her shoulders, was using men the way they once used her. Meanwhile, back at The Pad, Bill blamed me for Oppy and almost losing his home, but was addicted to the steady stream of girls I supplied. From that day on, rehearsing for I.U. Sing became an obsession, especially on the word that 'a major company' would be there. And I couldn't help thinking again about William Morris.

At The Pad a few nights later, answering the phone to the sound of stifled breathing, I feared the worst and braced for another explosion. Then a trembling female voice whispered, "I'm sorry... I can't live like this anymore... Please..." and the words cut off. I had to get Charlotte out of there, if it wasn't already too late. Flashing on the night the Jacksons performed, I had an idea... Masowski was caught off-guard when I showed up at his off-campus apartment. One of his football roommates, who recalled throwing me down the halls of McNutt howled, "Hey guys, look, we got our old ball back!" They also remembered Charlotte, and anyone who ever needed drugs knew Black. That night two carloads of testosterone barreled into the drug den like Viking warriors, on a mission to save the princess. Black was upstairs in bed with Charlotte when the stampede thundered through the front door, shattering everything in its path, trouncing the one bodyguard half asleep when Black appeared at the top of the stairs in his underwear and a shotgun. Before he could pull the trigger, Masowski caught him in the head with a flying table leg, storming upstairs as Black fell backwards to the hardwood floor, the shotgun discharging into the ceiling. Charlotte was only half conscious when we arrived at the hospital, where Hairy got her admitted to the Drug Detoxification Unit on an emergency basis. Masowski and a couple of the guys hung around until it was obvious there was nothing more we could do. The next morning Hairy called to report that Charlotte was a heroin addict, and would need some serious 'drying out' before we could see her again.

I.U. Sing was an annual competition of elaborate musical productions held in the main auditorium. When the judges left to tally their votes, the lights dimmed and the orchestra pit rose with me and The Sot-Weed Factory on Steppenwolf's *"Magic Carpet Ride."* The response was instantaneous. Moving non-stop from *"Knock On Wood"* to *"Jumpin' Jack Flash,"* everyone was on their feet when I took out the red twelve-string. Quietly finger-picking *"Don't Think Twice"* in a single white spotlight before gently moving into *"Sometimes I feel Like A Motherless Child."* Then Tony came in on the bass and Andy added color with the keys, before Jimmy's brushes and drums set the pulse. On the final downbeat it was into Oscar Brown Jr.'s *"Work Song"* and an abbreviated dance lesson as The Sot-Weed Factory set up to amplify my closing strip routine. Coming full circle to my first I.U. performance at Freshman Camp, this time when I ripped open my shirt on *"Twist & Shout,"* there were 3,000 fans on their feet, filling the aisles and yelling my name, with bras and panty's raining from the balcony. If there was a record company anywhere in that audience, I had a deal!

When the judges returned with their findings, the audience could care less, stomping and yelling for an encore. With my old beat up acoustic that had just seen the world, I retold the story of *"John Henry"* one last time. Backstage after the show, a girl with the biggest tits I'd ever seen asked for my autograph, accompanied by tall blonde guy in a sport coat and big-collared pink shirt who handed me a card. At first all I saw were those bouncing jugs, imagining the size of her nipples, before noticing the Chess Records logo on his card. The Chicago recording home of Rotary Connection with Minnie Ripperton, Ramsey Lewis, Chuck Berry, Howlin' Wolf and Muddy Waters, Chess was universally recognized as one of the flourishing roots of rock'n'roll. There were two after-show parties in my honor. We hit the fraternity first, where it was great to see the BAK House plastered with well-wishers slobbering through the halls again. Drew, the Chess A&R (Artist & Repertoire) guy, especially got a kick out of Useless, laid out on the floor with his mouth open under a beer keg, filling up like an arcade clown while pissing in the air at the same time. The brothers also managed to soak Zoey's blouse with cheap champagne when we arrived, leaving nothing to the imagination. By the time we left for The Pad, Drew was feeling no pain and I was feeling Zoey, squeezing the steering wheel with one hand and her full-size TV-dial nipple with the other. A little smoke inhalation at The Pad and Drew was gone for the duration. Then Zoey disrobed as even the girls applauded her monstrous oversized breasts bouncing off in either direction. Giggling, jiggling, and stark naked, the two of us grabbed a giant sleeping bag and headed out into the night. On the grassy slope in front of the Student Union, now shivering, our feet wet with dew, we dove into the felt lined canvas bag.

Unable to get both my hands around one of her breasts, it proved impractical to try and alternate between them. There was something primal in molding the massive mound into my mouth, her dark irregular areola tightening in a taught circle. But even with her nipple erect as me, Zoey was simply purring with her eyes closed, not overly turned-on. Realizing I was probably just repeating a perennial male preoccupation, there was a distinct change in her body language when I turned in the other direction, tongue trailing down to her navel. Her hips began moving in deep rolling breaths, pubic hair wet with acrid anticipation as I lightly licked the inside of her thigh. Briefly brushing the tip of my tongue across her clit, using my index finger to make her climax, she soaked my senses while sucking on me, saliva dripping from her mouth. But with my head clamped in her cunt and cock caught in her throat, neither of us could breathe. The sleeping bag rolled over as we tumbled out into the wet grass, gasping for air, but too hot to stop. Sliding back and forth on her slippery pontoons, my dick went skinny-dipping in the dark, right into the jaws of the snapping turtle, as she flailed helplessly on her back, lost in excitement.

Curled up in the sleeping bag, we woke the next morning on Dunn Meadow to the sound of students shuffling around us… stark-naked, in the center of campus, with no easy way out. Climbing into the bottom of the bag, we tried to stand up and discreetly ask assistance. But a talking, four legged, barefoot sleeping bag, standing on the lawn in front of the Student Union was hardly inconspicuous. In no time there was an accommodating crowd, happily 'guiding' us home, via New Jersey. First crossing the Jordan River that trickled through campus, we next toured the Student Cafeteria before a brief stint on the center line of 7th Street, with cars helpfully honking on all sides. Luckily the spectacle attracted Drew, who was out searching with a change of clothes. What a relief to see his blonde head pop into view at our feet, calling up to see if two of them belonged to Zoey. Over lunch, while she held his hand and rubbed my leg under the table, Drew offered me a 'development deal' with Chess Records. It meant moving to Chicago upon graduation where they'd cover all my expenses and put me in the studio to, "see what kind of music we could make together." Nothing would stop me this time.

After I.U. Sing, I couldn't go anywhere on campus without being mobbed by 'friends.' Unable to take a shit without somebody in the next stall asking me to sign his toilet paper, now I understood why starlets committed suicide. Then a dose of reality, when Hairy called about Charlotte. Although she was doing great and ready to see me, there was a problem that hadn't resolved itself during detoxification. Charlotte was just over a month pregnant by Black. The institutional green walls accented her eyes, unwilling to make contact as she sheepishly entered the room. Her black hair shorter, pulled back, and salted with thin stands of premature gray, despite everything there was still an elegance about her. Before she could sit, I reached out and we stood in tears, refusing to accept each other's guilt or apologies. But I knew it was my blind ego that almost killed her. Still weak, she collapsed into the seat-cover couch, confessing that dating Black was just to taunt me, unaware she was flirting with a poison spider until caught in the web of addiction and abuse. And even though abortion was illegal (and perhaps for her also immoral), the nightmare of his seed growing inside 'made her skin crawl.' With our democracy denying the religious 'right to choose,' hospitals in handcuffs, and girls shoving hangers up inside themselves or butchered in kitchens and bloody backrooms, there had to be something we could do.

Two weeks later, as the supersonic Concorde made its maiden flight and Golda Meir took a giant step for women's rights to become Israel's new Prime Minister, we were on the highway to Ohio in my 1954 Nash, Janet as co-pilot to an illegal abortionist from her past. In my role as catalyst, timing and fate had formed a bond between the former 'ugly duckling' and swan with broken wings. Before leaving, Polasky recounted how, avoiding surgery, 'The Doctor' would insert some sort of poison to cause her to double over in pain and abort. But Charlotte figured, after what she'd just been through, this would be a walk in the park. Worried it was too soon for another body-shot, I also knew the longer we waited, the more dangerous it would be. As sunset deceivingly colored Charlotte's sallow complexion, we pulled into a suburban split-level neighborhood, with little white mailboxes numbered at the end of each driveway.

At "252," Janet steered us around back to a private entrance. Waiting at a screen door next to a Formica MD placard tacked on a wooden shingle, a red plastic bubble on a converted station wagon/ambulance peered through the adjacent garage window. The Doctor's matronly assistant/wife then led us into a makeshift waiting room that smelled of roach spay, complete with copies of *Time*, *Look*, *The Saturday Evening Post*, and *Mad Magazine*.

Charlotte's hand wavered slightly as she filled out a form complaining of 'stomach cramps and bleeding,' holding The Doctor 'harmless for any possible complications' arising out of the 'D&C operation' he was about to perform. Returning a receipt for $150 of the $350 paid in advance, The Wife smiled more at the cash than Charlotte as she led us in to meet The Doctor. Standing in his white coat and gray hair, he looked like Marcus Welby (who didn't show up on TV until later that year), feigning recognition when Janet reminded him of her last visit. Knowing I would soon be ushered out, I backed up to one of the two windows of tightly closed blinds and managed to pull the chord raising one set a few inches above the sill. Janet excused Charlotte's shaken appearance as 'car sickness,' misdiagnosed as fear or pregnancy-related by The Doctor, who also seemed a bit unsteady on his feet. When I suggested that perhaps we wait another day, The Doctor deferred to Charlotte, who absolutely refused, demanding to "get it over with." A shell of the once vibrant beauty, Charlotte's porcelain skin, now devoid of color, her shimmering green eyes encircled in darkness, tried to smile as I squeezed her hand and kissed her forehead before leaving the room.

As soon as the door closed behind me, I was out feeling my way around the side of the house to a crack of light spilling into a flowerbed beneath the office window. Charlotte sat on the examining table, now in a white cloth dressing gown tied in the back, talking to Janet. As The Wife stowed Charlotte's clothes, Marcus Welby headed toward my window but stopped half way, taking a swig from a metal flask hidden in his coat pocket before turning back to the girls with a smile. Charlotte then stood while The Wife unrolled a long sheet of white paper for her to re-sit on, knees up, placing her feet in stirrups at the foot of the examining table. Following an injection from The Doctor, The Wife returned with a bowl of soapy water and a sponge to wash between her legs. Charlotte's tension seemed to ease, swaying and loosening her hair as The Doctor rolled over an IV (intravenous apparatus) but hesitated upon examining her arm, roughly pulling Janet aside. When Janet returned to hold Charlotte's hand, Welby took another shot from his flask, this time he wasn't smiling.

In the harsh fluorescent lights and whites, Charlotte appeared bleached and bruised, attached to an IV drip, her legs open in The Doctor's face as he sat on a small metal stool manipulating her last vestiges of pride. Then, after inserting a length of rubber tubing with a funnel at the end, he poured in a bottle of liquid, like emptying transmission fluid into a car, before temporarily removing the IV and helping her down from the table to a rubber mat on the floor. In a matter of minutes, Charlotte was in obvious pain, doubled over in the fetal position clutching her stomach as Janet joined her, entwined and crying together while The Doctor took another drink. This was barbaric! Forced to drive for hours and watch helplessly as a drunken quack used poison to provide deniability for an otherwise simple procedure, outlawed in the 'land of the free.' With each wave of cramps, Charlotte quivered, her veins and muscles stiffening and protruding, clenching her teeth and hands as Janet held on, reliving her own pain. When red ooze began flowing from her guts, Charlotte passed out and together they placed her back on the table, like a white bleeding Christ figure. Reattached to the IV, her feet returned to the stirrups, even though only semi-conscious, Charlotte's body continued to cramp and expel fluids, membrane and blood into a metal receptacle at the base of the table. With minutes passing as hours, it seemed as though the worst was over when The Wife returned from the sink with the wet sponge and The Doctor resumed his position on the stool. Then while probing with a thin metal tool, something went very wrong.

In an unexpected aftershock, Charlotte suddenly opened her eyes and lunged forward, in a nightmare scream before falling back into unconsciousness. The metal rod jammed deep inside, hemorrhaging renewed as The Doctor wrestled with the instrument. When it dislodged, deep red blood began spurting and gushing, spraying his face and clothes. As The Doctor froze dripping in panic, my foot tangled in a garden hose, throwing me face down in the grass, trying to run back inside. Kicking open the office door, the floor slippery with blood, Charlotte lay on a rolling aluminum table, her nails turning blue and skin pinched back in a skeletal stare. The Wife clearly in charge, had Janet wrapping ice from the refrigerator in wads of gauze, packing Charlotte in an attempt to slow the bleeding before slapping her husband and yelling at us to get out of the way as she wheeled the lifeless body out to the garage. Forcing The Doctor in back with Charlotte, The Wife was shrieking, "You See! You see what I've been saying!... Now look what you've done, you dumb sonovabitch!!" Then turning on us, "Stay here! The last thing we need is you two idiots at the hospital!" as she jumped in the front seat and peeled out, red light and siren screaming down the block. No way we were staying behind, gunning the Nash, we barreled across the lawn, knocking off the neighbor's mailbox in hot pursuit. Janet's dress and shoes covered in blood, transfixed on the flashing red light in the distance, part of us was riding in that ambulance.

As they wheeled Charlotte into the emergency room, we skidded up on to the curb. Intercepted at the doorway by The Wife, "You assholes! I told you to stay put!" Fuming in a furious whisper, "If that little junkie dies, we're all up for murder, so keep your goddamned mouths shut until we can get our story straight, or better yet, get the fuck outta here!" But we weren't going anywhere without Charlotte. Her tirade then took on volume, soon cursing at the top of her lungs, hysterically waving and blocking our path, when The Doctor appeared like a zombie in his blood soaked clothes with word that "Charlotte didn't make it." Probably sensing 'There but for the grace of God,' Janet sank to the pavement sobbing, while all I could do was stand in disbelief repeating into the flashing red light, "She wasn't a junkie…she was a dancer."

There was no investigation, just paperwork confirming the 'accidental death' and arrangements to ship her body home. A week later, Janet and I were half the congregation in a small town wooden church, with colored light streaming in through a stained-glass cross above a simple pine box on the alter. There was no music or singing, just her mother weeping into the arms of a neighbor and a minister, making up words. I'd never seen death before and how small and frail the human body becomes, drained of its life-force. A used receptacle dressed and painted up as an ironic reminder that none of our cosmetic skills can simulate life. Rather than stare at the crumpled remains, I closed my eyes and remembered. Sifting through the mental snapshots where Charlotte still lived, flashing those startling green eyes in the school bus window; or prancing into the BAK House foyer, her long black hair flowing behind; waiting for me in stiletto heels before making love in the loft; and oh, how we danced…

Death also puts life in perspective, forcing you to reassess your priorities. Ironically, Janet was 'born again' that night on her knees in front of the hospital, with a vow of celibacy, soon back in beige working full-time at The Bloomington Hospital next to Hairy and her God. With the first totally artificial heart implant declared 'successful' even though the patient died, I began to question my own ability to love, or truly care about anyone but myself. Afraid to hurt someone like that again, while at the same time bristling under the strain of celebrity, for the first time in a long time, longing for the simple, unconditional love of family and home. In a related incident, Phil was forced into a fateful decision when Pam came out from Boston with his parents for Little 500 Weekend, the annual bicycle race and campus celebration. When both girls showed up at the stadium, with an audience of thousands, sitting next to his mother and father, Phil had to choose between the girl they thought he would marry, and the one it turned out he really loved. As the crowd came to its feet for the first lap, he threw his arms around Ingrid, and shattered Pam ran from the stadium in tears… All part of the intricate balancing act of positive to negative, Yin and Yang, good and evil, black and white… living and life.

With Nixon in the White House, political satire was declared 'Un-American' as the *"The Smothers Brother Comedy Hour"* was cancelled for laughingly telling the truth, squashing the presidential candidacy of Pat Paulsen and my insightful friend 'Froggy' who first uttered "Ribbit, Ribbit" on TV. In Political Psychology, we studied an experiment where a subject was chosen by rigged coin toss, to administer shock to an apparent peer. Even though a sample jolt and reactions from the 'victim' confirmed the pain, each subject was willing to increase the voltage to a level marked 'lethal,' as long as the 'authority figure' in control suggested it was necessary, calling into question the entire concept of prosecuting 'crimes against humanity' by people just 'doing their job.' And as 'the job' in Vietnam dragged on, so did the protests, but without me. On the last day of the last final exam of my life, I just needed to get home. Not even waiting for graduation, every inch of the car stuffed with memories, I headed out past the plastic MacDonald's arches, now claiming sales in the multi-millions, and waved goodbye to a time and place I could never live again, except in the past.

There was something comforting about sitting at home in front of the TV, surrounded by family, when Neil Armstrong took that "one small step for man." Followed by déjà vu a few weeks later as the last Kennedy brother's political aspirations drowned with Mary Jo Kopechne on Chappaquiddick Island. In The Village, clubs like The Bitter End, The Gaslight, Café Wha?, and Folk City were still there but each a commercial copy of the original. With pictures from the 'glory days' of the folk movement shaking on the walls, neon signs and souvlaki stands reverberated to the feedback of Jimi Hendrix' guitar smoking in psychedelic lights at The Electric Circus, or Procol Harem and Santana at The Fillmore East. But that summer all the talk was about the upcoming "Three Days of Peace and Music" scheduled for Woodstock, where it was rumored the promoters were paying Jefferson Airplane, Credence Clearwater Revival, and The Who more than $10,000 each, and Jimi Hendrix something like $30,000 to perform. And the unbelievable list of performers kept growing. Originally a commercial venture masquerading as a festival of 'peace and love,' it ended up a financial failure and self-fulfilling prophecy.

Despite my aversion to the 'back to nature' bullshit, this was shaping up to be the mother of all rock concerts. Warned to arrive early, even the day before, Route 17B into Bethel was lined with abandoned cars. Pulling the Nash up under a tree, it was at least a three-mile hike to a chain-link fence with a gap in the center, kids pouring through, and no one taking tickets. Meanwhile, Abbie Hoffman and his 'Yippies' had pressured $10,000 out of the promoters to set up "Movement City," his festival-within-a-festival, passing out irrelevant flyers encouraging 'gate crashing.' Making a statement against the 'corrupt' materialism of our parents, with as much money as he could extort. The main stage still under construction, the field in front was already filled with blankets, tents, and kids dropping acid and dancing to music in their heads. The 'Hog Farmers,' brought in from a commune in California, had erected The Freak-Out Tent to deal with bad acid trips. Illegal drugs were another way of pissing off our parents, while they overpaid tobacco and pharmaceutical companies for theirs.

At the lake, kids were skinny dipping and taking in the sun while some old guy was running around trying to get them to cover up in front of the cameras. The whole 'free love' thing was disconcerting to the sexually repressed WWII generation, especially considering many of them had to get married to 'do it' and were now contractually stuck lying next to the same old nag every night. But the most difficult concept of all, for the veterans who 'fought to make the world safe for democracy,' had to be our rejection of the age-old political axiom that 'might makes right.' Whether in the long run, the moral imperative of non-violence could ever actually control the anger and greed and territorial tendencies of mankind, at that particular juncture in time, our entire idealistic generation wanted to try. As a practical matter it meant guys who got in fights didn't get laid. So everyone was 'turning their cheeks' (in every sense). Still encased in a self-protective shell, I walked back to the car alone that night, climbed into the back seat, and began working on a song before falling asleep.

Waking up the next morning to find the entire length of Route 17B now a double parked car lot, I couldn't help but get caught up in the smiles and hugs of complete strangers as we made our way back to the venue. By now the chain-link fence was a memory, trampled by a hundred thousand sandals, sneakers, and bare feet. It was late afternoon when Richie Havens began to play. The roads impassable, poor Havens had to just keep going until musical reinforcements could be flown in, ironically by army helicopter to save the 'anti-war' rally. But really, despite the slogans and 'peace-painted' faces, this was more about the music than politics. Later that night, with Sly Stone singing "I want to take you higher!" tens of thousands of matches danced in the darkness, most of them lighting up joints trying to comply. At about midnight, something in Ravi Shankar's sitar either annoyed or saddened the gods, as the sky began to weep and by the time Joan Baez finished *"We Shall Overcome,"* a full blown storm was thundering 'we'll see about that!' Under any other circumstances it would have been disaster, but we were all so high it just became an excuse to hug each other and get naked. It seems ludicrous, but for me, huddling that night in the rain and mud under soggy blankets and tarpaulins, somehow washed away layers of guilt and pain. When the sun broke through the clouds at dawn, for no reason, I just started to cry. And people I'd only known for hours wrapped their arms around and held me, probably assuming I was just coming down from a 'bad trip'... and in a way, I was.

Most of Saturday was a blur, stumbling around smiling and hugging people. Navigating through bodies and sleeping bags looking for the Food For Love stand, a guy smoking an Indian Peace Pipe told me it had been demolished, before offering a bite of his peanut butter sandwich. And everyone was sharing everything they had. I met Buddha, sitting in the lotus position, his stomach hanging out over his blue jeans; and Jesus, passing out bread from beneath a soaking white sheet; and Moses, leaning on his staff by the lake; and Mohammad, singing to his followers in a tent on the path to the portable toilets. The Gang of Four were out there preaching communism as army helicopters continued to airlift in musicians. Janis Joplin, Creedence Clearwater, the Grateful Dead, Canned Heat, the Who, Mountain, Santana and Jefferson Airplane, all converting violence into positive energy, pulsating through the massive body of disciples, 250,000 strong, becoming one with the music. Abbie Hoffman grabbed the microphone at one point in a political tirade, and Pete Townsend actually bopped him in the head with his guitar. And at sunup, with Grace Slick singing "One pill makes you larger, and one pill makes you small…" Some guy was yelling back "Hey man, stay away from the purple acid, that shit 'ill kill ya!"

By Sunday I was pretty burned out. With visions of dry clothes in the trunk and Twinkies in the glove compartment, I made my way back to the Nash, still wedged in under the tree, and slept most of the day. That night, too exhausted to make it back for The Band, Crosby, Stills & Nash, Joe Cocker, Ten Years After, and Jimi Hendrix, I worked instead on my own protest song. Actually more of an anti-protest, called *"Part Of It All:"* ♪

I have stormed all the walls burned by fiery speeches
  As I fought to change the laws but now time it teaches
I'm much too small
  And the walls are way too tall
And life's not for that at all

I have tried to mix the black and the white together
  For a time it was right, couldn't last forever
Lawyers would stall
  And fight over nothing at all
And life's not for that at all

Now those younger days are gone
  And the stars have left my eyes
And I feel a twinge inside
  As I begin to realize

Ain't no sense to watch the news at nine
  Can't change it anyway
For the people with the power
  Only live from day to day
So I close the door
  Ain't marchin' anymore
I ain't singin' no more protest songs
  Just sittin' on the floor
And I don't give a damn about your wars!

Now I stand on a stormy night and the sky excites me
  Or I walk through a flowing field and the wind delights me
I'm a waterfall
  Or a tree that's twenty feet tall
Now I'm life and now I'm part of it all

And as the last stragglers began to pull out on the dawn of the new decade, I tossed my guitar in the back seat of the Nash, rolled down the windows and turned up the radio, flipping over the hourglass, wondering where the sand would settle and what more there was to see on the other side.

♪ *Song available on iTunes & www.LEKalikow.com*

SEX, No Drugs & Rock-N-Roll
Memoirs of a Music Junkie
Part 2
The 70's

L.E. Kalikow

Please note that this autobiographical story, although based on true life, includes altered names, personalities and events, both for artistic and legal reasons and should, therefore, be considered a creative re-creation.

Copyright© 2016 L.E.Kalikow

Sex, No Drugs & Rock'n'Roll
Memoirs of a Music Junkie

Part 2: The 70's – The Impossible Dream

I. (1969)
(Chicago)

It wasn't just the gold records and photos lining the mahogany trimmed walls, or the plush amber carpet in the new offices of Chess Records at 320 East 21st Street. It was the history, and the thought that I might actually bump into Muddy Waters or Chuck Berry or Minnie Ripperton from Rotary Connection on the stairs to my first recording session. Actually it wasn't really 'my' session, but Drew assured me that with a little patience, it would be soon.

The control room was piloted by a long-haired freak toking on a joint while his free hand danced across rows of buttons, knobs, and faders, head bobbing to the rhythm of a Fender guitarist on the other side of the glass partition. Drew unsnapped his sax and began giving his reed a mini blow-job while silently loosening his fingers and valves. Two other horn players stood nodding at the console while I hid behind my insecurity in the corner.

Three days ago, after splattering off the mud of Woodstock, my old Nash seized up on US90, just west of South Bend. A full day of hitching with my knapsack and guitar, eventually got me to Loyola University, a few blocks from Drew's apartment, and the beginning of my life as a recording artist.

Drew Ambach was an A&R (Artist & Repertoire) representative for Chess Records. At least that was on the folded business card he gave me back in February, after my triumph at I.U. Sing and the night of debauchery that followed. In all fairness, he may have been a bit inebriated when he promised to sign me, which probably explained the look on his face when he opened his front door. Apparently,

Drew was about to leave for a studio gig with an alto sax strapped to his shoulder. So with my stuff stashed in his subterranean guest room/office, I was off to my first professional studio session. As it turned out, this would not be a normal recording date.

Even though *"Honky Tonk Woman"* was #1 on the Billboard Charts, somehow I didn't think *"When A Whore Falls"* was destined for Pop radio, or any radio for that matter, but it was definitely in the tradition of Chess Records. The leather trimmed console in the darkened cockpit, controlled a series of tape machines and communicated with the studio by means of a flip switch the engineer now used to call in the guitarist. The pumped up pilot then pushed some faders, and suddenly there was piano, bass and drums, and a slide guitar to match the Fender tracks just laid down. Monster speakers flooded the control room with down-n-dirty rhythm and blues as the horn players toked on another joint before heading in to the studio. While the mics were placed and tested and the horns belched in the background, two giant beer kegs were wheeled into the studio along with a large metal icebox as a precursor to the arrival of Tom Nance, the artist/songwriter, and his producer, Billy Birnside.

This entire session may have been an experiment in diversification by Marshall Chess, now VP of the label. Tom Nance turned out to be a white hippy, and Birnside, the owner of a Chicago jingle house... not exactly in keeping with the Chess heritage. Their arrival definitely dampened the mood in the control room, despite the beer. Then the girls arrived...At first I thought they were background singers... *very friendly* background singers. The tie-dye dirty blonde nudged herself next to me in the corner, while a bouffant-wigged 'Diana Ross' ran her fingers through the hair of the engineer. The mini-dressed Afro-Mulatto tried to approach Nance, but was rebuffed to the guitar player on the couch. Drew and the horn section cranked it up in the studio as the homely hippy's nipples convinced my dick she was really beautiful. And I almost went with it when the control room door opened again, and there was Zoey.

Memories of Zoey's massive breasts, rolling naked in that sleeping bag at I.U. had filled some lonely nights. With our simultaneous gasp of surprise, her un-tethered monsters bounded across the control room knocking me to the floor. Everyone cracked up, and the session was back on track as Miss Tie-Dye do-si-doed over to Nance, and the real background singers arrived. Zoey and I exited to a private office, to catch up.

After initial small talk, conversation became irrelevant. With the shades drawn and the office door locked, Zoey slipped off her panties, lifted her dress, and just stood there naked, looking down at me on the leather couch. It wasn't just the enormity of her breasts, but how shapely and full, bouncing with well-defined nipples that actually pointed up a bit and hardened as she touched herself, telling me how she'd masturbate thinking about our sleeping bag night. Remaining on the couch, I was also now naked, sitting facing her with my own fingers gently rubbing my penis in time with her. Staring at each other's crotch as her fingers got wet and began to probe, I couldn't help but shoot. Feeling my cum splatter on her skin, she threw back her head, eyes closed, pinching her left nipple with her free hand, while violently rubbing her clit, soaking her fingers, before suddenly opening her eyes wide, gasping, and violently jumping on my cock. With her thighs wrapped around me sweating and pumping, squishing my face between her massive soaking breasts it was all I could do to keep breathing. Another climax and now we were sliding and laughing on the sloppy leather couch, flopping off on to the carpet. With her legs wide open, and her right hand on my rear firmly pushing me inside, I watched a perfect bouncing nipple sticking up and inviting me down. Encircling her left breast with both hands, I began sucking as she grabbed my ass, squeezing and moaning. Then with her arms and legs clamped around me, we came together again.

By the time we made it back to the session the basic tracks had been recorded, and the beer blast was on, with microphones strategically placed in both the control room and studio. Apparently Birnside wanted the record to sound like a party, so what better way to achieve this than to get everyone drunk and record it! Now this was a career choice I could live with, even if I didn't drink or smoke. My personal proclivity to be in control didn't begrudge others the right to completely loose it. In fact it was fun to watch... While bouffant's head was bobbing in the pilots lap and the Mulatto bouncing topless on the guitarist, Birnside was smashing plates and glasses over a metal garbage can in the studio. Behind him, Drew and the horn section were clinking beer mugs and leaning on each other as the dirty blonde poured Jack Daniels on Nance's head and jumped him to the floor. Since Zoey was there at Drew's invitation, she figured she'd better get to him, and I headed back down the hallway to find a vending machine for dinner.

After a bag of potato chips, peanut butter crackers and a Snickers, back in the studio Billy was gathering everyone to sing the chorus line. In the pot permeated control room, partition framing the picture, the entire crew leaning on each other, the guitarist missing his pants, the Mulatto missing her shirt, everyone dripping from beer and booze, singing the line *"When A Whore Falls"* in drunken unison, here was my welcome to the music business.

At Drew's apartment the next morning, Zoey was gone and he was passed out in the living room. Tiptoeing toward the kitchen, suddenly a hand grabbed my ankle. For an unconscious instant Sergeant Drew Ambach was back in Nam, before releasing his grip and sitting up in a semi-comatose haze. Despite his return over a year ago, this soft-spoken musician was still reliving images that wormed into his sleep and seared the synapses to intimacy, blocking his ability to hold or be held. This explained why Zoey and I were no threat. And more importantly, why perhaps his having a sober, non-druggy roommate might be good, at least for now.

Drew only saw me perform once, and had a gig that night at a spot in Evanston, ideal for his covert reevaluation. The Chuck Lane Trio enjoyed a local musician following, eking out a living at weddings and dives like this. A typical hotel lounge with red plastic mesh covered glass bottled candles at each round table and a full bar, there were maybe three patrons when we arrived. Drew headed to the makeshift stage as I sat and ordered a coke I couldn't afford. Musicians straggled in as the night progressed until the original keyboard, bass & drum trio, was surrounded by a trumpet, sax, electric guitar, and congas that couldn't fit on the stage. And these guys could play! Waiting my turn was driving my butterflies crazy until Chuck finally signaled. We agreed on the Lenny Welch song *"Since I Fell For You."* As always, my voice took everyone by surprise. And with the final note suspended in blue, the players all nodded in approval with Drew looking like a proud father.

The next morning we were off to see Billy Birnside. It turned out that Drew wasn't really an A&R rep for Chess Records directly, but rather for Billy's label, Birnside Records, that had a production deal and was distributed by Chess. The office was a wing of Birnside's lavish suburban split-level home, lined with Clio Awards for the music behind everything from the ubiquitous Marlboro man to a "Think Small" Volkswagen. Despite his obvious wealth, Billy was insecure in his relative obscurity, and longed to see his name on a hit record. Based on Drew's enthusiasm and a few of last night's musicians, Billy hoped I would be his *"Ticket To Ride."* And the rush was on... They explained the advantage of direct access with no layers of secretaries, A&R, or business affairs people. And supposedly, Marshall Chess spent more time at Billy's place than in his own office. Whether all this was true was irrelevant. With no other options, I signed the 'development deal' that covered all expenses while working on my record, and marked my first official recording contract!

From soaking at Woodstock and hobo hitching to the Holy Grail in Chicago, now it was time to *"Let The Sunshine In."* The last week in August the scent of suntan lotion barely covered the smell of dead alewives washing up on the shore of Lake Michigan. A sanitation crew raked the patch of beach at the end of Drew's block every morning before sunbather's towels lined the sand. And I became a regular with my plastic pocket transistor radio playing *"Sweet Caroline"* by Neil Diamond, having *"Hot Fun In The Summertime"* with Sly & The Family Stone, smiling with Johnny Cash at *"A Boy Named Sue,"* and changing the station from the Archie's *"Sugar Sugar"* to ride the *"Marrakesh Express"* with Crosby, Stills & Nash, or to *"Lay Lady Lay"* with Bob Dylan. The beach also had its own *"Mrs. Robinson,"* an attractive Brunette MILF* who spent the day politely rebuffing male gadflies.

*(**MILF**) Mother I'd Love To Fuck, an abbreviation that didn't exist at the time but fit my fantasy.*

Possibly in her late thirties to early forties, Pamela Sayers was a former top model living on declining royalties and alimony from Tom Sayers, a popular WXFM radio personality. Drew knew them both but hated the sun and never came to the beach. He also assured me, with former lovers like Mick Jagger and Bruce Dern, and her ex still in the picture, his introduction would be irrelevant. But on my insistence, he found an old picture of the Sayers with him at the original Chess Studios, *"2120 South Michigan Avenue,"* an address immortalized by the Rolling Stones back when I was in high school. That evening, with the photo as *"My Way"* in, acting out the *"Games People Play,"* my finger was on the intercom at her beachfront apartment, when The Guess Who started *"Laughing"* on the radio and Tom Sayers answered her buzzer... not what I had planned.

As it turned out, the photo was a catalyst for an evening of insights. From the outset it was obvious that Pam and Tom were still close, despite the separation. They had also once been a circle of friends that included Drew, Billy and his wife Joanne, and Marshall. In fact Drew's A&R job and trip to Indiana with Zoey were engineered as a 'coming out' of the mental casket in which Viet Nam had shipping Drew home. It was Pam who found him the apartment nearby and, pleased that he now had a roommate, sent me home with a motherly hug... again, not what I had planned.

North along the beach, a park stretched for blocks that served as a game preserve for an assortment of colorful inhabitants. Barely noticed by the junkies hiding in the shadows, a bone fide member of the 'Peace & Love' generation in my bell-bottoms and dashiki, it was perfectly safe to inhabit the darkness in concert with the wild life. Strolling through *"Fellini's Satyricon,"* characters popped out of the darkness with distorted faces and bodies, jugglers and a unicycle, poets reciting, Haitian drummers, and the most beautiful black woman I'd ever seen, sashed in red satin, smiling as she passed. A guy claiming to be Gerry Ragni stopped to tell me he wrote *"Hair,"* while under a tree by the water an albino guitarist with fingers flailing non-stop over an unplugged electric guitar provided the soundtrack. And once again, having set out for a quiet walk in the park... this was not what I had planned.

Zoey was a receptionist at Chess Records during the day, and waitressed a few nights a week at "It's Here," a folk club on North Broadway near Loyola. Based on my credits, new record deal, and a blowjob, she was able to wangle a 'Special Guest' spot out of the owner. Overcompensating for his wife's brow-beatings at home, the club was his sanctuary and private fiefdom where turnaround was fair play. The fake Greenwich Village red brick walls lined with photos of artists who never played there, led to a minimal wooden stage with a single stationary spotlight. A sheetrock wall and black curtain separated the stage from the kitchen/dressing room, complete with a rifle used by the chef/janitor to pick off rats that sometimes dropped in from the alley. The owner made it clear, he'd kill the spot and yank me if my performance wasn't as advertised. Opening with the Zombies' *"She's Not There"* from my standard folk repertoire, the appreciative Saturday night crowd sang along with *"Puff The Magic Dragon"* and the chorus on *"Don't Think Twice"* before reverential silence in *"Just A Little Rain"* was shattered by two gunshots and a "Got The Fucker!!" from the kitchen. No place to go then but to *"Alice's Restaurant,"* from the just released film, to a rousing standing ovation and the offer of a regular weekly spot from the owner. Finally...something went as planned.

"Satyricon" Park was Cézanne serene in daylight, but some of the characters remained. Drew explained that both the albino and Black Goddess were neighborhood legends. The stark white speed freak

never left the park, except when locked up by social services, only to return within days to resume his frenetic death spiral concerto. The Black Goddess was either a porn star or virgin princess, depending upon the story. No one really knew, but even in sunlight she was breathtakingly beautiful. As the weather changed, sunbathing with Pam evolved into plutonic afternoons in her apartment. Seeking her 'parental' advice on the female orgasm, nipple sensitivity, clitoral verses vaginal stimulation, and mental keys to arousal. I knew it was just a matter of time…and timing.

It was a Tuesday night, when Zoey got a phone call that changed everything for us. A DC-9 mid-air collision over Indiana and her dad was suddenly gone. She'd have to support her mom in Boston, unsure when and if she'd return…another reminder of the frailty of time. Trying to refocus on my career wasn't easy when Birnside hadn't committed to a recording date. Perhaps as a distraction, Drew brought me to meet Chuck Lishon, a thin, short dark haired entrepreneur who, along with promoting local bands, had partnered with RCA artist Hans Wurman, to release *"The Moog Strikes Bach."* Following the wildly successful *"Switched-On Bach"* by Wendy Carlos, it was among the first albums to use the newly invented Moog synthesizer. By the time we left, Lishon had me convinced that the future was now…and time was ticking. Demanding to see Birnside the next afternoon, his wife Joanne shortstopped us at the front door. Behind her, I caught a glimpse of Marshall and Billy hunched over white powder on a glass table, with sheet music stretched out around the room. There would be no answer today. …Timing was everything.

That evening Billy invited us down to The Flower Pot, to see the latest Chess Records priority. Koffee was a fabulous looking white Aretha Franklin clone. If she could find her own voice, she'd be a star. And my project would have to wait. With Zoey gone, my career on hold, a chill in the air, and no progress with Pam, I began a sexual liaison with Ellie, a divorcee from It's Here. Recently out of an abusive marriage, on our first night, when I gently quivered just the head of my dick until she climaxed, she lost it. Grasping, crying and laughing at the same time, jumping in relief and disbelief, it was her first orgasm…and I had a sex addict on my hands… literally. Every night she came in a different outfit, sliding my hands up to her wetness before heading to the bedroom, or the kitchen, or the living room, or the closet, depending upon whether Drew was home. It was great fun…at first…until she asked to move in. And all I could think was, how the fuck do I get outta this? On a Monday night, when she arrived in a blue and white cheerleader uniform a year before Monday Night Football, I told her we had to talk. She wanted to fuck first and talk later, but I insisted. At the kitchen table under flickering fluorescent light, I told her I didn't love her and it was time to move on. Waiting for the obligatory tears and pleading, instead Ellie leaned back in her chair, lifted her cheerleader skirt and guided two fingers into herself, before looking back up to say, "OK, but fuck me anyway!"…So I did.

Downtown Chicago was still a police state in the wake of the Democratic Convention, and with photos of the My Lai Massacre on the air, 'tricky Dick' was trying to extricate us from Viet Nam without alienating his 'moral majority' backers. *"Butch Cassidy & The Sundance Kid"* jumped off a cliff running from the authorities as the media converged once again on Chicago for the trial of the Chicago Eight, soon to become The Chicago Seven when Black Panther Bobby Seale was bound and gagged by the Honorable Judge Julius Hoffman. Then fresh from Woodstock, Yippies Abbie Hoffman and Jerry Rubin appeared in mock judicial robes over fake Chicago police uniforms, all revealed while throwing kisses to the camera. The final autumn colors of the 60's had *"Come Together"* with The Beatles, along with *"Helter Skelter"* images of the Manson Murders, rumors that McCartney was dead, and pop reflections in Andy Warhol's new *"Interview Magazine."*

After weeks of sex education sessions, hands-on mentoring finally seemed possible when Pam answered the door in wet hair and a black silk robe. Apologizing for her appearance while drying her hair with a towel, she casually fell to the couch instead of heading to her room… and I got hard. Pamela Sayers, worshipped worldwide, and clearly out of my class, was practically naked on the couch in front of me. With Eric Clapton playing in the background, an autographed album cover on the coffee table, Pam asked my opinion. "On what?" I answered. "The record, silly... He's an old friend... It's so cool he's finally doin' his own thing." The words didn't register. "Did you ever pose nude?" I asked. "Where did that come from?" she responded. "Just wondering..." I replied. Wrapping the towel into a turban, she answered, "Once or twice when I was your age... in another lifetime..." She paused, then woke, "You know, I'm old enough to be your mother!" *"Well I'll be a motherfucker!"* I thought to myself, but said "Gimme a break, you could do Playboy tomorrow!" Half-laughing she pulled back the edge of her robe, "Not with this scar I couldn't." Immediately moving to the couch for a closer look, ever the teacher, Pam began explaining the horizontal versus bikini cut hysterectomy. Tentatively allowing me to touch the scar, the lecture continued even as my fingers moved on. Watching her eyes close and head tilt back, the words now cumming in broken breathy sentences, I came in my pants. *(I still get hard today thinking about it).* Despite the lecture, it would be years before I understood the meaning of 'hysterectomy', and why she laughed when I asked about protection. And even though her breasts were no longer perky, and she bikini waxed more than I might have liked, and the lovemaking wasn't as ardent as 'extreme sports' with Ellie, the fact that Pamela Sayers actually opened her legs, took me inside, and let me make her cum all over the couch... several times...will always be one of those valued entries in my memory book.

It turned out I should have been using protection with Ellie. When she didn't show up at the apartment for more than a week after 'cheerleader night,' I assumed it was over. But following the "Days Of Rage," when the National Guard stepped on Chicago's neck to squash the S.D.S. and cut off the city's circulation, Ellie reappeared. Disheveled and distraught, I assumed it was somehow related...no such luck...How the fuck could she get pregnant on the pill!! Sobbing that she needed money to 'deal with it,' unleashed images of Charlotte in another lifetime. Despite my relief when she refused escort to the doctor, Drew figured it was a scam. The $300 would wipe me out, but I rationalized, if she needed money that bad, so what... I was gonna be a star!... We never heard from Ellie again.

I was sleeping when the police arrived a few nights later. Drew was rocking in the corner of the living room in the lotus position in his underwear, blood dripping from the broken window where a junkie had picked the wrong place to rob. A blood trail running through the alley to the street, led to a flashing ambulance a few blocks away. Sergeant Drew Ambach had neutralized an enemy intruder and shut down. Apparently whatever body part protruded in the dark, was grabbed and sliced on the shattered glass, evoking the biblical image of a thief's severed hand. Appreciating the circumstance, the officer on the scene didn't press, even as Drew snapped out of his trance and began dressing. He said he was fine. We knew he wasn't.

Always soft spoken, he now responded in single sentences, never initiating conversation, except for occasional flashes of uncharacteristic anger. When he exploded on the phone with Billy, I finally got my recording session, not how I wanted, but I'd take it. The basic tracks had already been cut when we arrived at the studio except for an elderly Groucho Marx looking character sitting under a microphone surrounded by a pile of junk. Ira worked almost every session as the resident percussionist and sound effects procurer, presently scraping a hollow wooden gourd with a metal rod before switching to a bag full of marbles, clicking in rhythm to the tracks. On a metal rack in front of him hung a hodgepodge of pipes, bottles, lids and covers, rods and wands, a flexible saw, tambourines, and on the floor an assortment of pots, pans and washboards. Ira was a true sound artist. The song Billy chose for my first session was Laura Nyro's *"Stony End,"* as recently released by Barbra Streisand. Having never heard or seen me perform, Birnside assumed a hit song by a hit female writer, charting for a hit female artist, could be a surprise pop hit for me. After all, that's how they pitched commercials, and singers were interchangeable.

It would take years to later understand why Billy Birnside was my worst possible first producer. Creating a pop record, like any artistic endeavor, usually requires understanding the art form, often trivialized by the casual observer who sees a Jackson Pollock as 'paint splashed on a canvas that a kid could do.' And in fact, a kid might be able to splash paint in a form that elicits an emotional response and is considered art, but not know what the fuck he or she did. Which is exactly how most hit records are made. The professional however, must understand the why of it. In pop/rock music, it meant tapping into the teenage psyche, finding a string that resonates, and plucking it with an original twist, often with a simple melodic or lyrical hook. Singers were usually garage band graduates who didn't read music, but sang from their hearts. The voice need not be 'good' but rather unique, recognizable, and most of all, it had to be honest. Kids know when you're faking it.

Billy Birnside thought that making a hit record was like making a commercial, except longer, with no idea he was in a completely different medium. Having spent his career with studio musicians who played the notes exactly as written, every time I strayed, Birnside stopped the session. That was after ten retakes on the opening lines, popping my "p"s and hissing my "s"s, which was OK live, but not in the studio, he explained. On "poor mother" I had to hide the 'p' and lose the 's' on the end of "mines," not to mention burying it on "Stony End." Then my dynamics were all wrong. It was good to portray emotion, but not to get soft or loud, they did that in the mix. And so it went for more than two hours of retakes, until Billy threw up his hands and told me to forget about being a recording artist. "Maybe you should think about Broadway?" he suggested. Here was a dose of reality I didn't see coming... a respected, award-winning producer telling me to ditch my dreams. Actually, he was full of shit... Any real rock producer made allowances with proper mic placement, filters and a good sound engineer. But I didn't know that. As it turned out, Billy Birnside never did produce a hit record, although he eventually wrote a few and got to work with Barbra Streisand, who could sing the notes exactly as written and didn't pop her 'p's.

Drew had left the session early and wasn't at home. Neither was Pam, so I wandered into the park to sit by the water, the albino's guitar wailing in the background. The enormity of the *"Worst That Could Happen"* was still setting in when a velvet voice intruded from behind. Sensing a kindred spirit, The Black Goddess asked permission, before slipping into the lotus position on the rock beside me. Charmaine's red-satin sexuality was a lucrative look for photographers trying to capture *"The Age Of Aquarius,"* but beneath the makeup and false eyelashes was *"Something"* in the sadness that drew her to me. And I desperately needed to talk. It was hard to accept that my self-image was a fantasy, and the dream I had taken for granted, would never be. And it all came gushing out until *"Raindrops Falling"* forced us back to the apartment.

Initially I just needed to be held, but with the first kiss it was obvious that The Black Goddess was a hand painted illusion. I never knew that black models wore so much makeup. The caked, reddish-brown powder, that came off on everything, with a 'medicine cabinet' scent, made it difficult to *"Come Together."* With no evident sexual desire, she avoided my gaze in an awkward attempt to go down before I grabbed her by the shoulders. At which point Charmaine began sobbing uncontrollably, apologizing for a secret she couldn't reveal… just what I needed today! My vulnerability, she explained, brought down her guard, and now she was in uncharted intimate waters, smearing my chest with brown residue and cherry-red lipstick. After having spent hours in her arms, suddenly the tables were turned. Trapped in my own apartment, there was nothing to do now but hold on.

Even with constant reassurances, all she could tell me was she was saving for an operation in Australia. I had no idea what that meant, but needed to retrieve my sleeping arm from beneath her. Afraid I was giving up, Charmaine grabbed my hand, held my palm to her unresponsive breast and stared at me in silence. Then, with a frightened gaze, she trembled my hand down the length of her body and opened her legs. At first it felt like some sort of girdle. Closer examination revealed a strap between the lips of her vagina. The

Black Goddess had both a CUNT AND A DICK!! A perfect way to end a day of shocking disillusionment!

And that was just the beginning...Within weeks, and the confirmation that Chess Records had been acquired by GRT (General Recorded Tape), Leonard Chess, the label's founding father, passed away. After a brief stint as company President, Marshall jumped ship to head a new label for the Rolling Stones in London. Then "The Hawk" whipped in off Lake Michigan, forcing the city to install ropes along the icy sidewalks. With a dysfunctional label, producer and roommate, temperatures dropping and women growing dicks, it was time to leave Chicago. On Dec. 7, the anniversary of Pearl Harbor, while boarding a Greyhound home, came word of the murder at Altamont the night before. While the Rolling Stones sang *"Sympathy For The Devil,"* a Hell's Angel plunged a knife into the belly of a freaked out hippie, and so ended the generation of "Peace & Love."

II. (1970)
(Home)

Thomas Wolfe was wrong. Back home, the split-level in White Plains was empty with siblings gone, and mom thrilled to be cooking again. Dad accepted my need to fail as a musician before finding my true calling as a lawyer, and secretly looked forward to the assortment of woman who would soon be parading through. The downstairs wreck-room was converted to my private apartment, with sliding glass doors that opened to the weeping willows in the backyard and a side path up to the street. Not a bad place to write.

Taking the words of Billy Birnside to heart, if I couldn't be a recording artist, I'd write a Broadway musical. Adhering to the adage 'write what you know,' *"Where Has All The Ivy Gone?"* would be an election between the liberals and conservatives at a large mid-western university. The second act to close with an audience vote, and a finale based on the tabulation. Coincidently, the hippy liberal protagonist would look just like me. Now all I had to do was write it.

But January in New York is cold, and I needed a recharge. My tall dark prom date, Allison Pines, lived in a mansion on North Street with imposing white columns like those long legs I fantasized about. Feeling especially small, unsure if her family even lived there anymore, waiting in a cold rain for someone to answer, came a flood of high school memories, when all the girls were virgins and I was beaten for my long hair. The massive wooden door finally opened to Allison's mom, Ellen, holding a baby girl and a bottle. Apparently Allison was no longer a virgin. She also wasn't home. In the city on a photo shoot, the free-spirited single mother, was now a successful fashion model. Although taken back a bit by my afro, Ellen gave me their number to call later. Pulling into the driveway at home, I noticed a bright red Mustang next door at the McDermott house. Back in the day, the willowy blonde Rowena 'Ro' McDermott would sometime drop me at school in the morning, on her way to Briarcliff College. I'd try not to stare at her legs as she shifted gears.

There were nights I'd hide in the dark, peering through the attic fan to catch a glimpse of her changing, but to no avail. And suddenly there she was, waving from their living-room window. Nonchalantly heading to her front door, there was a brief glimmer that disappeared with her father's presence, as we exchanged pleasantries. Refusing Mr. McDermott's tentative offer to come in from the rain, I left wondering why she was still at home, and what was in that fleeting glance?

Having cast my preliminary female fishing lines, it was now time to get to work. The first order of business was a story line and characters. The election would be for Student Body President, with a long-haired hippy living off campus named Guy (an 'everyman'), running against a crew-cut ROTC Captain, from Sigma Epsilon, named Bud (named for the beer). Each needed a girlfriend. Guy's girl would be Zoey (after my Chicago lover), a towny who worked at Woolworth's to help pay her tuition as a poli/sci major. Bud was pinned to Allison (for my prom date), a tall glamorous Delta, majoring in home economics. As a subplot, I decided to have them switch partners somewhere in the midst of the election involving seduction and betrayal. With both *"Hair"* and *"Oh Calcutta"* on Broadway, sex and nudity would not be a problem, especially for me.

In real life however, it was too damned cold to go anywhere, never able to catch Allison at home and only occasionally waving to Ro, there was nothing to do but write and masturbate... both persistently.

The initial task was to block out the scenes and music. Act 1. - The show would open with a production number establishing the school election, each side putting up signs and tearing down the opponent's. "Go With Guy!" or "This Bud's For You!" appearing on large picture posters. I'd compose the music with my guitar and new Hitachi two-track cassette recorder, which allowed over-dubbing for harmonies. Although the sound deteriorated with each generation, the bigger problem was the inability to hear the old track while recording the new one. This meant 'flying blind,' relying on the odometer numbers to know when to start and finish, unable to hear if you're on rhythm or pitch until playback. But it was doable. However, attempting to find the notes, time signatures, and rhythms, and translating them to lead sheets was a lost cause for me, to be surrendered to a 'real musician' later.

After another series of calls, and probably coerced by her mom, Allison finally agreed to see me. Apparently she still imagined the skinny little guy whose head was shaved by the cops before the senior prom. When the door opened to my giant afro, dashiki, bell-bottom jeans, and tall black boots, Allison went from surprise to self-conscious in a palpable instant, suddenly running a hand through her hair and looking away as if she'd been caught naked. *"Whole Lotta Love"* was throbbing in her brother's room upstairs, ironically as Eva Von Zeppelin, heiress to the airship designer, was suing to stop Led Zeppelin from using the family name. Ellen Pines last saw me wrapped in the rain, hair matted and partially obstructed by an umbrella. As she joined us in the hallway, cradling Allison's baby in a fluffy pink blanket, the former dancer and choreographer was cool with the new me. But we all knew her TV producer father, would not be as accepting. With the gurgling little puffball now in her arms, Allison and I ducked into the den and closed the door. (*I never understood why people find infants adorable, puppies yes, but not babies. They're just chubby bald little spitting, pissing and shitting machines with bobble heads and eyes that can't focus.*) Little Jeanie was the product of a failed relationship, one of many Allison had been through since high school. It was soon obvious that with the baby, auditions and photo shoots, despite the newfound attraction between us, finding time together would be difficult.

Back in the basement, the next few scenes had to establish the characters and their relationships. The first would take place in Guy's pad, fashioned after my own off-campus apartment, complete with a sheepskin couch, red burlap window covers, a giant yellow beanbag, pot plants in the bathroom, and a red carpeted ladder leading up to the loft bedroom. After a song by Guy and the hippy crew protesting everything from the war to Playtex bras we discover that Zoey's a neat freak, picking up when everyone leaves, expressing doubts and the fact that she wouldn't mind wearing a bra occasionally. The next scene is at the Fraternity house, where Bud and the brothers sing about conformity and protecting American values. We then cut to Allison's room in the sorority house, where she's frustrated with her makeup, weight, and oh-so-proper clothes, envious of girls who can just get up and go.

With winter's bite releasing, it was time for me to get up and go. Crosby, Stills, Nash & Young were singing *"Déjà vu"* at the Fillmore East, as I headed down MacDougal Street, leather gloves clutching my guitar. The Café Wha? was now closed and The Feenjon had weird Israeli music downstairs. The Gaslight Café, a fake copy of the original, was still there but the Kettle O Fish was now home to a Psychic Tarot Card reader. Thank God, Gerdes Folk City was still around the corner on 3rd Street, where poker faced Mike Porco concealing the faintest smile of recognition as I walked in. Grumbling how The Village had "gone to shit," in the next breath I had a spot opening for Eric Anderson that weekend, with the coveted right to 'pass the hat.' From there it was up to Bleecker Street, lined with nameless bars and secular restaurants, until reaching The Village Gate on the right, and diagonally across the street, Paul Colby's Bitter End. Paul was a diminutive, long-haired, outspoken defender of individual rights, and the consummate promoter, vainly proud of the artists 'discovered' at his club, as depicted in the wall mural behind the bar. To the left of the venue, an unmarked door led up a narrow staircase to the sound booth and walk-in closet sized office where Colby conducted business. Always on the phone, a raised index finger had me wait for a slot that weekend opening for Jim Dawson. This was the West Village, where folkies like me could still find work, but the real scene was now the East Village.

Opened by Bill Graham in 1968, The Fillmore East was the primary rock venue of the day. With artists like Jimi Hendrix, The Allman Brothers, the Grateful Dead, Derek & The Dominos, The Chambers Brothers, etc, and where Neil Young & Crazy Horse just recorded a live album the week before. Around the corner on St. Marks Place was the Electric Circus, with flame throwing jugglers and trapeze artists performing between musical sets, strobe lights flickering over a huge dance floor, while multiple projectors flashed images and footage from home movies, a hedonist forerunner to what later would be known as 'Disco.' Just up the street on Park Avenue, was Max's Kansas City, the center of 'Glam Rock' inspired by Andy Warhol's entourage, who dominated the restricted back room with The Velvet Underground, while sequined black-leather patrons squished together in the earsplitting main hallway, blasted by the likes of Iggy Pop, Lou Reed, Alice Cooper, and David Johansen's New York Dolls. At twenty-three, I was obviously already the older generation.

"M.A.S.H." was number one at the box office as F. Lee Bailey defended Captain Ernest Medina for the 'My Lai Massacre,' with Edwin Starr's *"War"* on the radio. Simon & Garfunkel broke up on the *"Bridge Over Troubled Water,"* while The Jackson 5 sang *"I'll Be There,"* and 'women's lib' estrogen got a boost from *"The Mary Tyler Moore Show"* debut, against a shot of testosterone from the new *"Monday Night Football"* with Howard Cosell and Don Meredith. Then *"Marcus Welby M.D."* did a double take at cross-dressing Flip Wilson's Geraldine on prime time TV. In the midst of this *"Ball Of Confusion,"* with *"Gunsmoke"* still on the air, the film *"Woodstock"* was released and the country experienced some serious 'cognitive dissonance,' *(a concept I learned at I.U.)* and a perfect atmosphere for my musical.

The next scene would be a confrontation at the Student Union Candidates Meeting, with the two couples, in Howard Cosell's words, getting "up close and personal" to the song, *"You're An Idiot!"*

Years shrink as we age. Four years is half a lifetime when you're eight, but only ten percent at forty. Growing up, Rowena was way older, but now almost my age, chatting in her driveway, her repressive father at work. Ro's blonde hair and blue eyes now fit right in at IBM, where "Big Blue" was selectively breeding its image. Downstairs in my room, her Ivory Soap complexion blushed at the lyrics, but unlike Marilyn Chambers, tightly crossing her legs. Four years commuting to college from her father's house and dealing with her mother's secret dementia, her hormones were at odds with her head. Hiding behind innocuous hints, avoiding eye contact, longing for an intimacy she feared. Realizing her father would soon be home, when she got up to leave, her neighborly peck on the cheek morphed into a sensual embrace before pulling away to run for the door.

Staging the rock quarry scene would be tricky. Abandoned, deep blue water filled limestone cavities surrounded I.U. Perfect for skinny-dipping, and dumping old cars. I imagined the ass of Bud's new Chevy convertible jutting out on a rock formation, stage left, with the conservatives lounging in the latest styles. And Guy's peace sign painted old VW precariously perched stage right, the hippies joyously getting naked, Zoey surreptitiously flirting with Bud. Then both sides perform *"Don't Look Now"* before the hippies jump into the water and swim away. At which point, over Allison's objections, the fraters push the VW over the edge and drive off. Allison stays behind to apologize to Guy. That night, the hippies retaliate, stealing Bud's Chevy, and leaving it at the student union, sprayed with peace signs, a large "Go With Guy" poster in the front seat. After the commotion the next morning, Zoey apologizes to Bud. That's it for act one.

Deep in composing mode that night, I almost didn't hear the light tapping sound of Rowena at the sliding glass door. Neither of us thought she had the balls, her parents asleep next door. After a fake search for a misplaced purse, we settled on the couch next to my guitar, her right toe nervously shaking her knee, and forefinger tightly twirled a thin lock of hair. This would require a guitar-induced seduction. Inspired by Eric Anderson's *"Come To My Bedside,"* my *"Silhouette In A Negligee,"* ♪ ended with a quiet falsetto suspended in the air as I leaned over and kissed her. Rowena melted into the cushions, her mouth wide open, pulling me to her. Then suddenly we were in the 50's, saving herself for her husband, and pushing me away. Adept at undoing a bra snap with two fingers, her pointed pink nipples popped out, and once in my mouth, her scent permeated the room. That's when the phone rang. Who the fuck was calling in the middle of the night! Before I could get to it, they picked up upstairs and dad's groggy voice called down. We could hear Ro's father screaming through the phone line... her mortified and me with a serious case of blue balls. The next morning an invisible wall separated our two houses, never to come down, and I really needed to get laid.

♪ *Song available on iTunes & www.LEKalikow.com*

White Plains had become a shopping Mecca, with a new Macy's mall in the works. Cruising in mom's Ford Galaxie would be like duck hunting in a Harley. I'd have to park it before targeting prey. At least that was the plan, until prancing in white patent leather boots and a red leather miniskirt, nipples poking through layers of love beads on a pink braless tank top, a Clairol Herbal Essence blonde appeared, gliding just out of range across the street. No time to do anything but stop and take my shot. Leaving the Galaxie in park, traffic honking and fingers flying, I darted across Mamaroneck Avenue to confront the startled chick. Pointing to the traffic jam she was causing, in an unexpected stately British accent, Jennifer Winston playfully agreed to wait while I parked the car. Then, to my surprise, dashed across the street behind me into the passenger seat, to mixed reviews from the audience as we drove off.

Just out of town Milk Maid was the make-your-own-sundae shop, where custom once demanded teenagers leave rubber in the afternoon and rubbers at night. But 'The Maid' had matured, showing her age with cracks in the counter and chairs. Nonetheless, a unique experience for my proper British subject, whipped cream dripping over her hot fudge sundae with nuts, sprinkles, and two cherries. Jennifer was refreshingly uninhibited but also evasive, deftly changing the subject when I noticed the new Crowne Plaza Hotel key in her purse. Then, after an hour-long sugar high talking binge cuddled in the front seat, my hand under her blouse and hers caressing my hard-on, we needed that hotel. The full story came out when we couldn't park nearby. Jen was an exclusive London based call girl, flown over by a wealthy Connecticut businessman, who would soon be moving her into Manhattan. Sneaking through the parking garage entrance, not to be seen, I nonetheless couldn't resist pulling down her red panties in the empty elevator. Dropping to one knee for closer examination of the heart shaped coiffure then revealed, she was grabbing my head with both hands, leg wrapped over my shoulder, when the elevator door opened (*difficult to explain had anyone been there.*). The elevator closed twice before we made it out and down the hall. By the time her door closed behind us, we were half naked, rolling on the newly carpeted floor. Despite the fact that this was actually her job, Jennifer loved to fuck. At first it was just fun, like the 'helicopter' with her stretched out, legs closed, spinning around on my cock. Each climax however, became more extreme as we continued from the floor, to the couch, to the kitchen, to the bedroom. Then it was no longer a game. For the first time in her life, she would later reveal, Jennifer completely lost it, literally screaming 'Harder! Harder!" in multiple convulsive orgasms, to the slapping sound of our wetness in tides slamming against the headboard. At one point when I tried to pull out, she grabbed my cock and jumped back on, almost sliding off the soaking sheets, squeezing her nipples and begging me not to stop. And so it went until finally cool replaced warm, and we found ourselves shivering in each other's arms. Although not expected that night, it wasn't clear when her patron would show up. Having tempted fate enough for one day, I slipped back down and out the garage, already looking forward to our next rendezvous.

A blackboard in front of Folk City that Saturday night had my name scribbled in white chalk under the much larger 'Eric Anderson.'

Upon entering, the darkened bar room, where Dylan once hid in the corner, opened into a performing area with a foot-high platform stage against the right wall. Pictures of the great folkies who actually performed there *(unlike those at It's Here in Chicago)* filled both rooms. A rickety wooden staircase led down to the basement/ beer cellar/ storage shed/ dressing room, where at least there were no rats... that I could see. Jennifer, now at the Hilton on 53rd Street, was suggesting a night in 'The Village' to her friend as I tuned my guitar before stopping next door for the best baklava ever, thick with walnuts and honey. Back in the basement deciding what to play, my homemade material had moved from interpersonal to social commentary. With everyone 'getting back to nature,' this first day of spring had just been declared 'Earth Day' by Secretary General U Thant at the United Nations. (*Only to conflict with another 'Earth Day' announced a month later by someone else.*) In honor of the day, I opened my set with *"Corned Beef On Rye,"* ♪ my anti 'country living' protest song:

Everybody moved to the Country
    For a better place to be
Get away from the crime in the city streets
    Now all this may be true
But there sure ain't nothin' to do
    And I'm getting' kinda tired
Of talkin' to the grass and trees

Where can I buy
    A corned beef on rye?
Where can I see
    An X- rated show?
Can't get no eats
    'Cause they done rolled up the streets
And by ten o'clock
    Even the television shows are closed.

I remember the ladies
    In the black silk satin gowns

And the all-night bars
>	And the burlesque shows
Here they smell like horses
>	With calluses from working the ground
Lord I'm so tired of calico
>	And hearin' 'bout hogs on the radio

Where can I buy
>	A hot pizza pie?
Where can I get
>	A Chinese egg roll?
I like the birds and the bees
>	Listen to the wind in the trees
But I'd rather get tight
>	Late at night
Rock'n'roll into the morning light
>	Go out and find
A lady-of-the-night
>	Come back and walk up
Twenty-four flights
>	I don't care
It'll be all right
>	I just can't take
This country life no more!

>	♪ *Song available on iTunes & www.LEKalikow.com*

It wasn't until half way through my second set that Jennifer arrived with her patron. Unobtrusive as Inspector Clouseau, in his double-breasted pinstriped suit and wide silk tie, rudely maneuvering to a front table. Meanwhile Jen looked fabulous in a laced see-through top and bell-bottoms, completely diverting attention from the stage. Desperate to avoid the slightest glimpse of recognition, I stopped to retune my guitar. Now, with every man in the room staring at her, it would be obvious if I didn't look, but maybe a giveaway if I did? How long would be appropriate? Perhaps a passing glance? But they were sitting right there in front… fuck! Quietly finger picking and waiting for the room to subside, eyes shut, I acted lost in my closing number. Hearing me sing for the first time, I knew Jen was getting wet, hiding my hard-on behind my guitar, hoping 'the beard' didn't notice. Then that magic moment of silence before a burst of applause. Double fuck! Now they wanted an encore! Quickly closing with *"Don't Think Twice, It's Alright,"* Jennifer's hand slid to her companion's thigh under the table, casually looking at me.

Sunday night was rainy and cold, The Bitter End empty for the first set. But Jim Dawson's followers drizzled in while Jennifer's date took a limo home from The Hilton, and she opted for a well-earned night's sleep. That night, as I sang my ode to the *"Subway Rider"*:

♪ *Song available on iTunes & www.LEKalikow.com*

Subway riders sittin' in a line
    Faces all painted and pale
Young man sittin' with his face in a book
    Old lady hangin' on to the rail
Train keeps pickin' up people
    Like a vacuum pack can
Who's bitin' my hand!?

Suddenly flashing sirens from the street bounced off the iconic red brick wall behind me, and someone announced a bomb at The Electric Circus. The next day papers were filled with stories of the pipe bomb planted by a Black Panther as I headed back into the city for a meeting with Beechwood Music, a major music publisher.

Music publishing is a complex affair. When a song is created, it's automatically split in half between the writer(s) share and publisher(s) half. If you don't have a publisher when you write a song, you control the publishing half until it is assigned. If you can't or don't want to do the paperwork involved, you can assign the 'administrative' rights to another publisher for a percentage. Billy Birnside had such an arrangement with Beechwood Music, and had been sending them demos of my songs. Luckily, thanks to my attorney father *(who saved my ass more than once)*, my publishing was contingent upon a major record deal that never happened. So I still owned all my rights, and Beechwood was interested. Now, with my musical half complete, it was time to meet.

1650 Broadway, that housed Beechwood, was the songwriting 'sausage factory' annex to the iconic Brill Building diagonally across the street at 1619. Allegro Studios and its live echo chamber was in the basement where Katz & Kasenetz blew their 'bubble gum' blasts, Tommy James warbled *"Crystal Blue Persuasion,"* Dion sang a tribute to *"Abraham, Martin and John,"* and literally hundreds of hit records were created. Upstairs Don Kirshner's Aldon Music was the 60's songwriting assembly line of Neil Sedaka, Howard Greenfield, Carole King, Gerry Goffin, Neil Diamond, Paul Simon, Phil Spector, Barry Mann, Cynthia Weil and Jack Keller among others. Tenants also included Scepter Records, with Chuck Jackson, The Shirelles, BJ Thomas, and The Kingsmen, while Roosevelt Music, had the team of Feldman-Goldstein and Gottherer. In fact, as I walked in the front door on 51st Street, "O-o-Child" was on the radio by The Five Stairsteps, on 1650's Buddah Records and written by Stan Vincent, who I'd come to know years later.

When the metal wood-grained elevator clunked opened, to my immediate left was a door marked "Leiber & Stoller." Down the gray linoleum squared hall, the office of "Morty Wax PR" preceded Beechwood Music. Morty was a very large public relations guy, who years later would shed half his 250 pounds but maintain a substantial clientele. A glass partition in the nondescript reception area of Beechwood revealed a metal windowed executive office where GM, Jerry Simon, in a jacket and tie, Professional Manager Lou Ragusa, hair over his ears in a flowered silk shirt, and Lou's stunning 'little black dress' wife/recording artist Linda were waiting. The offices also included writer's rooms, one squeezing a small upright piano, the other with assorted guitars. From the outset it was clear they wanted to sign me as a songwriter. To my surprise, with Linda's encouragement and despite Billy Birnside, they also felt I could be a recording artist. With the script outline and a few songs from my show, the meeting stretched from the scheduled half-hour to an all-day affair and more complex negotiations than any of us expected. In the end, I agreed on a deal, once again contingent on a major record contract and/or production of my musical and 50/50 co-publishing on any covers (songs recorded by another artist). This called for a celebration, and I knew just where to go.

Two blocks up and one over in an executive suite at The Hilton, at precisely 6:30, Jennifer experienced a prearranged migraine. Waiting in the lobby, behind a pillar and reflected view of the elevators, I watched Clouseau disembark to a waiting limo before calling up on the house phone. The lobby froze when Jennifer emerged in a skin-tight white sequined jump suit, red stilettos and a flowing red scarf, as I ducked out the back door to wait around the corner. This was my first encounter with actual $100 bills, donated by her sponsor and put to good use at a lavish Persian restaurant and marathon night of debauchery. It was late the next afternoon when I caught the Stamford Local home, with a date to meet again that weekend.

Back to writing… after the first intermission, Act 2 would open with two simultaneous morning bedroom scenes. On stage right, Allison wakes with Guy in his loft bedroom, while on stage left, Bud and Zoey awake in a bunk bed in his frat house. Together they sing *"I Can't Believe We Did This!"* while they dress, an intricate musical quartet that would take the remainder of the week to complete.

On weekends Jen's benefactor was with family. So, what better place to spend Saturday night with my British import, than with *Mad Dogs and Englishmen,* at the Fillmore East? Behind Joe Cocker, a giant choir, horn section, multiple drummers and Leon Russell on keys. Unlike other bands, no original material, but a monstrous rock revival in praise of The Stones, Traffic, Dylan, The Beatles, Ray Charles, Otis Redding and other rock Gods. A Pentecostal experience, my pulse, breathing and consciousness lost in rhythm, this was my drug of choice. And when I came down, Jennifer was staring at me in wonderment and in heat. The taxi's eyes were in the mirror when she jumped me in the back seat. Then we shocked the shit outta the premature jocular cab doorman at The Hilton. No more anonymity for us! This actually worked out OK, since various hotel staff would later hide me from Jen's obnoxious benefactor and smile as he walked by.

At Beechwood there were other priorities, as they geared up for their first major artist release, soon to be announced. But it was fun just to cross-pollinate with other writers and a connection to backup musicians. That's how I found Jose Martinez, a conga player who could literally make his drums speak, wetting his fingers and massaging the skins in syncopated rhythms. All I needed was Jose and a bass player to work Lloyd Price's Turntable club a block away. 'Mr. Personality' had his name in lights above a smoked glass door on Seventh Avenue and 52nd. This led down a dark narrow stairway that, at the bottom, opened to a massive ballroom and stage, with state-of-the-art sound and lighting. Managed by future boxing promoter Don King, the place was clearly well financed. *(But not so clear as to where the money came from. Which could also be said for most of the record companies at 1650 Broadway.)* But Jose presented a unique scheduling problem… he was homeless. This meant taking abuse from whatever phone number he last gave me, when thrown out by his latest 'fiancé.' Although my favorite gig, with the guitar, bass and congas pulsating together in hypnotic rhythm, it just didn't *"Come Together."*

One thing that did, was opening solo for Van Morrison, with Jefferson Airplane and Hot Tuna at SUNY, New Paltz, arranged by the promoter, who saw me at The Bitter End and needed an acoustic act that didn't require much set-up. Hot Tuna was actually a diet version of The Airplane formed the year before when Grace Slick had throat surgery and couldn't sing. For the next few years they would open before Grace and the full group took the stage. I was then slotted to perform in front of the curtain, while Van Morrison's crew set up. A large tent was constructed behind the gymnasium to house the performers where that afternoon sultry Slick was tripping in a see-through tie-dye, spinning around the room. While Bailin yelled at the roadies to get control, someone stepped on Jorma's guitar and he freaked. Meanwhile, no one had seen Van Morrison. As we approached show time Morrison was still a no-show, and Grace was having trouble getting dressed and/or standing up. Taking the stage with Hot Tuna, Bailin mumbled that he couldn't live like this anymore. Meanwhile with a team of volunteers calling every motel and bar in the area, the promoter warned that I might have to 'stretch my set a bit.' Once in the spotlight, Grace came alive and performed with her usual flare. But it was literally minutes before my time slot when Van Morrison dropped out of a taxi, drunk and abusive. I opened my set with *"Corned Beef On Rye"* and *"Subway Rider,"* before slapping my guitar in rhythm to cover the gurgling and swearing behind me as they poured coffee into Morrison. *(Well at least they weren't shooting rats.)* When the curtain finally opened and he slurred through his set, the audience just assumed he was being artistic.

Over the next few weeks I finished most of the music for "Ivy", including a Woolworth's confrontation scene at Zoey's cash register, where it becomes clear that Allison is the liberal and Zoey, the conservative. Next comes the big pre-debate rally at the Student Union, where the remixed couples face off singing "We're Gonna Kick Your Ass!"

Meanwhile, the weekends were spent in the city on Jennifer's allowance at amazing restaurants like The Four Seasons and Lutece, before legendary sexual marathons eliciting smiles from chambermaids and doormen. In the real world everything was breaking up... Michael Nesmith left The Monkees and, while, singing *"Let It Be,"* Paul McCartney announced the end of The Beatles, days before an oxygen tank explosion on Apollo 13 almost ended in catastrophe. Fugitive priest Philip Berrigan was arrested for pouring blood over draft files while, standing in front of the American Flag, *"Patton"* broke all box office records. Johnny Cash sang at the White House as Nixon sent troops into Cambodia and told us it was "not an invasion" but an "action." When students protested at Kent State University, the Ohio National Guard opened fire, captured forever in the iconic John Filo photo of Mary Ann Vecchio kneeling over the body of Jeffrey Miller. And in the midst of all this, Beechwood Music announced the release of their latest artist, Orville Stoeber, on MCA's UNI Records. Despite major promotion, the artistic and critically acclaimed poet was out of sync with the times, and the record flopped. Unfortunately for me, now that Beechwood blew its wad, the parent company, EMI in the UK, wasn't investing any further in the States, especially as their affiliate DJM, was having local success with their new artist, Elton John.

With my album once again on the back burner, finishing the musical became a priority. For the big debate scene I pictured two podiums, center stage, facing the audience, with a professor between them as moderator, initially with his back to the audience and surrounded by the liberals sitting stage right, and the conservatives, stage left, each cheering their candidate. There would be five basic questions, the first two from the moderator, and the last three by plants in the audience that he calls on. These would be as follows:

1. Pro America *vs.* Anti War
Conservative: "Love It Or Leave it" – You should believe in our government and back the president, especially when at war.
Liberal: The Viet Nam War was immoral and to protest it, a matter of conscience, that personified America's democracy.

2. 'Right To Choose' in Campus Housing *vs.*
Anti Discriminatory Clauses and Practices
Conservative: Fraternities/Sororities should have the right to choose their membership, and not be forced to accept other races or religions.
Liberal: They absolutely have the right to choose their roommates, but not with written discriminatory charters of exclusion, preventing the choice of other races or religions.

3. 'Pro Life' *vs.* 'Right To Choose' on abortion
Conservative: All life is sacred, including that of the unborn child.
Liberal: A woman has the 'Right To Choose' as it affects her own body and well-being.

It's interesting that the 'Right To Choose' is a conservative stance on housing and a liberal one on abortion

4. Fair College Entrance Competition *vs.* Affirmative Action
Conservative: It's not fair and reverse discrimination to offer college acceptance to minority students over equal or better-qualified white students.
Liberal: Minority students handicapped by inferior inner-city education and poor living conditions, deserve a 'helping hand' in providing a path to higher education for the desegregation and overall good of society.

5. Anti Drug *vs.* Legalized Marijuana (and LSD)
   Conservative: Drugs are bad!
   Liberal: Drugs are good!

After these pre-arranged talking points, the audience could then ask their own questions, for the candidates to improvise in character. At the close of the debate, paper ballots, provided with each Playbill, would be collected and counted during the final intermission. For Act 3 – the election outcome, a large blackboard sits center stage at the Student Union where the final votes are tabulated. Two finales are prepared, each to the same music but different lyrics, so theoretically, the show could end differently each night, depending upon the audience.

While working on re-writes and finishing the finale, out of the blue the real Allison called asking a favor. Her family was Quaker, with another clan of Friends from Eastchester coming over that weekend. If I could find a date for their daughter, also Allison's age, we could double. A fellow train rider from Harrison, who suggested we 'get together sometime, 'agreed and I canceled Jennifer that weekend citing 'family.' When his silver Porche only sat two, I followed in mom's Galaxie to meet the Friends family of John Raitt, and his assertive, redheaded daughter, Bonnie. A recording artist in her own right, working on an album in some big wooden barn in the Midwest that supposedly had 'amazing sound,' Bonnie hopped in the Porche, and with Allison in the Galaxie, we took off for the Elmsford Drive-In. Unfortunately my friend thought his money compensated for an obnoxious personality, and the girls spent a good part of *"Airport,"* flying between our two cars, the snack stand, laughing and knocking on fogged up car windows until we were all asked to leave. The flight home then degenerated into a drag race that spilled off I-287 and on to North Street in front of General Foods headquarters when we saw the cop in our rear view mirror. Pulled over in front of the high school, the two girls jumped out to put on a performance worthy of an Academy Award (or at least a Tony). Crying with actual tears, that we had fallen asleep, missed our curfew and wouldn't be able to go to the prom, and how a ticket would be an embarrassment to their prestige's parents, fuck if it didn't work! If we were black, we'd be in jail instead, escorted to Allison's driveway, before the cop drove off.

In the city, Jennifer was moved from the Hilton to a brownstone in Chelsea, at 21st between eighth and ninth. Even without a doorman to report us, avoiding detection became more complicated with no 'house phone' or staff running interference. A red pay phone on the corner and a flowerpot on the steps, green line facing in or out, were our primary means of communication. Despite the initial smell of fresh paint, it was comforting making love in what felt like our own apartment, walking to the Empire Diner for breakfast holding hands. Meanwhile, I found Roeby Justice, who did things on an acoustic guitar that seemed impossible, fingers flailing with chord structures that made simple melodies sound like orchestrations. Pale and soft spoken, with thin wisps of blonde hair and a whisper voice, Roeby lived in a trailer in New Jersey on barely enough money for public transportation as a part-time carpenter. His Zen demeanor concealing a vibrancy that exploded off the strings when we played off each other in a cement loft on Perry Street that Richie Havens let us use. Like our acoustic jam on *"Ain't Gonna Look Back,"* ♪ recreated years later in the studio. Despite the cinder block walls, whenever Leslie West and Mountain cranked it up two floors below, we were no match for the noise and vibrations. But with Roeby, my live sets took on a new dimension.

♪ *Song available on iTunes & www.LEKalikow.com*

As graduation day hit in schools across the country, *"Where Has All The Ivy Gone?"* was complete, and from Beechwood, Jerry and Lou arranged a presentation at Columbia Records. Across from The Hilton, the "Black Rock" sheathed in Canadian black granite, housed the CBS Network, with three floors assigned to the record labels. Headed by free-spending Clive Davis, who famously had Blood Sweat and Tears play for his son's Bar Mitzvah, and A&R legend John Hammond, a former music critic and civil rights activist, who originally signed Dylan over the derisions of entrenched Mitch Miller era executives. Now the undisputed king of recorded music, Columbia included Barbra Streisand, Johnny Cash, Simon & Garfunkel, Miles Davis, Johnny Mathis, Janis Joplin, and literally hundreds of hit artists. Clive assigned my project to a new young A&R guy named Tom MacNamee and staff producer Ray Calcord and with the help of Jerry and Lou, we agreed on a 'development deal' for my show.

Next was choosing between ASCAP or BMI for performing rights collections. Whenever a song is performed in public, whether in an elevator, a concert hall, on the radio or in a bar, a performance royalty is owed to the copyright owners. These Performing Rights Organizations (P.R.O.s) collect that money for their publisher and songwriter members. The more members, the more they can collect, so they compete. Now I had a major publisher and record company, and decent live credits, the rush was on. Although ASCAP was larger and more established, BMI promised personal attention and better collection technology, while both claimed the other was a scam. In the end, when ASCAP offered a $750 advance, despite the fact I had no credits and nothing in the pipeline, that was it for me.

These were boom years, when even Moondog, the Viking helmeted vagrant, living on the corner of 52nd and 6th Avenue, got a record deal. For every twenty releases, one hit paid for everything and the money got silly. A non-stop party of concerts and groupies, booze and drugs, and company jets on 24 hour call for payoffs to radio DJs and program directors through a network of third party 'promotion' men (since direct payments were considered 'payola'). In this context it took MacNamee no time to assemble backers for my musical and I was soon in CBS Studios, recording demos. One morning, when a bass player didn't show, checking an adjacent studio for a substitute, Paul McCartney turned around with *"Oh Woman, Oh Why"* vibrating on the monitors, to reply "Well I'm a bass player, but I'm afraid I can't do it right now." That was the end of my session, until Linda arrived to throw us all out. It was amusing how star-struck, even professionals could be, when confronted with celebrity. At Columbia, the staff was in an uproar when Johnny Mathis walked in unexpectedly, secretaries swooning, unaware at the time that he was probably more interested in the new mail boy. In 1970, except for a few hippy freaks, gays were still in the closet. In fact the cover of the first Elton John album released that summer was a decidedly masculine facial profile hidden in black. And my mom still thought Liberace was just a sweet man who never found the right woman.

I never understood why girls loved giving blow jobs. Probably because orgasms are more in their real heads than in my little one. A combination of control and sensuality, feeling it stiffen in her mouth, siphoning my will power as it hardens and pulsates, the shaft plunging in her imagination. Feeling herself dripping as saliva soaks my cock until she also can't resist climaxing as it shoots, filling her mouth and panties with soft salty cum. On second thought, I guess I do understand. But when Allison came by with a thank you apology by blow-job for the Bonnie Raitt double date, it wasn't my first choice. For years I had imagined opening those long legs, rubbing that magic space between her thighs and sliding inside, her ankles up above my head. Instead here she was, using my dick as an all-day sucker, pulling it out to lick and tickle with her tongue, slipping the head between her lips while rubbing the crest with her forefinger before sucking it back into the warmth, prolonging every second until finally I was shooting everywhere. Then while smearing her breasts with my cum, as a reward, Allison leaned back and opened. Meanwhile, in the city, things were getting more complicated with Jennifer. The once independent, free-spirited sex goddess was displaying mood swings and flashes of jealousy.

Over the next month the show backers found a producer and leased an off-Broadway theater on Christopher Street in The Village while 'script doctors' were called in to 're-work' my book and dialogue and the music transcribed and copyrighted in the name of Beechwood Music in conjunction with my newly created Gold Cover Music. This was all OK until the backers began talking about replacing me as the lead with a 'name.' Everything came to a halt as I fought for control. Luckily Jerry and Lou provided legal support while the record company remained neutral against a few key backers who threatened to pull out. One such backer, Allen Goldfarb, was on the Columbia Record's guest list for Jimi Hendrix's Electric Lady Studio opening night party, just around the corner from our theater. Lou at Beechwood put me on the list in his place, so that perhaps I could meet Goldfarb without the lawyers around. Jimi and his manager Michael Jeffery, originally bought the defunct rock club Generation to reopen it, until demands from the local mafia and reevaluating the numbers, convinced them to convert the space to a private recording studio. Unfortunately, flooding, construction problems, and massive cost overruns now had them spending the evening at opposite ends of the room. Like Jimi's music, the John Storyk design was revolutionary with curved walls and windows, ambient light, and a Lance Jost psychedelic mural complementing the floating spaceship feel of the entire place. With state-of-the-art electronics and acoustics, after Electric Lady, recording studio construction would never be the same.

I recognized Goldfarb from a New York realty magazine, sipping champagne with Michael Jeffery across the room. Jeffery, a weasely Brit who also managed The Animals, scanned the room in his black-rimmed tinted glasses as I kept my distance and waited. When the two separated, I took my shot. Initially put off by the intrusion, Goldfarb gradually warmed as I gushed about the show, how much I appreciated his backing, and asked what I could do to smooth things. Apparently, although they heard me sing on the demos, he and few others had no idea if I could cut it live. A mention of my stint in the Catskills changed everything. Suddenly he was decanting memories of Grossingers and The Concord, the Rat Pack and Jerry Lewis at

The Browns. My connection to Totie Fields and her manager clinched it… he would have adopted me right then. We'd schedule a private backer's audition at our theater, to see if we could then all come to terms.

Ironically, when Jimi left that morning for England, to perform at the Isle Of Wight Festival, he would never again see Electric Lady and, other than some tracks laid down during construction, never record there. Less than a month later he was dead of a supposed overdose. Rumors of Michael Jeffery's unsubstantiated boast to a confidant, that he poured red wine and pills down Jimi's throat that night, dissipated when Jeffery died in a mid-air collision over France a few years later. Conspiracy theorists contend the crash might have been a political assassination of the sleazy suspected spy with ties to European organized crime. In fact the skies had recently become an arena of political discontent. In Jordan, Palestinian guerrillas hijacked and exploded three passenger jets, holding 150 passengers as hostages. Then a Pan Am 747 was blown up in Cairo, hijacked in flight from Beirut. Two commandos tried taking an El Al 707 in Amsterdam, but you don't fuck with Israelis. They didn't make it.

For the audition I tracked down Jose and paid Roeby's expenses to come in from Jersey to complement the house piano player. Strutting across the stage on *"The Right To Choose"* from the debate scene, with Goldfarb beaming in the front row, the result was a foregone conclusion. In fact the producer suggested maybe we use the guys for the actual show. *(I didn't mention Jose's living situation)*. Maintaining my Executive Producer position with the right to play Guy as long as we were off Broadway, we'd revisit the deal if Broadway became a possibility. But in the end, it didn't mean shit when everything fell apart.

Two weeks after losing Jimi, Janis Joplin was found dead in an L.A. motel and Jennifer proposed marriage… both events equally shocking. Apparently in a prior life, Jennifer was a well-paid draftswoman who also incidentally had a young daughter living with her parents in England. Now, in a letter dropped off at Beechwood, she suggested we all move in together in New York and live happily ever after. Then the other shoe dropped…out of nowhere, the threat of an unprecedented off-Broadway, Actor's Equity strike. Following a tearful confrontation with Jennifer, November's cold set in, along with the strike. After weeks with no settlement, we lost the theater lease, and even Goldfarb couldn't hold things together. Clive Davis was preoccupied opening offices and a studio in San Francisco and MacNamee left to join an investment banking firm. With the promise of a job gone, Roeby enlisted in the army band, and performing without him now felt empty. It was suggested I talk to a producer my age over at RCA named Stephen Schwartz, working on a musical at La MaMa Experimental Theatre or with Joe Papp at the Shakespeare Public Theater in The Village, but this all sounded too "hoity toity" for me and New York was fucking freezing! I just needed to get away… someplace warm… and sunny… with a beach… and cheap…

III. -1971-Winter
(Miami Beach)

Stuck in the 50's, Miami Beach was God's waiting room for old Jews to take their last rights at delicatessens like Wolfie's and Pumpernik's. I figured my Catskill's resume might land a job at the Fontainebleau, where James Bond and Goldfinger *(maybe Goldfarb's kin)* played poker, or next door at the turquoise Eden Roc. No such luck...my torn bell-bottom jeans and Afro scared the 'alta kackers' *(Yiddish for old farts)*, who shoed me away from their back doors with brooms and insect spray. Just north of the Eden Roc, metered parking and a stonewall bathroom bunker still sit at the entrance to a public beach, where I opened my guitar case, threw in some cash hints, and commenced busking. By mid-afternoon it looked like enough for a cheap motel and a hot dog, when a bushy blonde bearded, red nosed son of Santa Clause flopped down next to me in the sand. Phil was starting a commune down on 1st and Washington, and wanted a musician onboard. Why the fuck not? So we caught a bus down to a coin laundry and the bail bonds office of George Liebowitz for my introduction. George came right out of Central Casting, a heavy, bald, cigar-chewing toad in a coffee stained tank-top, who spent much of his day watching 8 millimeter porno's in his back room *(video wasn't invented yet)*. Our deal with George was simple, we would rent the top floor, consisting of 4 rooms, a bathroom and kitchen, for $75 a week, provided that he could visit whenever, and if he could get a blow-job from one of the girls, that was his business *(we kinda intimated that would be a possibility)*.

Phil had also enlisted one other partner in our venture. John was a dishwasher at Piccolo's, a terrific Italian restaurant nearby that provided sustenance spirited out sporadically in his tomato-smeared apron. With mattress pads lining the floors *(like La Senora's in Barcelona)* at $5 per night, and long-hairs barred or thrown out elsewhere, we had no trouble making the rent. *(Plus a free night to any girl that would blow George, and whatever extra she could suck out of him.)* Phil, John and I decided, by majority, who would stay or go, backed by George's, unique relationship with the cops, which also meant as long as we banned needles and hard drugs, there would be no busts. Like my previous college pad, even though I never did a doobie, the place provided a permanent contact high, and the persistence of pot permeating the premises, precluded preparing or preserving any food for the fucking fridge! *(try saying that twice).* Someone always had 'the munchies.' I hid Mounds bars in my underwear drawer while Phil filled his leather Bota Bag from wine jugs of Ripple or Bali High *(both a bargain at $3 a gallon)* and *"we all shined on"* in *"Instant Karma."*

Living with *"Everyday People"* forced me to face the pool of privilege I'd been swimming in, now sunbathing with the ones who built, and filled and repaired and cleaned that pool... or never came in contact with it at all. Timmy was a nineteen-year-old burn-out who worked for the city and loved my song *"Midnight Woman,"* ♪ written in Chicago about a hooker that lived upstairs. It was his standing *(or falling over)* request every night after a few joints. Mae, a waitress at Lum's *(known for their hot dogs cooked in beer),* was twenty-five going on sixty, a chain smoker already missing most of her teeth. British maroon-haired Marion was receptionist at The English Pub next to the surf shop, and constantly on a diet. We had no idea where Ted went every day, a loner who rarely spoke, except to ask where he could 'score some weed.' This was the base crew that paid the rent, the rest were transients who crashed and moved on. And although we were obviously not all created equal, it didn't matter.

South Beach's Ocean Drive was a series of dilapidated Deco hotels with rusted air conditioning units and laundry hanging from the windows. Their cement front porches were lined with concentration camp survivors rocking in folding chairs facing the ocean as ambulances replaced taxi's, cruising for their next pick-up. Despite the civil rights movement, there were no blacks on Miami Beach, not because they didn't tan. Refugees from Castro's revolution flooded Miami, filling entry-level jobs with skilled workers and

♪ *Song available on iTunes & www.LEKalikow.com*

forcing the black unemployed into a downtown ghetto called Overtown. Meanwhile the transplanted Cuban aristocracy cleaned up and governed Miami proper, from what came to be known as 'Little Havana.' Their influence trickled back across the causeway to the old Yiddish junk shop on the corner renovated in Spanish and the food-mart sanitized and remodeled to sell Cuban sandwiches.

At the end of Ocean Drive, in stark contrast to the neighborhood, and across from Lum's, The English Pub and the surfboard shop, sat a manicured dog track and parking structure. The street front dead-ended at a fishing *(and drug dealing)* pier, where a combination of currents and contours created the only surfing beach in South Florida. A fountain of youth bubbling with hippies, surfers, college kids and townies, all sharing sun, sand, waves, and unlimited weed, flowing into the U.S. under the auspices of The Black Tuna Gang, ironically headquartered in a suite at The Fontainebleau.

As a political system, Capitalism, based on wealth, power and greed, overcomes Communism everywhere, but that doesn't mean it's better, just more in line with human nature. Lions ate Roman Christians. But Christianity survived, The Roman Empire's gone, and lions almost extinct. Phil was a proselytizing communist who believed street begging an honorable profession. However, when circumstances required, as a part time garbage collector for a private carting firm, he'd retrieve cast-offs and converts... the practical practice of political science. In keeping with the course curriculum, my afternoons were often spent on the silent grass island of the capitalist dog track, reading *Siddhartha.* That is, when Man-Of-War weren't showing up on the beach. At first sight of the bobbing blue balloons, all but die-hard surfers scurried to the sand. Which meant surfboards to borrow and the only times I got to try it. Needless to say, I never became much of a surfer, eventually associating the sport with humiliation and stinging welts.

Like real estate, timing and location were essential to street performing. On sunny days, the public beach next to the Eden Roc was good for $25 in tips. But far and away, the Sunday Brunch line at The Famous Restaurant on Washington Avenue, a block past the seminal 5th Street Gym, was the weekly jackpot. Often generating more than $50 in two or three hours, enough to cover the entire week's food. Other than The Grove Pub, an hour away by public transportation, there were no decent nightspots. But it didn't matter since most evenings were spent above the coin laundry, singing, laughing and fucking *(usually in that order)*. Giant flying cockroaches called Palmetto Bugs *(the Florida state bird)* also took up residence. To identify the regulars, we named and spray-painted each in distinctive fluorescent colors. A little disconcerting to anyone tripping, but fun at night when a red dot moved across the ceiling and someone called out "There goes Hymie!"

Maid Marion was soon making enough at the pub to move into her own place, replaced by Barbara, a cute little Cuban with short black hair who, after a few joints, would climb on whoever was closest… male, female, didn't matter. She also helped save the commune by doing George at least once a week. The image of toothless Mae going down on me in the darkness was a recurring nightmare until luckily, she and John became 'a thing' and I was free to seduce the newbies. Marilyn wore a Ball State sweatshirt *(what a cool name for a college)* that I kept when she left. Candy was an off-pitch soprano, who climaxed in a squeal that caused Hymie and Ethel to run for cover. Then there was Jan, a female jockey with an attitude, in tight jeans and a tank top I met at Lummus Park. She barely spoke, but didn't tell me to fuck off and actually followed me back at the pad. Upstairs while I talked to fill the gaps, she commandeered a room, closed the door and unzipped her jeans enough to reveal the prominent pubic mound between her thin muscular thighs. Then forcing her jeans to the floor and tossing the tank top, she stood in silence, touching herself, almost annoyed, waiting for me to undress. The images still linger, the afternoon sun beaming between torn, fluttering, pink and white flowered curtains, her sweat glistening as she rode me into dusk.

Jan was the first and only female jockey at Hialeah, and not welcome. Afraid of the precedent, the little guys would blackball any trainer to let her race. Relegated to morning workouts, ridiculed, ridden into the rails, ice water tossed at her horse's legs or riding implements tossed at her, a pioneer catching the arrows. But she loved horses and riding, refused to be intimidated, and surprisingly, was not gay… also not big on conversation. When the spirit moved, usually late afternoons, she'd come by, get on me, get off, get off again and go. *(Lucky she never brought a whip!)* But Jan had a secret. The last and only night at her apartment, I caught a glimpse of her in the bathroom… shooting up. *(I have this thing about needles… can't even watch them on TV. Slicing off an arm with a machete, no problem, just don't stick it with a needle. I'm not big on mosquitoes either… same image.)* Not more than a week later Jan was busted, jailed and, unlike certain male jocks with similar problems, banned from the track, and gone.

Timmy's bed came available when he was busted for dealing at the pier and we faced our first voting dilemma. Michael was a fake hippy from Canada, in pre-torn designer jeans, who just wanted to get laid. John and I figured what the fuck, at least we'd have a stable contributor, but Phil didn't want him. Majority ruled and Michael moved in with his Gucci suitcase that disappeared a day before Phil somehow came up with an extra pound of weed… communism at its best. Meanwhile, someone was sneaking into my underwear drawer and chewing on my Mounds bars. This pissed me off until I discovered the culprit one night, caught in the act, his beady little eyes shooting back in the dark… a communist brown mouse!

In keeping with the theme, following the release of *"Steal This Book,"* Abbie Hoffman was invited to the University of Miami and I arranged to open the show. *(Ironically, so many potential buyers actually took his advice that many bookstores refused to stock it.)* The outdoor audience, was a mix of New York 'party' students that couldn't get into Syracuse; curious onlookers; high heeled husband hunters teasing their hair; ROTC candidates in military garb; recent Cuban refugees; foreign exchange students; liberal and conservative faculty; and a crew of cameramen and reporters. The seated congregation was backed by the varsity football squad and bordered on the right by a line of cheerleaders, all standing in uniform, complete with shoulder pads and pompoms; while the ground in front of the stage filled with Hoffman 'Yippies.' After a few songs went over pretty well, I hid behind the backdrop allowing a brave college official to apologize for Hoffman's delayed appearance. When he finally arrived by police escort and took the stage, the Yippies went crazy, jumping and cheering before he uttered a word. At first the applause was unanimous when Abbie opened with the unexpected…"I'm telling all of you out there, avoid all needle drugs…" then went on…"The only dope worth shooting is Richard Nixon!" and bedlam ensued. A cacophony of boos and hisses matching the cheers and Hoffman realized he was in for some fun. Suddenly on cue, the cheerleaders broke into calisthenics, pompoms flailing, chanting "Love It Or Leave It!" spurring Hoffman's antiwar rhetoric. From the rear, the football players began tossing talcum filled sweat socks exploding on stage in bursts of powder while an ROTC captain argued with Hoffman from an audience microphone. With Abbie's mere mention of the word 'communist' a Cuban refugee grabbed the mic, screaming from the floor in Spanglish. Then Yippies began throwing the socks back at the players, seats toppled, hairdos fled and the police forcibly removed Hoffman from the stage. In the end, two foreign exchange students sat stunned, "In Germany we hear about America freedom of speech… but never understanding what means this…is maybe too much speech, not so much listening."

Back at the pad a transformation was taking place. A few weeks prior, two relatively straight coeds from Ohio University came by and to our amazement, the best looking blonde bonded with Phil and stayed. This resulted in a frightening *"Invasion Of The Body Snatchers"* when Phil shaved off his beard, cut his hair and began to shower regularly. An omen of things to come as the dictator in Woody Allen's *"Bananas"* reserved a room at The Fontainebleau and the city brought in bulldozers to dismantle the pier and plow the ocean bed to stop surfing. Then the ambulance came to remove Ted's body from the back alley, executed as an undercover narc. Friendly Ted, always looking to score, was the cop who busted both

Jan and Timmy. Here was some serious cognitive dissonance. The two bullets in the back of his blood-soaked head marked the literal coup de gras to my flight from reality. It was spring in New York and time for a new beginning.

In the TWA lounge at Miami International that morning, the only passenger of interest was a decent looking hippy chic carrying a sheepskin coat. With an assortment of love beads dancing on an oversized tie dyed t-shirt, she bounced to a red plastic seat that matched her bright pink panties when she sat and crossed her legs. Making my way to the vacant seat next to her, she stared at my 'aura' totally stoned, before confessing a fear of flying and asking if I'd hold her hand for takeoff. These were the years before computers when seating was basically on the honor system. I figured what the fuck, she had to have a better seat than my last minute ticket in the rear. When she presented her first row, first class stub to the stewardess, I just held on and followed. Refusing to release her grip, even while downing glasses of champagne, everyone just assumed we were a couple as she cuddled up and pulled over the sheepskin coat. It seemed irrelevant that I still didn't know her name, when she slipped her tongue down my throat. Whispers rustled behind us as the heat increased, her thighs and panties soaking, my fingers sliding inside her while she unzipped and squeezed me, throbbing under the sheepskin. Unable to consummate at our seats, the stewardesses giggled in the galley as the first class passengers watched us attempt to sardine can into the lavatory together. Snickers gave way to outright laughing when once inside, we couldn't close the fucking door. When it finally snapped shut, the light flipped on to a challenging game of *Twister*. Sliding her pink panties to the floor, at first she sat on the sink and opened her legs. With one foot on the toilet and the other wedged against the door, I'd still need a three-foot dick to reach her. Arching her back and shimmying to the edge of the sink was just enough for my little head to slip in when my foot slid off the toilet seat slamming my other head against the folding baby shelf which flopped down to hit me again as I fell. The commotion brought a wave of laughter from the cabin while undeterred, my stoned and slightly inebriated partner pushed off the sink and sat on my face. Grabbing my throbbing big head with both hands, hips gyrating, my nose and mouth stuck in her soaking cunt, I thought I was gonna die. *(How would they explain this to my mother!)* In a panic I gathered my sprawled legs and leveraged against the wall, pushing up with all my strength while supporting her rocking ass, trying desperately to pull my nose out enough to breath. Once deposited back on the sink she rocked on, completely oblivious while I gasped for breath and slid my hand in to keep her 'occupied,' as it proclaimed on the door light. At this point I'd be damned if I was gonna leave without joining the mile-high club. In a masterful maneuver over the toilet, slipping in doggie style while rubbing her clit, she howled "don't stop! don't stop!" for the audience outside as we climaxed. When the bathroom door opened the entire first class cabin broke into applause. They definitely got their money's worth on this flight. At baggage claim a chauffeur holding a nameplate I never saw, whisked her away as a turbaned man tried to lead me to his unmarked cab greeting "Welcome to New York my friend."

IV. -1971-Spring
(Another Shot at The Big Apple)

They played musical chairs while I was away. Beechwood Music folded into the parent Screen Gems/Colgems glass skyscraper on Sixth Avenue, and Jerry Simon and Lou Ragusa moved into the less impressive new U.S. offices of Dick James Music off Seventh Avenue. Dick James was a colorful, cigar smoking character who made millions in the 60's with Northern Songs, the Beatles first publishing company he set up with Brian Epstein. Now DJM was about to launch Elton John in The States while trying to hide his gayness. But despite their best efforts, Elton's flamboyant persona poked through the pounds of fluttering confetti on stage. *"All In The Family"* was also poking through America's morality on TV, but without cigarette commercials, now banned while the National Institute of Mental Health reported a third of US college students were smoking pot. In Washington, the 26th Amendment, allowing 18 year olds to vote, was on the verge of ratification while 200,000 anti-war activists rallied. This included 700 Vietnam Veterans Against The War who tossed their metals in protest as, on the radio, Marvin Gaye sang *"What's Going On."* And off-Broadway, *"Godspell"* opened by Stephen Schwartz to rave reviews.

My Beechwood situation now lapsed, Jerry and Lou offered another one-year co-publishing deal, like before, contingent on a major record contract and/or production of my musical. Despite the potential, my priorities had changed along with the staff at Columbia, which meant starting from scratch on *"Ivy."* But Broadway had been a detour. Once signed to Dick James Music, based on Jerry's personal relationship, my next audition was for a record deal at Capitol with Noel Sherman. Noel and his brother Joe co-wrote a number of hits, most notably *"Ramblin' Rose"* for Nat King Cole. Probably in his 40's with thinning red hair and white freckled features, he rearranged everything on his desk while listening to my demo and popping what looked like antacid tablets. With Grand Funk Railroad supporting the label, Noel was looking for a new Pop MOR (Middle Of The Road) artist, and encouraging when he gave me his card.

The Mercer Arts Center was a complex of live venues cut into the backside of the broken down Broadway Central Hotel, which also housed Art Bar, frequented by the glittering Max's Kansas City crowd. On stage that night with just my acoustic guitar, it was hard to hold the audience, especially when a tall blonde pranced in wearing nothing but gold spray and pasties. Noel was squeezing to the exit when I pulled her up onstage to sing along on my latest composition, *"Wish I Was A Lady So That I Could Be A Whore."* ♪ Suddenly the whole room was that Austrian Beer Garden, spilling their drinks and singing along on the chorus as my partner twirled her tassels, and Noel stayed... My career saved by a naked exhibitionist... God bless the sexual revolution!

Of course for every movement, there's a counter force. Shannon Hanlon was a stunning auburn-haired Catholic-school neighbor, I'd fantasized about from a distance. With Rowena moved out and Allison usually unavailable, I figured why not take a shot? After a brief introduction in her driveway, at the front door her starched mother was less than ingratiating. Twenty-three and still at home under a strict dress code and curfew; her daughter would take no part in the sexual revolution while she was alive! Wilting in her confinement but brainwashed by the Catholic Church and her mom, this beautiful *"Green Eyed Lady"* was forced to support the family when her dad died. Overcompensating, her all day smile in a clean white dental office had become a permanent mask. On our first date, after *"Willie Wonka & The Chocolate Factory,"* we sat under a streetlight in the Ford front seat and talked. Behind the exquisite facade was a depth of intelligence and wit that understood her mother's fear of losing her to a husband, the inconsistencies of the Catholic church, dueling with her pent up sexuality and longing for release from responsibility. Shannon desperately needed just to talk, and at this point it was all she could handle. So, despite her mother's

♪ *Song available on iTunes & www.LEKalikow.com*

best efforts, we became good neighbors, but it would be months before our first kiss. Meanwhile, a few weeks after Sinatra gave his retirement appearance in Los Angeles, Joe Columbo was gunned down in Columbus Circle, kicking off a mafia war *(and affecting certain record companies and nightclubs)*. A few days later three Soviet cosmonauts were found dead in their Soyuz spacecraft, Jim Morrison took an overdose in Paris and 'Satchmo' Louis Armstrong left the stage for the last time. For Shannon, it was all God's will.

No longer a student radical but not yet a 'Mr.', my self-perception was in transition. More spectator than participant, I watched the balance of power shifting with Communist China joining the U.N., as we sold tons of grain to the U.S.S.R. and Nikita Khrushchev died in relative obscurity. The secret Pentagon Papers were printed despite the government's legal blustering about 'national security' proving the government had been lying to us about Vietnam and Northern Ireland was exploding. Meanwhile, my world was rocked by news that Mayor Lindsay was having a political sex change to Democrat and the New York Football Giants were moving to New Jersey. Then came Attica, the prison riot where, ten years earlier I might have been demonstrating... and I could hear the Byrds singing, *"Ah, but I was so much older then, I'm younger than that now."* Then *Look Magazine* closed its eyes and disappeared.

Opening for Tom Rush at The Bitter End, I really missed Roeby. Noel stayed through the set but wasn't ready to sign me. I needed to kick it up a notch. That Wednesday night, on the grass outside Wollman Rink, with the Allman Brothers onstage for the Schaefer Music Fest, a tall weird looking long hair in purple bell bottoms plopped down next to my closed guitar case. Having never heard me sing, nonetheless Bob King was convinced I looked like a star, and he was gonna be my bass player. Who could argue with that? The next day, over the George Washington Bridge to a working class neighborhood in Teaneck, his distracted three-hundred pound Italian mother greeted me at the screen door. Past the plastic seat covered living room, a shaky wooden staircase led to a cardboard box filled basement space beneath the kitchen. An avid Dickie Betts fan, Bob tended to overplay, but the electric bass added a new dimension. Now we needed to plug in a guitarist. Weeks of excruciating auditions followed until quiet, unassuming Carl Addanisio took out his red Fender Stratocaster and blew us away. Like Bob Dylan six years before at Newport, shocking his fans, I was going electric.

It would take months of rehearsals before our first gig, amplifiers competing with heavy metal thrown by Bob's shrieking Italian mother at her cursing Irish husband to the smell of garlic and tomato sauce cooking upstairs. At Capitol, I continued to visit Noel, stoking his interest in a concept for my first album… 'my generation and sex'… With songs like *"Red Light, Green Light," "What Kinda Girl Do Ya Think I Am?," "If I Had It To Do All Over, I'd Do It All Over You,"* and *"Get On The Pill Or Else Get Outta My Arms!."* However he seemed more nervous and preoccupied with each visit, swallowing handfuls of antacid and plastic prescription bottle pills. Meanwhile in the next office, producer Terry Knight, in a tirade that often lasted all night, was yelling into multiple telephones, promoting Grand Funk Railroad at radio, and berating *Rolling Stone* for their miserable reviews.

With a perfect turned up nose, dimples, deep green eyes, and an Ann-Margret figure, Shannon Hanlon was a classic Irish beauty, experiencing withdrawal from years of religious indoctrination. Simply being held, a bout of conscience, requiring my continual trust building assurances. Then, from the other end of the continuum, came Constance Patrick. Celebrating the Joint Resolution of Congress declaring "Women's Equality Day" and bored with the guys she'd been meeting, my sister's Chapel Hill roommate simply got in her red MG and drove to White Plains. Praying she wouldn't look like Bella Abzug, how cool to see those long legs and flaming red hair dance out of that sports car. Helen Reddy sang *"I Am Woman,"* as she slid her index finger down my chest before the flowing silk dress brushed by, settling in the living room easy chair. Gracefully placing her legs on the ottoman facing me, Constance sighed, closed her eyes, and without a word, pulled up the hem to reveal those long white thighs gradually opening. If this was the new *"American Woman"* the Guess Who were singing about, I was all over it! That weekend, my parents away, we fucked non-stop accept for occasional bathroom breaks and PB&J *(for which we also found some original uses)*. Constance fit her name, climaxing to a plateau of multiple-orgasms, undulating in rhythm as long as I stayed hard, little pink nipples pointed up. And watching my shaft sliding in her red vagina, lobster sauce beading on the surrounding whips of pubic hair and dripping down her swelling crotch, I stayed hard. Moving from one room to another, like most redheads, her lightly freckled skin, blotched and bruised easily, marking each position until she looked like *"Lydia The Tattooed Lady."* Not into in love, marriage, kids or entanglements, liberated Constance just loved to fuck, and for years thereafter, would intermittently return, to renew her tattoos.

Although Mike Porco was still at Gerdes Folk City, Allan Pepper and Stanley Snadowsky had come over from The Village Gate to book talent. On Mike's recommendation we auditioned for them on a Monday, and were slotted to open for Buzzy Linhart that weekend. The former roommate of John Sebastian, Buzzy was a crazy songwriter, vibes and guitar player, who went on to co-write *"(You've Got To Have) Friends"* with Moogy Klingman, flashed full frontal in *"The Groove Tube,"* and attracted a perfect audience for my new incarnation. Now I needed to electrify *(in more ways than one)*. Local singer/songwriter Eve Moon turned me on to a guy who installed something called a 'penny pickup' in her acoustic guitar, but to my shock, when mine came back, instead of using the existing peg hole for the chord, he put another hole in the curve of my new Martin D28... FUCK!!! *(still there to this day)*. The crowd that night included Art Kass from Kama Sutra, Buzzy's new label, Neil Bogart from Buddah Records, their new distributor, the entire crew from Dick James, and Noel Sherman with a promo guy from Capitol. *(Not too much pressure!)* Opening with *"Wish I Was A Lady So That I Could Be A Whore,"* like the Mercer Arts Center months earlier, the whole place was soon singing along, and on the second encore *(unheard of for a 'warm up' act)* I was pretty sure we had a deal. Especially when Noel saw Bogart slip me his business card.

The next afternoon at Capitol, Bob and Carl in tow, Sherman was all smiles, and there was my contract. In fact there were two… One, a production deal with Noel… the other, a Capitol Records contract, subject to the production deal. I needed legal advice. As my father read the recording contract, he just kept shaking his head. To him it bordered on legalized slavery. We needed a consulting opinion. Patent Council for GE, dad requested professional courtesy from the co-author of *"This Business Of Music"* and within days we were in the unpretentious offices of Bill Krasilovsky. A tall, thin, fatherly figure, his book, the standard to this day, and clientele, a 'who's who' of composers, artists and publishers. More professor than attorney, Bill made the distinction between legal and practical in the high-stakes music business, with one-sided contracts that reflected the risk. On the other hand, once successful, everything was renegotiable *(at $300-$400 an hour)*. But the 'keyman clause,' asserting that if Noel left Capitol, so would I, should actually give me the option to stay. This type of clause was usually to protect the artist, not a means of executive extortion. Bill also pointed out that signing the production agreement did not guarantee the record deal, which still needed Dick Asher's approval, as V.P of East Coast Operations. We left with Bill's offer to represent me at a 'highly discounted' rate until something happened.

Sherman agreed to the keyman modification but, as a sign of good faith, wanted me to sign the production agreement to protect him, with the stipulation that if he didn't get me a major deal in a year, it would terminate. So I signed with Noel, who suggested we tighten the act before a formal presentation to the label. Continuing to rehearse in Jersey, we performed wherever, including a gig opening for Elephant's Memory (later known as The Plastic Ono Band behind John Lennon & Yoko Ono) at Bananafish Park in Brooklyn. Almost missing our time slot while Bob got a blow job in the basement. Meanwhile I began to see more of Noel outside the office. Appropriately, at Sherman Square, on Broadway and 72nd, he introduced me to his favorite Orange Julius before heading west to the 23rd floor apartment at Lincoln Towers. A grand piano dominated the living room lined with gold records, celebrity photos, and a panoramic view of the Hudson, his 'ulcer' getting worse with each visit. Grimacing in pain, he was often unable to finish a sentence, cursing business associates and 'friends' who weren't returning his calls, bitterness festering. At the time unaware rumors of cancer had spread, his days supposedly numbered, no one had the guts (or good sense) to broach the subject, it was easier just to avoid his calls.

Back at home, an unexpected call from Allison. She had moved into a house in Brewster they were converting into a candle store, and asked if we'd like to play for the Grand Opening. The Honeysuckle House was a large white colonial with bright yellow shutters, impossible to miss from Route 22. Arriving that morning the circular drive, already speckled with vehicles, included a psychedelic VW bus, its artwork matching the logo stretched across the veranda. White tables, desks, and cabinets filled the entrance rooms, bursting with brightly colored shapes and sizes, kids running between them, ignored by the few adults present. Allison greeted us in a full-length tie-dye, tugged from behind by a little person she now referred to as 'the bean.' Piles of color-sorted crayons, slabs of paraffin and two double boilers complemented other cooking utensils in the kitchen, shelves lined with wax filled aluminum molds, pick-up stick wicks hardening in each. A communal effort that included two other couples (marriage status unclear) and their three kids, an antique cash register in the foyer was now ready for business. With a rock band already on the porch, Allison had something else in mind for us. Above the third floor bedrooms, a large beamed attic accessible by wooden ladder, would host the late night celebration. With candles lining the room, an ornate Indian water pipe the centerpiece, for me it was college *"Déjà vu,"* before Crosby, Stills & Nash. On a contact high back up in Fireman Bill's attic bedroom, with local musicians joining the séance… once again the music was magic.

By the winter of 1971, my recording career was frozen as Carole King sang *"It's Too Late"* and Noel went into *"The Hospital"* for tests at the same time George C. Scott was running them on the screen. With the graphic sex, drugs and violence of the 60's no longer filling our daily lives, filmmakers provided replacement therapy. In *"The French Connection,"* Gene Hackman brutally shot up everybody, including himself, while Malcolm McDowell raped a British housewife *"Singing In The Rain,"* in *"A Clockwork Orange."* In retaliation for two explicit rape scenes in *"Straw Dogs,"* Peckinpah had Dustin Hoffman slicing off limbs while *"Dirty Harry"* blew away bad guys to the cheers of the NRA. On a lighter note *(couldn't resist the pun),* Sean Connery, still 007 in *"Diamonds Are Forever,"* couldn't prevent a fan of Frank Zappa and The Mothers Of Invention from firing a flare gun into the rafters and burning down The Montreux Casino, while members of Deep Purple watched from across Lake Geneva, inspiring *"Smoke On The Water."* And so the year ended *"full of sound and fury. Signifying nothing."*

V. (1972)
(Timing Is Everything)

As Noel entered the hospital, there was a shakeup at Capitol. Dick Asher returned to Columbia Records, to run their international division out of London, and Artie Mogul was brought in to clean house. As Sherman was being prepped for life threatening surgery, Mogul called his hospital room to tell him someone had to come pick up his things, he no longer had a job...Noel never recovered. At Dick James Music my deal lapsed as Lou and Jerry moved out, so with my group now ready to record, I had no publisher, no producer and no record deal.

My first thought was back to Neil Bogart, but Buddah was going R&B, signing artists like Bill Withers and Curtis Mayfield. Norm Racusin, a former neighbor and family friend, had been President of RCA Records back in the 60's. Now at Readers Digest, he arranged a shot at his former label. When the A&R guy said my material was "too commercial," I knew the confidence inspiring adhesive tape with his name on the door would soon be gone. Meanwhile, a complication at home... When a nasty divorce forced family friends to sell their house, recovering from back surgery, their chopped off brunette daughter moved in with us. A God fearing right winged conservative, every prefab thought from Miriam's oversized mouth provoked an argument. Bedridden in pain, at first she enjoyed a tactical advantage... but fair game when she began to recover. Although unable to penetrate her psychological defenses, I was soon fucking her brains out whenever mom and dad left. Before long an addict, her monstrous mouth or bobbing bush would ambush me around the house... a sexual Frankenstein... I needed to move out.

Just off University Avenue in The Bronx, a Russian neighborhood of single family homes rented rooms to students. For $65 per week, I was able to share a two-room basement apartment with a grad student from Trinidad. Aside from the paneled rooms, a cement cellar sink, toilet, shower, gas range, refrigerator, and a single pull-chain light bulb complemented my new bachelor pad. With advance monies gone and no publisher support, responding to an ad in *The Times*, I was soon working for a film company... holding lights at weddings and bar mitzvahs. The trick was not tripping the guests with the electric wire snaking the aluminum dish lights through the room. My dark suit pockets lined with plastic bags for sliding food off unfinished plates, since the caterers weren't paid to feed us. At $25 per 8-hour event, packing, unpacking, lifting, pulling, and taking abuse from the photographers and guests, a double-header would knock me out. But I needed at least three roast beef and rubber chicken banquets per weekend to make the rent. Often counting coins on the bedspread for the subway, driving and parking mom's Ford Galaxie into the city was out of the question, besides, I needed the gas to get to work and rehearsals.

Within two weeks of moving into my new apartment, I almost burned the place down. It wasn't until half way to Brooklyn for a Sunday morning gig that I remembered the boiling pot of water in the cellar. Picturing the empty pewter pot glowing over the blue flames, the landlord's family and my roommate away, it took three tries to find a working payphone, to reach the neighborhood firehouse. But they wouldn't enter until the place was burning and said to call the cops. Without probable cause, the police said to call the firehouse. All I needed was someone to go in and turn off the fucking stove! After leaving a message at work, out of quarters and options, dodging finger pointing pedestrians and red lights, by the time I made it back, the blackened pot was actually vibrating on the stovetop. So was the phone, the production assistant yelling in my ear while I pulled a change of underwear from the drawer that also held my red leather lined I.U. diploma, obviously serving me well in my chosen career.

Back in Brooklyn that night for a bar mitzvah, another 'lighting technician' *(the title we gave ourselves in place of 'cord schleppers')* told me of a cash prize amateur contest at the Gil Hodges Lanes & Cocktail Lounge on Ralph Avenue nearby. My greasy dark suit a perfect fit for the mafia run bar adjacent to the lanes, weekends an Italian *Ted Mack Amateur Hour*, winner chosen by drunken applause. Complete with professional lighting and state-of-the-art sound, Bob Gerardi, the versatile piano player/MC could handle any request. An accomplished accompanist, he allowed me to improvise, change tempo, dance, or talk to the audience mid song. Life was a *"Cabaret"* like the Catskills once again, and Peggy Lee's *"Fever"* provided a terrific added income whenever a lighting gig ended in Brooklyn.

Nixon was in China when the government finally granted copyright protection to sound recordings and Paul McCartney launched his new band, Wings. On national TV, Sammy Davis Jr. kissed Archie Bunker while Elvis and Priscilla went their *"Separate Ways,"* and on screen Barbra Streisand asked, *"What's Up Doc?"* when Terry Knight brought a $5 million lawsuit against Grand Funk Railroad, one week after being fired as their manager. Against my advice, with the winter's thaw, Bob decided to try his hand at concert promotion. Booking Edgar Winter & White Trash into the Capitol Theatre in Passaic, he assumed we'd open, despite the fact we had nothing in common. Now we needed a drummer and new material. Bob's concert promoting career washed out in one night, butterflies too gentle a metaphor for my reaction to the small rowdy rain soaked audience of bikers and stoners. To avoid standing on an empty stage, we used existing props, including a large fake boulder as my throne (to double as shelter from flying debris if necessary). In deference to the audience, rather than original material, we opened with the Allman Brother's *"Midnight Rider,"* moving seamlessly into Blind Faith's *"Can't Find My Way Home,"* then back to the Allman Brothers to close… They fuckin' loved it! After that we could do no wrong, impressing three noteworthy spectators… David Krebs of Leber-Krebs Mgmt., who handled Aerosmith, Alison Steele, the "Nightbird" at WNEW-FM, and Arnold Maxin, the former President of MGM Records.

The day after Alison's mention on her late night show, at David's picture windowed upper west side apartment I was greeted by Denise, his breathtaking California blonde girlfriend, in pink hot-pants and a braless white tank-top. Now this was success... David was in the process of establishing Contemporary Communications Corporation with partner Steve Leber, including their management division handling Aerosmith and The New York Dolls. Meanwhile at MGM since the 50's, Arnold Maxin had been responsible for such hits as Sheb Wooley's *"Purple People Eater,"* Connie Frances' *"Who's Sorry Now?" "It's All In The Game"* for Tommy Edwards, and the career of an ex-Army baseball player named Conway Twitty among others. But in the late 60's when MGM tried to hype local Boston bands, dubbed "Bosstown Rock," the company lost $18 million and Maxin was out of a job. So with Krebs acting as manager and Maxin my publisher, our next meeting would be with producer Jerry Ragovoy. As in the past, everything subject to a major record deal.

Ragovoy, writer of soul classics like *"Time Is On My Side," "Stay With Me," "Cry Baby,"* and *"Piece Of My Heart,"* had recently opened his own studio, The Hit Factory. Known for his years with Janis Joplin, this would be a dream come true. After a brief audition and considering David and Arnold's involvement, Ragovoy agreed to produce an album on spec, working on studio downtime. The entire project a result of timing; David just setting up his management company, Arnold's career in transition, and Jerry looking to expand his production credits. This also meant sacrificing my 'lighting technician' career, especially considering my roommate had disappeared. Combing the Reporter Dispatch for a flexible waiter's job in Westchester that might pay more than The Bronx *(and wouldn't require a concealed weapon)*, I found something completely different... The town of Scarsdale needed mail carriers.

You have to get sick to appreciate how good healthy feels. It started with a runny nose, dry hacking cough, and watery eyes. I just figured it was a cold when Shannon arrived for her regular visit. Like the Virginia Slims ad *"You've Come A Long Way Baby,"* by not inserting my dick, technically maintaining her Catholic virginity, she gymnastically did not sin all night. But the bed was soaked when she left me shaking and running a fever the next morning, and it wasn't from not sinning. As the day progressed one eye developed conjunctivitis and white spots populated my mouth. Over the phone, the family doctor suggested aspirins, plenty of fluids and bed rest. Constantly refilling the pitcher of water on the bed stand, I shivered, sweat and slept through the next day and night, gradually finding it harder to get out of bed when a rash appeared behind my ears then down my neck. The only doctor who would come was my gynecologist uncle, but as Randy Bachman would later sing, *"you take what you can get."* By the time he arrived the rash had spread, I was running 104 temperature and hallucinating. The red spots on my legs were the key to what turned out to be a masterful diagnosis… No longer able to stand, and barely conscious, I looked like another OD at the Bronx hospital emergency room. The X-ray technician flopped me up on a machine and let me fall as she read the chart and laughed before helping me back up. The hospital room nurse attached the I.V. assuming this wasn't my first needle, until she read my chart and laughed. And for the next three days of doctors, nurses, interns, and candy stripers, everyone found it amusing that I almost died… of the measles.

After passing the civil service exam and providing my fingerprints, I was officially a Scarsdale postal employee. With overtime pay, it was the best gig ever! Shifts ran weekdays and Saturdays, 10:00AM to 6:00PM or 4:00PM to 12:00AM, thus allowing for studio sessions and, like college, no early mornings! Before computers or scanners, starting at 5:00 AM the sorters would sit in front of a honeycomb of wooden mail slots, working from memory. The fastest was Angelo, a thirty-year vet, tossing the envelopes with gunfighter speed. The entire process completed for the carriers to leave by 9:30. At first my job was placing canvas sacks on metal racks and stuffing them with others of the same size from a giant pile of empties. In the evenings we'd load trucks with the empties and collected mail, to return to the sectional center in Mount Vernon for sorting. No sweeping or cleaning allowed… that was another union. The first month was a trial period after which Harry, the Assistant Superintendent, decided which new employees to retain. Making the cut to sub-carrier, involved covering the routes of absent mailmen. In a mini jeep, armed with a map, instructions from the regular carrier, and a can of Halt! dog spray, I set out on my daily adventures.

The first challenge was finding hidden mailboxes. Many of the large estates felt it unseemly to make their receptacles obvious, hiding them behind bushes or cleverly disguised like the golf ball washer mailbox, a wooden lion's head door slot, or the mouth of a porcelain cow. These little details often omitted from the carrier's notes, both as an initiation prank and to insure that the sub-carrier never finished the route faster than the regular mailman. In fact we were privately warned not to return early, with a list of safe bars to hide from postal inspectors. Although my fantasy involving horny housewives never materialized, confrontations with mailman eating attack dogs were a regular occurrence... learning the hard way, not to shoot pepper spray against the wind. By far the most memorable such face-off was the day I attempted a Special Delivery...

Approaching from the opposite direction, I didn't see the large brown dog asleep in front of the garage. As my tiptoe touched the front stoup a barely perceptible growl had me praying someone would answer the doorbell before it was too late. But no one came, and suddenly there was no place to run when the drooling monster charged. Desperately pressing the bell and jerking the handle, I kicked the unlocked door open and slammed it back against the flailing body of the beast outside. Standing in the ornate hallway, the rabid animal bouncing off the front door, I held the official envelope above my head and yelled "Special Delivery!!" to avoid being shot by the homeowner. But no one came. Tentatively stepping into the plush living room, hands up and still calling out ...nothing. Next, to the carpeted stairs and then half way up... no answer. Reaching the office from the kitchen phone, Harry's response was "I never got this call (click)." Fuck!... now what? It took a while to devise a plan, making my way to the basement and the electric garage door opener. Pushing the button, I then ran upstairs and sprinted from the front door, the dog now tearing out from the garage, it was a foot race to the jeep. No time to open the door I jumped on the roof, snarling teeth snapping at my boots, then viciously circling the vehicle, drooling, barking and lunging for my legs. In a window across the street three kids were pointing at me and laughing when their mother came to the front door… to take a picture. Great, once again I was gonna die and everyone found it amusing. Luckily still armed with my trusty can of mace, a direct spray in the monster's face gave me an instant to slide down into the driver's seat. Avidly chased for the next three miles, I imagined the homeowner's puzzlement at the Special Delivery letter on the kitchen table.

Downtime at The Hit Factory was rare, with Jerry producing Paul Butterfield, J.Geils and others. Meanwhile Bill Szymczyk, his former chief engineer now at ABC Records, recorded B.B. King and The James Gang, and Bruce Teregesen, the current chief engineer, worked with Terry Cashman and Tommy West and their pet project, Jim Croce. Although Croce's first album had flopped on Capitol and his recent material was rejected at Columbia, Ragovoy allowed spec time to finish *"You Don't Mess Around With Jim."* When the LP was completed, every major label passed until ABC agreed to take it as a favor for getting the new Cashman & West album, *"A Song Or Two."* Thus accidentally signing one of the best selling records in history with singles that also included *"Operator"* and *"Time In A Bottle."* Meanwhile, I only got time in the studio *(and no bottle)* at weird hours with Joe Finelli, the maintenance tech who kept the equipment running, with Jerry's assurance that my time would come, as he began construction on a new studio downstairs.

Back in Jersey, always the entrepreneur, Bob had a new plan. Apparently his father's boss wanted to finance a rock band. Carl and I had no idea what was coming when the car headed back across the George Washington Bridge and down toward the Brooklyn docks. As we pulled up in front of a columned restaurant that looked like something out of *"The Godfather,"* an elderly Italian gentleman limped to greet us at the curb, and all I could think was 'Bob, what the fuck did you get us in to now!!' Having just seen the movie, Carl was afraid to get out of the car, and headed straight for the bathroom as we followed the old man up a staircase to a balcony above the expansive dining room. Told to set up at the other end of a long mahogany table, sweating bullets *(and watching for them)*, Carl came out long enough to plug in his amp and headed back to the toilet. A heavily embroidered curtain was drawn across the balcony banister *(probably to muffle mob murders)* as we waited for our benefactor.

Hearing footsteps on the staircase, instead of a panel of hitmen, what emerged was a large Italian family surrounding a silver-haired grandfather. Now we were really screwed… what to 'frigging' play for The Don's grandkids from my 'sex' album? With *"It's Kinda Nice,"* ♪ our only innocuous unrehearsed song we had to wing it when, from the other end of the table, his family around him, fingers together, palm facing up, Mr. Pannini gestured 'Play!' Half way through, he held up his hand and said 'basta' (enough) and we thought we had dodged a bullet…Until they opened the curtain for us to play for the restaurant and Carl almost collapsed. Mr. Pannini, it turned out, was cousin to "Crazy Joe" Gallo, and responsible for the Brooklyn docks *(where we could easily disappear)* and we only knew one fuckin' song that wouldn't offend everyone! Then from the far end of the restaurant, seated with his family at a large round table, disregarding other diners, Pannini once again gestured and called out "Play!" This time we got through the whole song, then immediately packed up, praying we had gotten away with it. Within minutes Carl and his equipment were downstairs and in the car as Bob and I attended the round table with The Don.

In an elegant understated sport coat and open handmade white linen shirt, with manicured nails and perfectly coiffed silver hair, Mr. Pannini was actually warm and charismatic. Much like a loveable grandfather, doting over his family and proud of every dish that came out of the kitchen, it would have been easy to accept his help, if I didn't know better. No business was discussed until after the meal, the family dispersed, and a care package sent out to Carl, who

♪ *Song available on iTunes & www.LEKalikow.com*

I explained was not involved in decision making. "Personally," he began, "I no like-a your music. But the family, they tella me izza good." As he continued, all I could think was *'How the fuck am I gonna get out of this?* "You donna know me, but I canna tell you dis, tomorrow I canna have Frankie Valli right here atta dis table....Joe," referring to the old man who greeted us, "You calla Frankie and tell him amma wanna see him." Looking back at me, "You know Roulette Records? Morris Levy izza my personal friend. I canna getta you a record deal like that..." snapping his fingers. At which pointed I needed to speak up. "Mr. Pannini," I began, " I very much appreciate your making the time for us and absolutely believe that you can make things happen. But I'm a young kid just getting started and would really like to try and do it myself first, on my own if I can." Staring at me in silence for a moment *(hoping he couldn't hear my heart pounding)* he answered. "OK, I respect dat. And I tella you dis... I like-a you. You looka me straight inna de eye and tella me what is inna your-a heart. Now amma here forra you. Anyting you need... even justa to talk. You-a calla me, huh?" "I really appreciate that" I said, and as he hugged me goodbye all I could think was "Holy shit! We're actually getting outta here in one piece." Two weeks later 'Crazy Joe' Gallo was gunned down at Umberto's Clam House in Little Italy, not far from my apartment, launching another gang war. Then, driving to work on the Major Deegan, news radio announced that Pannini was shot in the head having breakfast in the chair where I last saw him. And I thought, 'What if I'd been more naïve? Who would own me now?'

Whether on a mail route or stuffing sacks, the occasional studio session with Finelli kept me believing even though Ragavoy never seemed to make it and reaching Krebs had become problematic. With his new offices still not completed, after a showcase at Max's Kansas City, Clive Davis signed Aerosmith to Columbia, and David had his hands full. Meanwhile Arnold invited me to his Long Island home to hear all my material, and fell asleep. In retrospect, today I might have done the same since, at the time, most of my repertoire was 'in development.' But Maxin also, perhaps prophetically, observed that maybe I didn't have the personality to be a star. As he put it, "You wouldn't kill my mother for it." While there, on the nightly news five men were arrested breaking into the Democratic National Committee offices in Washington's Watergate apartment complex. Part of a messy presidential campaign that began with segregationist Governor George Wallace gunned down and permanently paralyzed. He still won six states in the Democratic primary. Shirley Chisholm ran as the first black person and first woman and won New Jersey. Of the Democratic contenders, Nixon's people saw Ed Muskie as the biggest threat so, just prior to the New Hampshire primary, planted fake letters claiming he dissed French-Canadians and that his wife drank and swore. In a snowstorm speech defending his wife, what Muskie claimed were melted snowflakes, reporters saw as tears. No one wanted a crying president so, in a split decision, George McGovern got the nomination with Senator Thomas Eagleton of Missouri as running mate. Afraid Eagleton might influence southern voters, two weeks later Nixon's 'trixters' leaked that he'd once undergone electro-shock treatments for depression...there went Eagleton... and the election.

That September, American Bobby Fischer won the world chess championship over defending Russian master, Boris Spassky. Then at the Munich Olympics, although Mark Spitz (*so obnoxious at I.U. we refused to rush him*) won a record seven gold medals, our basketball team lost to the Russians in the most controversial final in Olympics history. But that paled to the controversy when eight members of the Palestinian terror group Black September scaled the walls of the Olympic Village. After an aborted airport standoff and 14 straight hours covering the story, newscaster Jim McKay announced, "There were eleven hostages. Two were killed in their rooms' yesterday morning. Nine were killed at the airport tonight. They're all gone." A line had been crossed... which is not to say hijackings wouldn't continue. A month later with the three surviving terrorists awaiting trial in West Germany *(the wall had not come down yet)*, a Lufthansa jet was hijacked by another group of Palestinian guerillas and the hostages immediately exchanged for the three murderers. Returning as heroes to Libya, some theorize the

West German government arranged the whole thing to get rid of them.

Having written off a career on Broadway, I still couldn't turn down an audition arranged by Arnold for the lead in the new Ragni/MacDermot musical *"Dude."* After gutting the Broadway Theater to the tune of $800,000 to create a circus in the round, complete with fake dirt (real dirt became mud when wet), firing the original director and choreographer, and spending liberally on electronics to compensate for the acoustics they destroyed, it turned out the lead couldn't sing. With only weeks to go, still recasting in her east side townhouse, preoccupied producer Adela Holzer impatiently waited as I tuned my guitar. Years later, the overly tinted red haired matron would be jailed as a con artist, but at the time was one of the most successful producers on the 'Great White Way.' Luckily, I didn't pass the audition. Dude opened and closed in a week, the most disastrous debacle in Broadway history.

With the Hit Factory rhythm section that included Dave Spinozza on Guitar and Rick Marotta on drums, Joe Finelli had been working on a pet project with synthesizer pioneer Kenny Bichel. *"Sweet Sadie Simpson"* was a Blood, Sweat & Tears type rock anthem, for the first time replacing live horns with a synthesizer. With my lead vocal laid in, our first shot was Columbia Records, where it looked like I was about to have my first major label release… until the lawyers got involved. Business Affairs were afraid the musicians union would freak at replacing musicians with electronics and killed the deal. Meanwhile Ragavoy turned out to be a better songwriter than businessman, with complications and cost overruns on the new studio wiping him out, both physically and financially. Then Arnold Maxin was indicted for misappropriation of funds during the Bosstown disaster at MGM. And so ended another year as Dick Clark celebrated the first televised *"New Year's Rockin' Eve"* and I watched the ball fall on my recording career. At which point my parents suggested I stop signing deals with anyone I cared about since they either lost their jobs, faced prison, bankruptcy or died.

VI. (1973)
Chateau D'Vie

Jeep sliding up Ardsley Road clad in my official mail-carrier uniform, complete with fleece-lined boots and a runny nose, my music career looked bleak as the stars realigned. In Rowe v. Wade (and companion case Doe v. Bolton) the Supreme Court struck down state laws banning abortion as heavyweight George Foreman did the same to Joe Frazier and fighting finally stopped in Viet Nam with the Paris Peace Accords, just as we said goodbye to long-haired Lyndon Johnson for the last time. With the first planeload of Viet Nam POW's arriving home, Roberta Flack sang, *"Killing Me Softly With His Songs"* when a band of Native American POW's took hostages at the Wounded Knee reservation, demanding fair treatment. On TV the year before, during the Dick Cavett time slot at 11:30 PM, Don Kirshner hosted the first live rock *"In Concert."* on ABC-TV. Now NBC was competing with *"The Midnight Special"* at 1:00 AM. Originally rejected by the network, Burt Sugarman bought the time with sponsor Chevrolet, and proved good enough ratings for NBC to buy him out. Following a Noxema commercial with an unknown Farrah Fawcett shaving Joe Namath, a local ad spot dropped in that night caught my attention. The Chateau D'Vie was to be a 'Catskill' type country club, but for singles only, just over the Tappan Zee Bridge in Spring Valley, perhaps a base to re-start my career.

Renovated on the site of the original Spring Valley Country Club, complete with 18-hole golf course, tennis courts and oversized outdoor pool, The Chateau D'Vie was to be the first and only such club designed for singles. Stocked with attractive models to sign up new members, it promised to be the ultimate catnip for affluent female pussies and their horny male counterparts. Threatened by my resume Gary, the closeted gay Entertainment Director, denied my job application on the spot. But the attentive blonde cougar who took down my details suggested I hang around. I figured at least I'd get laid, but Helen had something else in mind. That evening a microphone was set up in the downstairs bar for an impromptu performance for the staff. When finished, Helen introduced me to Nancy, fiancé to one of the owners, and the next morning I gave my two-week notice at the post office.

Hired for looks and talent, the staff would be a self-contained theater company designed to both service and entertain the membership. As *"The Young And The Restless"* premiered on daytime TV, potential country club members were screened for 'image' and single eligibility *(adultery could mean a lawsuit)* by the primary recruiters, Helen, Kaye and Peter. Helen a classy Chanel No.5, Kaye, a Jacqueline Bisset type beauty, and Peter a sandy haired Aussie heartthrob; our own in house 'soap opera'. Consensus had both Peter and Helen hooked on Kaye, and there was the rub *(unclear who was rubbing who)*. The principal partner and visionary behind the club was Harvey Klaris, a lawyer/investment banker who co-owned Sardi's, and years later would produce Broadway's *"Nine"* and *"The Tap Dance Kid."* Klaris was joined by investor/dry cleaning magnate, Arthur Nadaner, and C.P.A./partner Richard Kovner, who literally picked pennies off the floor *(probably why his shirts always hung out over his well-fed figure)*. There was also a rumored silent partner *(perhaps of Italian descent)* providing other 'unspecified' funding and support, including the liquor licenses.

Prior to opening, membership drive open houses showcased the elegant central wood-trimmed showroom/lounge with full stage lighting and sound, an adjacent bar, and restaurant/dining room. Downstairs, a late-night café/bar, sauna, locker room and showers, with a path down to the cabana lined pool. The golf course stretched out behind the main building while a second facility for staff and overnight room rentals was in the final stages of completion. As we all met to work out systems and plan activities, Gary kept his connections private to protect his position *(and emphasize my irrelevance)*. But for the time and place, gay was not cool. As he feared, despite my inexperience, armed with Harvey's list of agency contacts, Gary's closet became my room.

Members were each issued a gold-chained medallion for access to the facilities (to be relinquished in an elaborate ceremony if they married). By opening week, over a hundred medallions had been issued, sparkling in the lights of news crews and reporters from Rolling Stone to Playboy. After Sha Na Na packed the main room that weekend backed by our house band Hard Candy, just me and my guitar in the downstairs bar, felt like *"This Could Be The Start of Something Big."*

Like running a summer camp, my responsibilities ranged from setting up volleyball schedules, to coordinating with the tennis pro, maintaining the music and sound equipment, providing board games, running special events like scavenger hunts and raffles, producing staff talent shows spoofing members and events of the week, booking all talent, and going out of my way to insure that certain attractive female members didn't go home horny *(poor me)*. One such member was a blonde bombshell named Rene, who never paid to join, always on someone's guest pass. In my room, her favorite position a split, right ankle pinned up against her head and left leg straight out beneath me. A redhead named Sandy liked giving blowjobs where she might get caught. Head bobbing, eyes darting while I stood at attention watching her play with herself behind the dining hall, in the parking lot next to her car, out on the golf course, etc. Mary was a tailored brunette stockbroker who liked stripping while I thumped my guitar... and then her, and heavyset Elaine, large breasts flopping, could only cum doggy style *(A tough job, but someone had to do it!)*. In the dining room Dyhna, a free-spirited bohemian blonde dancer with great natural breasts, completely comfortable in her bisexuality, was secretly in a relationship with Ronnie on the athletic staff... and both fucking me... at first separately, then together. One long afternoon, the three of us were entangled in my bed when the phone pulled me away. On my return Dyhna had to check in with Klaus, the head chef, returning in time for Ronnie to cover her yoga class while the O'Jay's were singing *"Love Train"* on the radio, followed by *"Tubular Bells"* on Richard Branson's new Virgin Records.

While Watergate hearings monopolized the news, *"Match Game"* was the number one daytime program, recreated on weekends at the Chateau. Like amusement park tickets, the club issued unique plastic beads as currency, strung together and exchanged for food, drinks, and various 'pay-per-play' activities. Initial club visitors included Rocky Aoki, owner of Benihana's, and his entourage of female remora, model/actress Lauren Hutton, Norman Mailer, 'Breck Girl' and future Charlie's Angel, Jaclyn Smith, and a mysterious 'investor' name Frank Calzone. Once sent to deliver documents to Calzone's fortieth floor office on Fifth Avenue, although not listed on the building directory, "National Kinney Corporation/ Warner Communications Inc." was embossed on the smoked glass doors. Due to a parking garage scandal, Kinney had spun off its non-entertainment assets and, under former 'connected' funeral home owner Steve Ross, changed its name. Warner Communications was now the secretive parent company to Warner Brothers Films, Warner Music, Atlantic and Electra/Nonesuch Records, DC Comics and Mad Magazine. *(How appropriate that, originally handling dead people, Steve Ross would eventually represent thousands of such artists and composers... and double as Alfred E. Newman).* Probably from the parking garage side of the company, Calzone may have been that rumored 'silent partner.'

With a stock market crash, stagflation, Nixon's Watergate cabinet dropping like flies, the country headed into recession… probably not the best time to launch the club. After the promotional blush, recruiters found it had been easier selling the dream than reality. Shifting from screening applicants to trolling reject lists, soon our most glamorous members were Dovima, a 40+ supermodel from the 50's, and Judi, a high heeled, gum chewing 'Bronx bomber' who looked best from a distance (or from behind). As members got uglier, so did the finances. Without families using the facilities like a normal country club and despite Hard Candy's terrific nightly performances, other than weekends the place was empty. Every department began losing money, except the bar, where Slicked-Back Paul, with shiny Brylcreemed hair, bartered his membership for mix tapes and speakers that fell off a truck, then bartended for tips. To maximize profits we air-conditioned and expanded the room only to discover that barflies swarmed later and drank more when sweating and squished together. So Paul sabotaged the air conditioner and a wall was reconstructed. And sure enough... liquor sales came back *(confirming barroom drinking a punishing team sport serving the insecure)*.

When Rich Kovner suggested I book The Platters, every agent had their own version. I chose The International Platters, with original lead singer Tony Williams and his wife Helen. In the dressing room donning their lime green jump suits, years of addiction had taken its toll on Tony. Guiding him up the stairs, Helen recounted his support in the early years... now it was her turn. Onstage, unsteady on his feet, she leaned against him as if part of the act. But when the lights came up, that familiar crystal clear voice on *"My Prayer"* had me subconsciously muse that perhaps Tony Williams was the Jacob Marley to my future and wondered if anyone would be there to hold me?

By far the most memorable club performance was Screamin' Jay Hawkins. Budgets slashed, I had to pick him up in my Galaxie *(no longer mom's car, now mine)* at a midtown hotel/boarding house just off Broadway, along with his props, including a collapsible coffin. Unaccustomed to daylight, slouching in the passenger seat behind oversized dark glasses he fell asleep, his hair smearing the window with a thick layer of grease. Afraid to wake him when we arrived, I just slipped out, hoping as night fell he'd come back to life... and did he ever... When the smoke bomb went off onstage that night and his coffin opened, first he scared the shit out of Hard Candy. Staring at them before turning to the audience, he swore he would kill them if they stopped playing... and they believed him. In his black cape amidst colored lights and contortions, in a sinister beat he turned wide-eyed to the house pointing and hissing *"I Put A Spell On You!"* As the music built, he'd occasionally stare back at the band confirming his threat until he was jumping up and down on the stage sweating and screaming the line "I can't stand it!" *(exactly how the band felt)* the entire assemblage cheering him on. As he climaxed on the final, *"Because your mine!"* and fell back into the coffin, the room erupted *(and the band must have felt like the night we escaped The Don alive)*.

As fall slipped in, the pool no longer an attraction, membership dropped further from losers to degenerates, mirrored in Washington as 'Law and Order' Vice President Spiro Agnew was charged with extortion, tax fraud, bribery and conspiracy and replaced by Gerald Ford. Faced with impeachment, President Nixon was forced to turn over the Watergate tapes after the 'Saturday Night Massacre,' firing the Special Prosecutor, Attorney General and Deputy Attorney General when they refused to cover his ass. A social worker member from the Bronx was paying his club expenses with welfare checks for dead people and hit man Sal made no bones about his profession. For extra income the club rented numbered shower room lockers. When it became common practice for members to disregard the rules we began snapping off illegal locks. In Sal's case, the offending locker only contained a jockstrap and towel but he also claimed a Rolex and $500 cash, in effect calling me a thief. Backed into a diplomatic corner in Harvey's office, the club couldn't afford the negative publicity or extortion, and Sal wouldn't back down. Harvey made a call to his 'silent partner' and put Sal on the phone. Snake eyes smiling as he hung up the receiver, suddenly Sal remembered leaving the Rolex in another jacket and offered to accept $100 to close the matter. Glancing back like Screamin' Jay Hawkins as he left the room, it wasn't clear if this was really over.

Earlier that month, on the Jewish high holiday of Yom Kipper, Egypt and Syria, encouraged by other Arab neighbors, attacked Israel. With U.S. support, the little country turned around and beat the crap out of them all. OAPEC (Organization of Arab Petroleum Exporting Countries) retaliated with an oil embargo on the U.S., gas prices spiked, and club traffic slowed to a trickle. By now Hard Candy, no longer in residence, was relegated to alternate weekends with a band called Killroy sometimes filling in. On one such night, a sudden explosion shocked the room. A smoldering cigarette, the delayed fuse for a powerful M-80 firecracker. But the band played on until a half hour later, and another blast. With so many smokers in the room, there was no way to tell when or where the next one would detonate. Within minutes, a shattered window finished the festivities. Whether a stupid prank gone too far or sabotage, the result was the same *(I don't remember if Sal was there)*. Within weeks, down to a skeleton crew, I was one of the last pink-slipped amidst rumors the 'silent partner' had taken a nose dive off a Manhattan roof... perhaps a parking garage? Although short lived, the club resulted in a number of lasting relationships. These included exotic beauty Alana, and co-owner Art Nadaner, who in the end, apparently got what he paid for.

Although tucked up in Spring Valley, the permissiveness of the Chateau D'Vie was not an anomaly. In fact Screamin' Jay Hawkins was nothing compared to bawdy Bette Midler with Barry Manilow at the piano, boobs bouncing out of her towel at The Continental Baths, where New York gays streamed out of their closets to get naked. On Broadway *"Behind The Green Door," "Deep Throat"* and *"The Devil In Miss Jones"* heralded 'The Golden Age Of Porn'... The sexual revolution pushed to its illogical conclusion in the midst of government corruption and questionable individual morality, all testing the boundaries of 'freedom'... shades of a once disintegrated Roman Empire.

VII. (1973- Fall)
(Now What?)

Having lost my Bronx apartment, there was no place to go but home. Bob King was working construction for his non-English speaking Italian brother-in-law and Carl at Sam Ash Music. Both would be happy playing The Village again, but the Mercer Arts Center had since collapsed and NYU moved from the West Bronx, ripping up the neighborhood with dormitories and a student center under construction on Washington Square. Over on The Bowery, Hilly Kristal opened what was supposed to be a Country, Blue Grass and Blues club (CBGB) but had become a loud underground Mecca for 'Punk' acts like Suicide, Television, Angel & The Snake (later to become Blondie), Joey Ramone, Patti Smith, and not for us. All we had left was Folk City, The Bitter End, and if really desperate, The Back Fence for tips, so no giving up day jobs, and I needed to find one.

Luckily, heading into holiday season, Harry was open to temporary help at the post office. Stuffing sacks, Charlie Rich singing *"The Most Beautiful Girl"* in the background, there was Linda Ragusa on TV with Phil Donahue. Now Lyn Christopher, with a new album on Paramount Records. Unfortunately Gulf & Western was dumping the label, so she wouldn't get much support (and no place for me). But Head of A&R, Mike Barbiero, mentioned Lou was over at 'Black Rock.' Hair trimmed, and flowered shirts replaced with a conservative sport coat, Lou Ragusa was now V.P. of Music Publishing for CBS International, while privately managing Linda. But even having just signed Bruce Springsteen, Aerosmith, and Billy Joel, the idiots at Columbia fired Clive Davis for financial shenanigans (for which he paid a $10,000 tax evasion fine). Replaced by aged Goddard Lieberson, with millions in profits, Columbia was creatively crippled.

At The Bitter End that weekend we opened for jazz guitarist Larry Coryell and acoustic rock band The Braid, both managed by Tom Payne and Vince Cirrincione. Vince wasn't interested in unsigned artists but Tom suggested I come by the office anyway. Through Contemprocon Productions, they booked acts like Captain Beefheart, Ry Cooder, Chic Corea, and Coryell, filling such mid-sized venues as The Anderson Theater, The Beacon, and Town Hall. Watching expenses and cross collateralizing, they survived despite the competitive market, unions, transit strikes, unpredictable weather and a tanking economy. Soon, when not at the post office, I was running errands from their 57th Street apartment/ office. In the bowels of the Time-Life Building, Wagner Photoprint handled artwork for the magazines upstairs, through a plastic tube circulatory system. After hours the manager would reduce and enlarge our concert posters for cash and at Postal Instant Press we printed flyers I'd stick on walls, bus stops and telephone booths throughout the city, taking full advantage of my sociology and political science degree.

Post Chateau, Dyhna and I were among the only white people attending a late night downtown showing of *"The Exorcist."* With audience participation, years before *"The Rocky Horror Picture Show,"* spectator lines better than anything in the script. When Linda Blair grabbed the psychiatrist's leg, a woman yelled, "Break dem balls bitch!" complemented by an exuberant laugh track. Following a doctor's onscreen stupidity, "Fuckin' doctors don't know shit!" a chorus agreeing in colorful expletives. On the head spin we heard, "Damn, I can do that if you fuck me good baby!" Then there was "Watch it… watch it… she gonna do that pea soup shit again!" met with unified revulsion as the priest wiped the slime from his face. Lame responses soundly ridiculed by the assemblage, the author often pummeled by his compatriots *(something I'd regularly like to do to the TV)*. And so it went. Looking forward to each outburst as much as the next scene. The only way to ever see a horror flick! Afterwards, with Marvin Gaye singing *"Let's Get It On,"* Dyhna reserved a room at The Chelsea to try out a sex cream purported to enhance the experience. Personally, I liked the movie better.

Other Chateau relationships included blonde bombshell Rene and ugly Judi from the Bronx. Despite her playmate appearance, at thirty Rene's time clock desperation scared men off, compounding a growing insecurity. At four years her junior, I was a non-threatening incestuous little brother. Which was fine with me, but not Kitty. The jealous black cat skulked under the bed waiting for Rene to fall asleep before flying up to hit me in the face then darting back under the bed. This made sleeping there next to impossible, which probably made Kitty very happy. Judi was strictly a late night 'booty call,' sneaking out of her family's row house, usually after midnight. We'd park in dad's station wagon on air mattresses in a dark alley behind the A&P. Thin and muscular, with long straight hair, a reddish blonde mound in that space where her thighs didn't meet, a firm tight ass, and small, perfectly upturned breasts, cherry topped with dark pointed nipples, Judi was both athletic and sensual...in the dark. Kissing was minimal, but everything else extreme as she'd multiple orgasm, wildly vibrating, changing positions, louder and more voracious with each climax. A terrific partner if not for the chewing gum Bronx accent and the Edvard Munch face.

Popular club member Betty, was an elementary school principal in Kingsbridge, still sending me long handwritten letters... red flags to stay away. Unlike the dictionary definition of love, for me, 'a monogamous malady that, if allowed to fester, usually results in disillusionment and pain.' The first signs of this disorder, 'infatuation,' the irrational anticipation of love... to be avoided at all costs. Suffice it to say, we never became pen pals.

Usually at the pool, Barbara was an attractive six-foot tall, long straight black haired suburban divorcee with great legs who had no idea why men all wanted to fuck her. There had been something about her I couldn't put my finger on... so I did. After an hour's drive to her split level Parsippany neighborhood, a day listening to complaints about her ex, and hours of procrastinating, we finally made it to her bedside. Where she assured me I was in for a major disappointment. Convinced she was frigid, and unwilling to let me go down, she opened her legs and waited for me to imitate her ex-husband. Her lips and breasts unresponsive, trying to prove her point... this would be a challenge. Quietly turning her over, I began messaging her back, and shoulders, and neck, gradually feeling the tension release until a slight sigh signaled it safe to begin running my hands down the length of her body, awaking her senses. Then back to her neck and shoulders with one hand while exploring with the other, gently probing between her thighs and feeling the ice melt. With one hand concentrating on the wetness and the other running through her long black hair caressing her scalp, her scent on my fingers, her body began moving with the rhythm of my hands. Rolling her over, her nipples now hard, quivering when licked, her mouth and eyes wide open, she grabbed and sucked me in. Sliding my arm between us and cupping her cunt with my hand, middle fingers probing, messaging, and soaking, her breathing and hips became more violent. Eyes closed, she pulled me on top, wrapping me in those terrific long legs. With a sudden pumping thrust, she yelled as her body took off into a gallop, bucking and spraying. Holding on for dear life, when the ride ended, curled into the fetal position she whispered what sounded like "Oh my god...I never knew..."

After almost a month as an unpaid intern at Contemprocon, Tom promoted me to Administrative Director, paid with a share of company stock *(that I still have in the drawer with my diploma and worth as much today as it was then)* and an opening slot in the upcoming show at Town Hall. How cool to see my name on the poster at Wagner Photoprint along with The Braid, Oregon and Larry's newly formed Eleventh House. Comprised of I.U. alumni Randy Brecker on horns, blind keyboard wizard Mike Mandel, bassist Danny Trifan, flamboyant drummer Alphonse Mouzon, and Coryell in front, the Eleven House, was on the cutting edge of the new jazz/rock fusion phenomenon.

Ethereal jazz group Oregon, formed a few years earlier by Ralph Towner, Paul McCandless, Glen Moore, and Collin Walcott, enjoyed a dedicated underground following. With woman's rights NOW (National Organization for Woman) in full bloom, *'Ms.*

Magazine' in its second year on newsstands, *Mary Tyler More* threw her hat in the air, as Bobby Riggs was soundly defeated by Billy Jean King in tennis' *"Battle of the Sexes."* A large contingent of radical feminist Oregon fans filled the audience at Town Hall that night. Opening with *"Wish I Was A Lady So That I Could Be A Whore,"* elicited an immediate audience response... men cheering and women offended, fists in the air, rowdier with each repetition. Backstage security moved to the front. Then came my latest composition, *"Get On The Pill Or Else Get Outta My Arms!"* They went fuckin' berserk! By the second verse, screaming vein-popping feminists stormed the stage, clawing over security guards as someone pulled the plug. 'Escorted' from the doused spotlight as the curtain fell... all documented the next day in *The New York Times*... my first national publicity.

That Christmas, Dyhna won a 'Night On The Town' raffle that included a private stretch limousine, red carpet tickets to the premiere of *"The Sting,"* and a night at the Waldorf Astoria, in the 'Premier Suite' complete with working fireplace... all firsts for me. As the now late Jim Croce's *"Time In A Bottle"* reached number one, cuddled in the antique four-poster bed's night of lost virginity, I watched the embers die on another year... wondering if my career could ever be rekindled.

VIII. (1974)
(Where Has All The Music Gone?)

A glacial shift was taking place in the country. In *"Where Has All The Ivy Gone?"* the sixties civil rights movement, assassinations, Vietnam fiasco, drug culture and sexual revolution had the left brain of the country at odds with the right. Now Nixon and his executive branch cronies' petty paranoia, hypocritical criminality and economic mismanagement had both sides questioning whether the recession crippled body politic could still function, circulation strangled by gasoline lines bloating the veins of Exxon. As films and TV desperately looked back to *"The Way We Were"* and *"Happy Days"* with *"The Walton's,"* *"The Brady Bunch"* and *"The Partridge Family,"* in Billboard, *"Time In A Bottle"* was replaced at number one by *"The Joker,"* then Ringo's remake of the 1960 hit, *"You're Sixteen."* It felt like our entire generation just gave up, wanting everything back the way it never was.

At CBGB's a new generation believed if you could play at least three chords loud and expectorate emotion, it was still music. This 'democratization' spawned bands like The New York Dolls, Blondie, The Dictators, Untravox!, The Patty Smith Group, The Saints, The Ramones, The Stranglers, and Talking Heads, all swimming through the Bowery underground. Where, coincidently, naked pictures of Dyhna now plastered the walls… a cast member in *"Let My People Come,"* a full frontal production at The Village Gate. In the midst of all this, Allan and Stanley left Folk City to open The Bottom Line. Not just another club, but a 400-seat state-of-the-art sound system musical oasis. The culmination of their years 'paying dues.' A service bar filled the wall to the left of a fully equipped raised stage, dressing rooms behind. Long perpendicular candlelit tables lined the tiered, columned expanse. An elaborate soundboard and spotlights on a rear black-iron balcony, while two massive mirrors were constructed to accommodate the few partially obstructed views. At the far end of the room, an unobtrusive kitchen access and hidden stairs led to the business offices above. On opening night Dr. John jammed with Johnny Winter and Stevie

Wonder to an audience that included Mick Jagger, Bette Midler, Carly Simon, Ripp Torn, Janis Ian, and Charles Mingus, to name only a few... not a venue for me to play (yet?).

In fact there was virtually no place for me to play The Village any longer. That's when singles bars, primarily on the Upper East Side, found they could cash in with cheap live music that wasn't too loud for the neighborhood. There was Brandy's, a basic watering hole, and Dr. Generosity's, with unshelled peanuts at each table and a sawdust floor for the shells. The one 'musical' club in the group was Kenny's Castaways at 211 East 84th, where Irish owner Pat Kenny booked artists like Professor Longhair, Willie Dixon, David Amram, and Bill Chinnock with a standing invitation to the Irish Rovers whenever in town. Starting there for $10 and 'tips,' it was raised to $25 when I learned *"Danny Boy."* On the Upper West Side was a strange club called The 3rd Phase, designed to mimic a cave, complete with stalactites and stalagmites built into the ceiling and floor around a five foot square fake stone stage. Now it was back to just me and my Martin.

At Rose Cleaners on Mamaroneck Avenue in White Plains, the perfect 36 D's of the braless *"Brown Eyed Girl"* behind the counter joyously bounced beneath her loose fitting T's. Hit on by everyone, including her boss, Jill embraced her sexuality like my music, allowing her to control her audience... But although blatantly advertised, selectively shared. In my case it took more than a few flirtatious visits and finally fingering my guitar while waiting for my plastic covered clothes, to convince her to join me after work. Once in my room, a single song and her blouse and panty less jeans hit the floor, the dark nipples I'd been staring at for the past month, staring back in full bloom. Jill loved being naked and my fixation on her perfectly formed natural breasts *(the fake ones might as well be plastic blow-ups for horny old men that smoke cigars)*...One of the few women who would actually climax when I gently squeezed and sucked and licked them *(most need to be touched elsewhere first)*. In fact every inch of her was sensitive to touch, the slightest scratches forming thin welts that would then disappear. Both vaginal and clitoral, her climaxes built to extreme multiples then subsided before gradually climbing again... purring, licking, stroking and tumbling beneath the sheets, completely lost in the moments... In fact, that's where Jill lived... in the moment. I'd write a song about our next date, when I arrived to find she'd left an hour before with another guy. Not that she meant to stand me up. She just went with her feelings at the time... But left me wondering what the fuck happened?... A long overdue blow to my overblown ego *(giving 'blow-job' a new meaning)*. In another of life's ironic twists, of all the relationships at the time, this one still survives.

Catering to the lowest common denominator, Neil Bogart launched his new Casablanca records with comic book simulated Kiss, whose self-titled debut album flopped, too 'musical' for Punk and too insipid for Top 40. Somewhere between the two, David Bowie released *"Diamond Dogs"* after having retired *"Ziggy Stardust"* the year before. Speaking of insipid, the *"Sonny & Cher Comedy Hour"* imploded when Cher dumped Sonny. Counter balanced by the since forgotten marriage of Captain & Tennille, as inane Top 40 Radio vacantly OD'd, *"Hooked On A Feeling"* with *"Benny & The Jets,"* on *"The Streak"* along with McCartney's innocuous *"Band On The Run."* Exactly where my band was. With no place to play and no income from Contemprocon, I needed a job.

Off the Cross Bronx Expressway *(like Greenland, probably so-named as a public relations gimmick, its traffic barely moving)* at the end of Castle Hill Avenue in view of The Whitestone Bridge, I found a gig as music director at The Castle Hill Day Camp. Catering to and supported by the local community, this wasn't the Catskills. The only other white faces were the two left-wing Jewish owners and Jeanie, the spontaneous northern Italian, natural blonde, green-eyed swimming instructor *(easy to see why she was hired)*. The kids, ranging from five to twelve, naturally related to exotic rhythms and drums, and the American Indian Lore I once taught in another life. This, along with late night skinny-dipping and sex with Jeanie (and Jill), made for a memorable summer.

Even before somersaulting with the kids, the outside world had turned upside down. As kidnap victim Patty Hearst, now Tania, robbed banks with the Symbionese Liberation Army, overseas the Portuguese military overthrew their dictator, Golda Meir was forced to resign in Israel, President Georges Pompidou died in France, Chancellor Willie Brandt was thrown out in West Germany, an underground nuclear explosion announced that India now had 'the bomb,' while in London the I.R.A. bombed The House of Parliament, President Juan Peron died in Argentina, and Generalissimo Francisco Franco stepped down in Spain, all leading to the final resignation of "I Am Not A Thief" President 'Tricky Dick' Nixon. And on the Billboard charts, The Hues Corporation sang *"Rock The Boat."*

Out in Jersey, Bob found local clubs for us to play, including The Soap Factory, where I met Lisbeth. Beth was a soft-spoken neonatal nurse with light brown hair flowing to her waist when unpinned. Her sparse conversation belied a sardonic wit, unnoticed unless paying attention. Coping with her chain-smoking mother and cop brother in the family home in Hackensack, despite amazing patience with her preemies, she had very little for her brother's macho friends. Locked in her room, sublimating with intricate pen & ink drawings or romantic novels, it was probably my lyrics that peaked her interest. Our first day together was spent in effortless conversation wandering through the state park as the leaves changed, sharing each other's dreams, culminating with unexpected oral sex under a tree at sunset. This was more than another sexual encounter and it didn't make sense when she later refused my calls. After a Jersey rehearsal, I drove over and waited with her frail mom in their cigarette smog living room for Beth to come home. Hidden in her surprise-party face, reticent acceptance before leaving with me to talk. Given my promiscuity, Beth was hesitant to 'get involved.' I pleaded she come out and live life, rather than hide in her room and read about it, for fear of being hurt somewhere down the road. Why not give us a shot, and quit if and when my infidelity became too high a price to pay? She said she'd think about it, and asked to be taken home.

Back at 1650 Broadway that fall, Bob Reno and Eddie O'Loughlin formed Midland International Records and signed Carol Douglas to cut a U.S. club version of the U.K. hit *"Doctor's Orders."* With the production aid of Meco Monardo, who at the same time worked with Tony Bongiovi and Harold Wheeler on Gloria Gaynor's version of *"Never Can Say Goodbye."* Exploding New York club sales on both records heralded what would come to be known as 'Disco.' Also nearby, Walter Sears, a porno Walt Disney complete with the same moustache, sat amidst the largest tuba collection in the country, editing low budget 'skin flicks' for the burgeoning commercial market. Walt loved my music, constantly asking to include *"Corned Beef On Rye"* or *"Subway Rider"* in one of his films. But I just didn't think it was the right career choice.

Meanwhile at Contemprocon I learned that a talent manager is really a glorified baby sitter that everyone resents. You're fighting with the record company over royalties and support, with booking agents over gigs that might destroy your artist's credibility or lose money, with your publicist for lack of or negative stories, with club owners and promoters concerning contracts, non-payment, or canceled gigs, while trying to keep the band members from killing each other over girlfriends, groupies, and gripes. In our case, every time Billy Cobham bought a drum, Alphonse needed two, until soon there was no room in the truck and it took the roadies an extra half hour to set up. Meanwhile, jealous of her husband's notoriety, Julie's outrageous behavior and demands led Larry to drink and the other band members to fall out. And there were always emergencies like a van breaking down in the snow hundreds of miles from the next gig, or losing Mike Mandel in the airport. While the money just seemed to evaporate in telephone calls, stationery, cab rides and couriers, electric bills and business lunches, guitar strings and drumheads, equipment repairs and truck rentals, rent hikes and daily annoyances. And in the end the artist doesn't know where the fuck it all went or why you deserve your commission. All of which explains the dearth of decent talent managers.

After a series of extended late night phone conversations, Beth finally agreed to come out with me on Thanksgiving night to see Elton John at Madison Square Garden. When surprise guest John Lennon stepped out to join him on *"Whatever Gets You Through The Night," "Lucy In The Sky With Diamonds,"* and *"I Saw Her Standing There,"* we couldn't know he would never again appear on stage. As the lights came up, Beth turned and kissed me, agreeing to a relationship that would last another twenty years. That New Year's Eve we froze together watching the ball fall at One Times Square while Guy Lombardo played *"Auld Lang Syne"* at the Waldorf Astoria still competing with Dick Clarke's *"New Year's Rockin' Eve"*... And I saw my dream slipping farther away.

IX. (1975)
(Going Commercial)

As the music went through what I hoped would be a temporary stupid phase, playing the businessman was a mind reset, no longer waking to sing subliminal lines into a tape recorder or rehearsing with the guys. After his firing at CBS Records, Clive Davis was hired as a consultant at Columbia Pictures and soon president of their record and music operations. In late '74, Davis folded the various Columbia legacy labels (Colpix, Colgems, and Bell Records) into a new entity named Arista Records (after his high school honor society). In early 1975, most of the artists signed to Bell were let go. Others, like Suzi Quatro and Hot Chocolate, sent to Bell/Arista-distributed, Big Tree Records. Several Bell acts, including Barry Manilow, the Bay City Rollers, and Melissa Manchester moved to Arista, where Tom and Vince were then able to sign Larry Coryell's Eleventh House as well.

Despite the new deal, keeping everything together wasn't easy. For a key showcase at My Father's Place, 'Eppy' Epstein's legendary club in Roslyn, at show time constructing Alphonse's massive drum set and Julie's shenanigans had everyone yelling and Larry passed out drunk on the dressing room floor. Even with the noise and vibration of the impatient crowd stomping upstairs, we couldn't wake Larry. Following a bucket of ice water, three of us carried his soaking semi-conscious body up the wooden staircase while Eppy tried to pacify the audience. On a chair backstage, force-feeding black coffee with an actual funnel, the animals were again growing restless when Coryell found his feet. Unstable on his own, the road manager held him up at the microphone as the curtain opened. And then suddenly, magic… When the spotlight hit, Larry's switch turned on, fingers flying through his patented guitar runs with every note distinctive and clear, like no other jazz guitarist in the world. For an hour, seamlessly moving from one composition to another, the performance was flawless. And when the spotlight cut off, Larry keeled over and hit the floor.

During the reign of the Fillmore East, Bill Graham's exclusivity clauses meant no act could play a 75 mile radius within four months. In 1971, when Graham closed the Fillmore and dropped out, Howard Stein, son of notorious loan shark Ruby Stein, opened the Academy Of Music on East 14th Street with his own deals. Ron Delsener, who produced the Schaeffer Music Festival at Wollman Rink with Hilly Kristal, controlled Broadway and above and John Scher took New Jersey. This meant Contemprocon could never book a major act. Managing one jazz artist without the resources to take on another, all suggested little upside, but gave me a New York office, and the legitimacy to apply for a gig at Don Elliott Productions.

Don had been a major jazz innovator in the 50's on brass, vibes and vocals. Working with everyone from Dizzy Gillespie, Miles Davis, Benny Goodman and Buddy Rich, to Coleman Hawkins, Billie Holliday and Stan Getz. From 1953 through 1960, winning the *Miscellaneous Instrumentalist* poll in *Down Beat* magazine. When rock pushed jazz out of the mainstream, experimenting with multi-track recording in his Weston, Connecticut studio, he collaborated with Quincy Jones, on such films as *"In The Heat Of The Night," "The Getaway,"* and *"The Pawnbroker"* and began a lucrative career writing jingles. Eventually, with literally thousands of commercials on the air, he also built a New York studio at 40th Street and Sixth Avenue, across from Bryant Park. While his wife Doris ran the business from Weston, they needed reps in New York. This meant making the rounds on commission and a draw, trying to convince Creative Directors to use Don on their next commercial. It wasn't much, but more than I was making at Contemprocon.

Whether blatant or subliminal, advertising was an industry built on sexual manipulation. Every relationship, image and message a double entendre. 'Windsong stayed on your mind while striptease music lathered Noxema shaving cream. Susan Anton was turned on by a phallic Muriel cigar on soft Corinthian leather, as a graceful cougar jumped an erect Mercury sign.' With a growing number of female Creative Directors, I was hired by Doris to complement

Maureen O'Neil, already there. Compact and aggressive, Maureen was a contradiction. Doris knew she needed a female rep, but didn't want competition or temptation for Don. Intelligent and articulate, but not especially sensual, Maureen was more her confidant. Doris, already in her mid-forties, was still the seductress. My job was the women.

But getting in their doors was a challenge. Making appointments by phone or just showing up didn't work. Even when Doris called ahead, they were usually 'in a meeting' by the time I arrived. Following a week of rejection, while leaving the second floor offices of a particularly snooty receptionist, I scouted the rear entrance on Vanderbilt Ave. for an alternate staircase. As expected, the exit door was locked, but before leaving a delivery guy arrived and entered an unmarked door to the left. There, an open-faced dumbwaiter shuttled packages upstairs and I figured what the fuck? So I scrunched in, pushed the button for the second floor and ended up in the ad agency food room. In the hallway, acting as if I'd just come through reception, I asked directions to the Creative Director on my list and introduced myself at the office door of Mitzi Adams. Surprised and then impressed with my 'resourcefulness,' I finally got my first appointment.

Mitzi was an attractive thirtyish Hampton's blueblood with Cleos on the wall instead of gold records. After a brief flirtation she explained why I was having trouble getting meetings. Apparently Don's lush productions and rich multi-layered voices were now, for the most part, passé. On the other hand, in the few cases where appropriate, he was the best. She promised to let me know when a possibility arose, and more importantly, to help me connect with a few other ad agencies. A follow-up box of Godiva chocolates with funds from petty cash, and so it began. A little over a week later the formerly dismissive receptionist was suddenly my best friend when Adams called. Closing her office door behind me, Mitzi pulled her chair away from the desk, aware I was watching her tightly crossing her legs as she spoke. Apparently Cottonelle toilet paper was losing share to dirty old Mr. Whipple squeezing the Charmin and wanted a new campaign based on their cotton ball soft image... perfect for Don. But she needed the demo by the end of the week. No problem I thought.

Thrilled with my first lead. I literally ran back to the studio to an unexpected reception. Up in Weston, weary of the jingle business and with delusions of being a recording artist again, Don balked at the pressure of another deadline. Doris lost it, screaming into the phone. Furious, she assured me it would get done, her fur flying out of the office, heading back up to give Don a 'dose of reality.' Maureen conceded that without the past income stream, the current overhead was crushing them. Despite the drama, by 4:00 o'clock Friday afternoon, I was headed back to Mitzi's office with three well-crafted soft and soothing odes to toilet paper. As the Grateful Dead mused *"a long strange trip"* for the student radical who once demonstrated against 'the establishment.'

The receptionist gone, and most of the offices empty, Mitzi still locked the door behind me, and this time also closed the blinds. Again pulling her chair away from the desk, she closed her eyes as the demos played, and demonstratively crossed her legs. When the music ended, with both her eyes and legs wide open, she was clearly not wearing panties. Without leaving my chair I unzipped, my cock staring back at her from across the room. With a Cheshire Cat smile she fell to all fours and stalked her prey. Her large diamond ring and speckled wedding band glimmering when she pounced, grabbing and devouring my defenseless dick. Head bobbing in my lap, fingers stuck in her over sprayed bottle blonde hair, I held her head firmly in place to shoot in her mouth. Purring with a self-satisfied grin, mascara running and cum dripping from her lips, she was surprised to see my dick still standing. Climbing up to drown it in her panting pussy, when I ripped open her blouse and nursed on her nipples she began to multiple, literally screaming in my ear. Needless to say... Don got the gig.

Maureen was more intrigued with my radical student past then my sexuality. Having graduated college a few years before everything exploded in the 60's, she was both an animal and women's rights activist *(not to imply they were the same)*, and piqued by my glib attitude. Cat and dog arguing in the office, she still laughed at my lyrics and flippant approach to life. In her rent controlled penthouse apartment on the Upper West Side, Maureen actually had a dog and two cats that lived together better than we ever could. But spent most of her time in court fighting the landlord trying to break her lease by any means necessary. This included turning off the water, sabotaging her electric system, breaking locks, and destroying property blamed on her. Bravely fighting back, Maureen organized both the tenants and the neighborhood and held on. Nerves always on edge, she wasn't easy to seduce, but late at night, after herbal tea and some quiet, she'd violently fuck and fall asleep.

Unable to pursue a musical career, I simply substituted with my other passion, regularly stopping at the Oyster Bar in Grand Central Station on the way to work. Up in White Plains, when the spirit moved, Jill would sneak out of her bedroom across town, shimmy down off the roof, drive over, get naked and fuck all night before heading to Rose Cleaners in the morning. Thankfully Shannon had married a good Catholic dentist and moved away and Beth lived over in Jersey, relegated to weekends, avoiding any 'conflict of interest.' In the city, along with Maureen, one-night-stands filled the gaps after occasional clubs gigs, just for variety.

When I wasn't fucking or facing rejection at the ad agencies, every day was spent at the recording studios in New York and Connecticut. Where I began to learn what I had previously taken for granted. A single note is created by a wave that has a top, mid-range and bottom and can sound very different, depending upon what part you emphasize. Then there are textures, vibrations. That note on the piano sounds different on a trumpet or violin. That same note on an acoustic guitar differs on electric, and varies from one amplifier to another. Understanding and manipulating the sound waves creating the notes is the art of audio engineering. Back then, electrical impulses of those waves were sent to magnetic tape to record. Don was using 2 inch Ampex 456 that ran about $100 per reel and could accommodate 16 tracks. This meant, for example, you could record a flute on the first track and a trumpet on the second. Then merge them on the third and record over the first track with a sax and the second with a trombone. With all four instruments on the first three tracks, you'd still have thirteen to fill your 'master' recording. However in so doing, the flute and trumpet were married, limiting your flexibility with those two instruments when 'mixing' that 'master' tape for your final recording.

A recording session involves both planning and reaction. Which tracks to merge, which takes to save, do over or edit. What mics to use and how to place them. Watching the sound levels, adjusting the inputs while appraising each performance. In Don's Connecticut studio, the soundboard included a patch bay of chords like an old-fashioned switchboard, for assigning microphones to tracks and tracks to each other. Whereas in New York, the console came from The Record Plant when they upgraded, and was 'automated.' Each demanding a different skill set.

Once the master is complete, the producer selects, filters, and applies the sound paint in 'the mix.' A 'dance mix' for example, might change the tempo, drop the strings, emphasize the bass and drums, and repeat a single vocal line. On the other hand, 'easy listening' radio could require dampening the drums, the strings and background voices blended up just behind a full rich lead vocal. The top of the sound waves then emphasized for Pop radio so the snare drum and vocals cut through. Also, occasional 'overdubs' might replace a track or add new colors to the palette. Much of the process is counter-intuitive. You might expect two voices to be stronger than one, when in fact a solo voice has more impact. A specific drum sound, great on its own, may need squashing to fit with the others. Mindful that most music was heard on shitty radios, the ultimate test of a final mix came when switched from the studio monitors to small Auratone speakers on the console, confirming hours of sound masturbation lost in translation.

Mitzi, like most ad execs, music and studio illiterate, overcompensated in front of her clients. The New York console, equipped with useless 'ad agency dummy' knobs and buttons, was in full working order for the Cottonelle commercial. Jeremy Harris, the tall, thin, soft-spoken sound engineer and part time drummer, knew to open the session at a low level. With every demand from Mitzi or client suggestion, he'd adjust a few dummy knobs, up the volume, and someone would say "Yeah, that's better." An hour later, the sound blaring and everyone pleased, unaware the real mix was done the day before. Having avoided me during the session, Mitzi casually suggested we meet for drinks to discuss the spot. Unclear whether that night's hotel room was to be her reward or mine, all I could picture was *"Jaws"* opening that week around the country... very scary.

As Saigon fell, completing our defeat in Viet Nam, with the economy here and UK in the toilet, the anti-establishment Punk disease spread. Seymour Stein signed The Ramones and Talking Heads to his Sire records, re-branding it as stylish "New Wave." Inspired by the Lower East Side infestation, British sex shop owner Malcolm McLaren flew back to infect England, forming the Sex Pistols with lead singer Johnny Rotten *(so named for his rotten teeth and attitude)*. And soon there was Cherry Vanilla, Teenage Head, The Undertones, The Boomtown Rats, The Runaways, The Screamers, and who could forget Throbbing Gristle? Now I understood how Don felt when rock replaced jazz. He loved my analogy that jazz was 'gourmet' to rock's 'fast food.' Now Punk was just 'bad food.' And the new generation was eating it up.

A kindred musical spirit, Don supported me, gradually converting the best of my rehearsal tapes to 16 track masters. After years of listening to my voice through a cassette player, it was a revelation when patched through a Pultec equalizer, suddenly with a 'presence' on tape, that previously lived only in my head. It also meant working with gifted musicians like keyboardist/arranger Pete Levin. With perfect pitch *(drop a coin and he'd tell you the note)*, I watched Pete write out all the charts for a commercial session, including an elaborate four part horn section, an hour before the musicians arrived. It also astounded me that studio singers would actually hit the wrong note if incorrect on the charts. I couldn't sing the right ones exactly as written.

Hidden amidst the cacophony of Punk and the *"Hustle"* and *"Jive Talkin'"* club noise joining Glen Campbell's *"Rhinestone Cowboy"* on the radio, there was an almost unnoticed new musical form finding its voice. First uncovered by Chris Blackwell's Island Records with Jimmy Cliff a few years earlier, and exported here with Eric Clapton's cover of *"I Shot The Sheriff,"* now Bob Marley's *"No Woman, No Cry"* added reggae to the musical dialogue. I could hear it in my head, and hit the offbeat rhythm with my guitar as I wrote *"Marianne,"* but couldn't explain it to Don. When the session finished we had a very nice calypso.

While Buzzy Linhart's dick flopped around on the big screen in *"The Groove Tube,"* Sony introduced Betamax, and the porn industry got an international erection, no longer zipped behind seedy X-rated walls. Bette Midler's boobs graduated from the Continental Baths to Broadway, with Ron Delesner's *"Clams On The Half-Shell Revue."* On the 'boob tube' at ABC, Fred Silverman took the reins, soon to unleash sexy, stacked, scantily dressed superwomen doing stupid things for big ratings, beginning with Lynda Carter's *"Wonder Woman."* Not to be outdone in silliness NBC launched *"NBC Saturday Night"* (becoming *"Saturday Night Live"*) with George Carlin as the first host and guest Andy Kauffman, accidentally becoming the most intelligent show on TV. Meanwhile, after two good albums failed, Bruce Springsteen dumped manager Mike Appel in favor of producer Jon Landau, and with a promotional push from Columbia, *"Born To Run"* exploded. Despite the live pyrotechnics and flaming guitars, spitting blood Kiss couldn't give away their records. With Casablanca on the verge of bankruptcy, Bogart pumped up the audience noise and overdubbed guitars to produce Kiss, *"Alive!"* And suddenly the public got it. They also got Disco, when Neil signed Donna Summer and released producer Giorgio Moroder's orgasmic *"Love To Love*

You Baby," with international repercussions. But for live performance, nothing could match the *"Thrilla In Manila,"* Ali and Frazier's final clash in one of the greatest heavyweight bouts of all time.

At home, despite my full dance card, I couldn't help noticing Rowena's occasional visits next door. The long legged fluffy blonde and fantasy unfulfilled, when she waved from the driveway one sunny afternoon, I scampered over like a tail-wagging puppy. No longer a secretary, now an IBM executive with an apartment in Hartsdale (near a bar I once hid from postal inspectors). Quickly jotting it down before her father returned, we agreed to catch up that evening. Served my first homemade pork chops *(never in my house growing up, more bland than expected)*, after initial fumbling on her couch, we entered each other's fantasy. Although dreamed about, no one ever went down on her. First pushing away then violently grabbing my head, no time for licking or tonguing, just clicking her clit between my teeth, nose imbedded in her soaking bush. In the bedroom, a sheltered puritan with no rhythm first trying to dance, lovemaking was a challenge. Overcum by the fact that, after all these years, I was actually fucking Ro McDermott *(imagining a Betamax to her father)*. Once again believing anything was possible.

X. (1975-Winter)
(A New Path)

Despite hitting the charts with *"Mandy,"* Barry Manilow continued his lucrative career writing and singing commercials. But when Doris suggested I contact him or his producer Ron Dante, it wasn't easy. *Billboard* had a *Buyer's Guide* that listed managers but not their clients and his booking agent wouldn't tell me shit, afraid to be cut out of a commission. There was no directory of producers. Luckily, since Coryell was also on Arista, I was able to get Barry's Product Manager on the phone. But at Contemprocon I faced a similar problem when Tom asked me to contact Dr. John (Mac Rebennack) about a possible recording date and he wasn't on a label. Luckily one of the guys had his home number. Another problem arose when a local car dealership wanted Don to do a commercial using the song *"Chevy Van."* This meant determining if the copyright was with BMI or ASCAP. Then phoning the research department for the publisher's info, to get permission to use the song and for what cost? None of this was easy, each piece requiring special knowledge and contacts… and I had an idea…

With no future in talent management or concert promotion, I was also fed up with ad agency assholes believing their shit didn't stink because they controlled $200,000 worth of toilet paper spots. Punk bands were multiplying like cockroaches and Midland International's *"Fly Robin Fly"* incessantly beating on the radio. Like Nicholson in *"One Flew Over The Cuckoo's Nest"* I needed to break out before my brain was fried. But stay close enough to the asylum so when it cleaned up its act I could sneak back in. How about servicing the sanitarium to make their jobs easier, while also expanding my contacts? … It was a no-brainer.

Building a cross-referenced music business directory from scratch with no financing sounded daunting. But I realized by simply researching the new songs hitting the charts each week, within a few months I'd have most of the Top 100 covered. Also, in printing and distributing my monthly research as a subscription based newsletter, my subscribers would pay to build the directory. With 3"x5" index cards coded (T)Title, (A)Artist, (Pro)Producer, (P)Publisher, (L)Record Label, (BK)Booking Agency, and (M)Manager, I began an alphabetical master card catalogue. Initial information garnered from *Billboard*, supplemented by scanning the back of record jackets at Tower Records along with days on the phones, where at first I encountered some resistance. After a series of collection society and record company meetings, and assurances that my information was not going to the public, but for professional use only, a network of phone informants was in place.

That's when Bill Krasilovsky presented a serious legal problem. By relying primarily on *Billboard*, they might demand a license or even steal my whole project. Luckily at the time, both Cashbox and Record World also had Top 100 Singles charts. Bill suggested that I track the new songs breaking each, without referring to specific chart numbers. Providing an 'after-the-fact' comparative analysis of the three trades, not competing but supplementing their already published information with my additional research... Fucking Brilliant!

After contriving a system, color pencil coding my cards for each monthly issue, printing and laying everything out by hand on work sheets, then came typesetting. Told the cheapest were Hasidic Jews on the Lower East Side, like the curl dangling Catskill kin I once entertained. There I discovered my ten-page booklet would cost ten times what I expected, not to mention printing and mailing. Without a real job, a bank loan was out of the question *(and Pannini was dead)*. With no place else to go, luckily dad backed my move from musician to publisher with a cash infusion.

Next I needed an identity. A directory was boring. The format had to imply magazine/newsletter hybrid, and the title get music execs to open it. After initial names, *"New On The Charts"* captured it. Unable to afford four-color glossy printing, the cover still demanded a picture, probably an attractive female. Conceiving "Research

Assistant Of The Month," maybe my subscribers could supply the photos? But I still needed that first cover. Finally using something from college, my photography course Pentax, striking Greenwich Village actress, model, and friend, Erle Bjornstad posed as my harried secretary. The tall dark Norwegian also had no topless qualms, so we shot all afternoon, for both her portfolio and mine.

Using press-type, I chose an intricate title font like the *"The New York Times"* but updated. Filled the background with chart paper squares, including a boxed descriptive paragraph, all held in place by a thick black border *(hopefully not an obituary)*. Going for 'underground' legitimate, I named my parent company Music Business Reference Index, and designed a logo to fit. And on the seventh day I rested. And it was good.

www.notc.com

XI. (1976)
(The Launch)

I needed a legitimate looking New York City address to print in the publication. Although still repping Don, when Conteprocon moved from 57th Street to 1500 Broadway in Times Square, Tom offered shared office space. But I couldn't commit, choosing instead to rent a mail drop and phone service at 521 Fifth Avenue, with access to a conference room and small offices for future expansion. The trades published a double issue at the end of each year, giving me two weeks for typesetting, printing and mailing the time sensitive promotional issue. Combing through the *Billboard Buyers Guide*, checking off potential customers, through an ad in the *Reporter Dispatch*, I hired new mom Louise 'Lu' Pollak to type the mailing list. She would be with me for the next four years, typing, stuffing, stamping and mailing *New On The Charts* from her Elmsford kitchen table.

While waiting for the first business reply envelopes, I pollinated the city with sample copies, including every office at 1650 Broadway. Although thrilled by the first few responses, it was painfully clear I couldn't afford the cost, and more importantly, the extra week required for typesetting. With oversized sheets in Lu's IBM Selectric, Photostatted down after hours at Wagner, the small type was unwieldy. Painstakingly throwing in lines between each record with a Rapidograph, the result lacked aesthetics but was functional. Reasoning the contact information compensated for appearance, with Erle's picture again on the cover and Lu's help, I made deadline for the February 'Premiere Issue.' Then, an intriguing call from Herman Steiger, head of Big 3 Music, the print division of United Artists Music Publishing.

The entrance at 729 Seventh Avenue, next to the infamous Metropole strip club, upstairs Herman greeted me in his wood-paneled office smoking a cigar *(reminiscent of George Leibowitz)*, with 'an offer I couldn't refuse.' Big 3 was in constant competition with Warner Brothers and Columbia Pictures Publications for the sheet music rights to the latest hits. Concluding my research would give him an edge, Herman posed a consultancy, my publication kept separate, with an office, phone, secretary and expense account. If he wasn't blowing cigar smoke up my ass, mind blown, I expected Allen Funt to jump out and yell, "Smile, You're on *Candid Camera*!" The next day I met Phyllis, my new secretary, gave notice to Don and Doris, and also initiated confidential correspondence with Joel Novak, V.P. of Special Projects for Billboard Publications. Now my newsletter was attracting attention and endorsements, I figured it made more sense for *Billboard* to acquire me than compete and over the next few months explored the possibility.

It was also time for my own apartment again. Seeing Beth every weekend had been difficult. But there was something special about her soft sensuality, intuitive nature, and the way she reveled in my weekly misadventures. I needed someplace to take her besides back to Hackensack, close to Lu and with an easy commute to the city. Down the street from the Mamaroneck Metro North station, set back on the roof over Tony's Pizzaria, was what looked like an empty apartment. Apparently, once livable, Tony never had the time or inclination to refurbish but was happy to discuss it with me. After some haggling, he agreed to cover the supplies if I'd renovate, with a fantastic $325 a month rental agreement the next three years. We shook hands and I went to work, replacing broken stairs, covering the gray Linoleum kitchen floor with bright self-adhesive tiles, painting the studio walls yellow and the hardwood floors red, with a plush swirling brown area rug. Three rear windows and a door leading out to the rooftop porch overlooking Mamaroneck Avenue in front, provided cross ventilation and light. But the first Saturday night with Beth led to a rude awakening…literally… Directly behind was the volunteer fire department, which meant at any time, without warning, an ear-shattering alarm would blast through the apartment. Startled, shaken and sprawled out on the floor, it was now clear why the place was abandoned. That week I installed heavy sound muffling curtains *(like the ones at Pannini's Brooklyn restaurant).*

Without a picture for the next cover, Tom volunteered attention-starved Julie Coryell. Meanwhile Bob King fell out with his brother-in-law, and I found him a place in phone sales at Big 3. After helping secure the print rights to *"Right Back Where We Started From"* by Maxine Nightingale and Dorothy Moore's *"Misty Blue,"* Steiger sent me in to meet the Chairman of United Artists Music Publishing. Off to see the wizard, as the impressive door opened a voice bellowed, "Tell Paul Anka to blow it out his ass!!" from the jowls of the oversized troll behind the mahogany desk, as he slammed down the phone and growled, "Now what the fuck do you want?" Looking more like a patron of the Metropole than the executive suite, offensive even to his 'friends,' it was my first and last visit with Mike Stewart.

Herman didn't care about my hours or habits as long as I showed results. Now in his seventies, he sold sheet music from a pushcart as a kid, knew every permutation of a deal and his bottom line to the penny. A master negotiator, chewing on his cigar with a wry smile, I'd watch him run circles around hotshot lawyers. Turning deals around ten ways before closing with "But obviously the best deal for you would be..." His proposal, then the pregnant pause, a deafening silence, the confused attorney embarrassed into agreeing, usually to the best deal for Herman. Closing every contract with a reassuring smile and a kosher salami, cherubic Herman Steiger was the consummate con artist *(or great salesman, depending upon your perspective)*.

The deconstructed Beatles never worked. McCartney wrote cutesy melodic pop that said nothing, Lennon, annoyingly repetitive lines that said everything, while Ringo got his tongue stuck in his cheek and George subconsciously plagiarized The Chiffons. On April Fool's Day, *"Oh What A Night"* was bumped off the radio by *"Disco Lady"* (soon to be followed by McCartney's *"Silly Love Songs"*) when Dyhna invited me to a midnight movie down on West 3rd Street. The Village was always strange, but that night The Waverly Theater looked like a copy-cat-costume party. The *"Rocky Horror Picture Show"* bombed at the box office, too outlandish for middle America, but perfect for The Village *(and the times)*. Everyone yelling in unison and dancing the *"Time Warp"* to soaring streams of toilet paper rivaled our night at *"The Exorcist."* Worldwide audience participation, would make the initial flop one of the most successful pictures in history.

Correspondence with Novak, including a detailed confidential business plan outlining *Billboard's* possible use of their new Cincinnati computer operation, bought me a ticket to L.A. In the airport, my initial conversation with great tits attached to a long-flowing brunette seemed wasted when seated in separate rows. But a faulty engine offered the opportunity to squeeze in next to them as we changed planes. Goal posts in mind, but careful never to let Gloria catch me looking at them, the sunlit flight warmed conversation. On touchdown, she offered a ride to my hotel, stopping first at her apartment. Her two roommates later confessed complete surprise. Gloria never brought anyone home. Another case of time and place, bored and alone, Gloria was desperate for change. Inspired by my energy and risk taking, she resolved to help chase my dream in L.A. and find one of her own. After a night of cathartic lovemaking, those large natural breasts dancing in the darkness, she let go for the first time in years. Glowing at the morning breakfast table, Gloria laid out her bank work schedule, offering to drive me in between. I had no idea you needed a car to get anywhere in L.A.

After a lifetime in New York, Los Angeles was culture shock. In *"California Freeway Goin' South"* ♪ I'd later write:

Never been out of New York City
  But I heard a lot about the coast
Flying on in to L.A. Airport
  Got myself a lethal dose
Step out into the California weather
  Funny you can taste the air
Fog on the freeway
  They say is getting better
But my eyes get red when I stare

♪ *Song available on iTunes & www.LEKalikow.com*

Despite the smog, everything was sunny clean, even the streets. Smiling faces made eye contact on sidewalks without swearing or 'fuck you fingers' flying. Friendly namedropping salespeople, secreting their headshots, all had something 'in development,' a script, record deal, a callback. Fame analogous to cash, the foundation of the fragile value structure. Unlike New York, if you were rich in L.A. it didn't mean shit unless you knew someone famous.

A struggling musician's life never included more than two-star hotels, so the Sheridan Universal, where *Billboard* placed me, was another new experience. In place of the usual moldy rubber curtains and grinding metal air conditioning unit, a clean, picture windowed room with central air. Before seeing *Billboard* the next day, Herman set up a meeting with his son-in-law Jack Keller, in the creative department at U.A. Music Publishing. A veteran of 1650 Broadway, Jack wrote more than fifty top 10 hits, including *"Everybody's Somebody's Fool," "Venus In Blue Jeans,"* and *"Run To Him."* Open and unassuming, after listening to my demo, Keller suggested we 'do lunch' soon to discuss a possible deal. Jack was actually more intrigued with Gloria than my music, stretching our meeting until she showed, just to see what she looked like. Years later I'd warn artists coming from Europe not to be deceived by L.A. In New York it was hard to get a meeting, rarely lasting long. But if they smelled money, a deal was negotiated. In L.A. everybody 'loves' everything and wants you to meet the family, but won't remember you next time or make an offer until someone else does… a glass half full/half empty scenario. Despite the praise and promises, the chances of an outside band with no local following making that first deal in L.A. was slim. On the other hand, an initial New York offer could be doubled on The Coast. As for rejection, in New York, muggers stare and stab you in the stomach, in L.A. they smile and stab you in the back. Either way you're dead.

Gloria confirmed there was no *"Seventy Seven Sunset Strip,"* as we drove through the opulence, celebrity and sex, plastered posters along the way to *Billboard Magazine* at 9000 Sunset Boulevard. The impressive panoramic penthouse offices immediately had me thinking *"Earthquake"* when the receptionist introduced Bill Wardlow. The effusive, used car dealer friendly, white haired Wardlow controlled the charts, second in command only to Publisher Lee Zito. Apologizing profusely, he explained they were 'backed up' and needed to postpone another day. Offering a car back to The Sheraton, and pick up for our next meeting, Bill nonetheless emphasized how much they 'loved' *New On The Charts*.

With Gloria at work and Keller 'unavailable,' my only other West Coast acquaintances were the Harris family. As a child in West Hartford, I vaguely remembered them staying for dinner on weekends or surreptitiously bringing food when visiting their cramped apartment. Where I played magnetic football on the dining room table with their soprano voiced older son Robert, little yellow rubber players vibrating across a green metal screen. Their handlebar mustache father Mark, a very British humored, eye twinkling storyteller, was having trouble finding steady work. When we moved to White Plains, they packed their beat-up blue Rambler station wagon and headed west to make a new start. Now Mark was a 'tailor to the stars' at an exclusive British men's shop in Beverly Hills, and Robert, an executive at Universal Pictures. With mom and dad on the phone after dinner that night, there were tears all around.

Like the Italian restaurant in Brooklyn, the *Billboard* conference room included a long table where I sat at one end waiting for the Publisher to arrive. To my right, Bill warned me not to use Zito's first name, to me he would be Mr. Zito. The pompous little Hercule Poirot then arrived, complete with thin, waxed, pointed moustache. Neatly laying out his papers, including my plastic covered business plan, before inserting a smile and raising his head to make eye contact. My detailed proposal suggested a computerized cross-referenced database, splitting their *"Buyers Guide"* into separate directories, all linked to *Billboard* credits. Also, with advance chart knowledge, we could publish the newsletter more efficiently, no longer waiting for the printed issues to begin research. Mr. Zito opened disarmingly acknowledging how impressed they were, immediately followed by an offer I didn't see coming... "We'd like to bring you out to be part of the *Billboard* family and run *New On The Charts* from your own office here. *(Holy shit! This guy wasn't so bad after all I thought. This was better than Herman's deal)* Trying to conceal my excitement, in a businesslike manner I responded, "That sounds great Mr.Zito. Can you tell me please, what kind of salary are we talking?" Then came the first punch... "We'll start you at fifteen thousand plus expenses" He didn't just say that? "Excuse me sir, did you say fifteen or fifty?" Next, some bullshit about *Billboard* being a 'steppingstone' to the future and all the executives who started there. Even in 1976, that was less than an executive secretary made. "Well if that's the salary, how much equity will I maintain in my company?" Then the final kick in the balls... "No, this will be a *Billboard* publication. In fact we've already initiated a 'New On The Charts' feature in next week's issue. So this is a 'take it or leave it' situation." Talk about 'stabbed in the back!!' I could feel the blood draining as they sat there smiling.

I don't remember much after that, other than calling dad from my hotel room, who suggested I come home immediately. Quickly packed, fat bald Telly Savales sat puffed up in the Sheraton lobby, his pinky ring stuck in the hair of one the silicone stuffed debutantes fawning over him... my parting image of L.A. before Gloria tearfully dropped me at the airport. I guess they figured an ex-musician living on top of a pizzeria that couldn't afford a car rental, would put up much of a fight. Apparently unaware dad was Head Patent Council at G.E., with a world-class staff of attorneys specializing in intellectual property. In his office the next day I met brilliant, deformed, Dr. Stangelove looking George Elgroth and rabbi Sam Helfgott, the two attorneys assigned my case. Within days *Billboard* was served papers threatening an Unfair Business Practices suit, including Beach of Confidentiality and possible Theft of Intellectual Property and demanding removal of 'New On The Charts' from the publication. *(Surprise! And Fuck You Mr. Zito!)*

When their lawyer's response claimed the case had 'no merit' and that my proposal contained 'nothing new of value,' Sam explained this was just legal posturing and why, in the end, we'd settle:

First - The optics in court of giant *Billboard* trying to squash little entrepreneur me.

Second - The public relations nightmare, rallying my supportive subscribers, the story probably to be exploited by the other trades and news media.

Third - Possibly exposing the correlation between full-page ads and chart positions, and the fact Zito and Warlow were skimming thousands in weekly extortion.

And Finally – The undisclosed conflict of interest at the law firm representing *Billboard,* not wishing to piss off the lawyers at G.E., to the determinant of other more valuable clients.

After legal papers ping ponged, the case finally hinged on the fact that *Billboard* paid for my flight and hotel, thereby admitting perceived 'value' and forcing a non-financial settlement. For the next five years they were restrained from pursuing anything in my outline, not documented before receipt thereof. Allowing time to build *New On The Charts* without competition and fucking up plans for their entire computer operation. Zito, devastated by his loss of 'face,' would thereafter go red with rage at the mention of my name. Although too powerful and connected to fire, Chairman William Littleford was furious with him. Had he only dealt honorably, everyone would have won. Both Apple and Microsoft were born that year, but my card catalogue wouldn't be a 'database' until the PC was introduced seven years later.

Before leaving for The Coast, I did get a subscriber's decent looking female photo for the cover, but with another deadline looming I had nothing. Down to the wire, I simply inserted a picture of Bob for Big 3 Music *(incidentally indicating I wasn't a male chauvinist pig)*. At the strong suggestion of George and Sam I also incorporated, now with enough income to rent a small room adjacent to Tom and Vince at 1500 Broadway, with access to their Telex for international correspondence.

The Mamaroneck apartment, it turned out, included another hidden feature. A dark musty attic, rusty nails sticking through splintered wood. On one side, a Mexican couple constantly fighting, then lights on apology fucking, projected through my cobwebbed attic window. While on the other, a partial bedroom view of three British lesbians in various combinations… my own private peepshow booth. On Mamaroneck Avenue, like the magical beauty floating through Fellini's *"Amarcord,"* I'd catch the occasional glimpse of a black wigged seductress I could swear was the *"Summer of '42"* blonde from my teenage Rye Beach memories. Feigning interest in her Baha'i ramblings, the religion shared by *"Summer Breeze"* Seals & Crofts. Fixated on the full imprint of her nipples through the sheer yellow bikini top. A full-figured siren in her twenties implying there could be something between us. The next day, waiting for hours with my bicycle, for a dream date that disappeared. Now years later, still out of reach, never visible long enough to confirm her identity (or existence). One neighbor that was real, spunky little Dorothy 'Dot' Jonas, great legs bopping through town in her colorful miniskirts. Making a point to meet her, it was hard to reconcile her appearance and the communal Christian house shared with five other devotees. Something didn't fit. She believed it her duty to convert me to Christ, mine to introduce her to sex. Guess who won?

In July, as the tall ships blew in to New York Harbor celebrating the country's 200th Anniversary, a team of Israeli commandos flew into Entebbe Airport under the nose of Uganda's Idi Amin, guns blazing, freeing hostages held by pro-Palestinian hijackers. Once again proving you don't fuck with Israel. In Canada, the Montreal Olympics were launched, where Bruce Jenner would win decathlon gold, and appropriately my cover that month included a picture of good-looking blonde Canadian agent, Doug Brown. Sex role's evolving as surgically reassigned Rene Richards, tried to enter the U.S. Open as a woman, and Elton John admitted his 'bisexuality' in *Rolling Stone*. Then everyone got confused watching Saturday Night Live's Joe Cocker/John Belushi duet, unable to tell 'which was real and which was Memorex.'

It became obvious that summer, subscriber photos weren't happening. With a final August issue shot of Linda Ragusa, now at A&M Records, out of friends to promote, it was time to reformat. A redesigned glossy black & white cover could add panache and not cost much more. But it had to be distinctive, something to stand out on a desk full of papers and definitely NOT a magazine (which implied gossip & cheap). Any photo couldn't take up the entire cover or cater to celebrity. Until then, record producers had been anonymous names on the back of record jackets. But production based Disco was changing that. Their cover stories would be new. Highlighting records that hit all three trades simultaneously would also reinforce my comparative position. White-framed black & white photos popped on a black background. Additional type floating within a white holding line emanating from the new solid, clean, rounded font almost achieved a three-dimensional effect. That September, with United Artists' Brass Construction producer Jeff Lane on the cover, a revised *New On The Charts* was mailed.

www.notc.com

There was also more than a new cover and producer bio in that September issue. With my list of contacts, Lu took over the basic research. Backing her up when necessary, along with the producer interview, I began phoning managers and record company subscribers. Looking for artists open to original songs and permission to list them. Artist song leads in that first *'A&R Newsletter'* section of *New On The Charts* would include Anne Murray, Brown Sugar, The Bellamy Brothers, Hank Williams Jr., Vicki Sue Robinson, Rick Dees, John Travolta and Black Oak Arkansas. If "imitation is the sincerest form of flattery," I was soon getting 'flattered' all over the place. The first 'compliment' came from the L.A. *"Songplugger,"* printed in my format on stapled red sheets to prevent photocopying (probably how he got mine in the first place). Next came Nashville, then some idiot in the Midwest. Eventually one of my subscribers moved to London and launched *"UK Songplugger,"* then picked up in Germany called *"Songs Wanted,"* and "Tip Sheet" became part of the music industry vernacular.

When Kenny's Castaways left the Upper East Side to a block away from The Bitter End, in a Village revival sparked by the influx of NYU students, my guitar was stuck somewhere behind boxes in the office. Herman thought he'd won the 'championship' with the print rights to the inane United Artists' *"Theme From Rocky."* While the country elected wholesome 'Howdy Doody' peanut farmer Jimmy Carter to replace 'Nixon pardon tainted' Gerald Ford. I didn't vote or give a shit. The year closed with The Eagles' *"Hotel California"* summing up my feelings about L.A. and for me, analogous to the business world I had entered.

XII. (1977)
(The Biz)

A counterpart to the Cannes Film Festival, in January MIDEM was a glamorous international music marketplace. Proudly founded and choreographed by French bon vivant, Bernard Chevry, pocketing rumored ubiquitous kickbacks from bars, restaurants, taxi drivers, even the attractive 'working girls' he flew in from Paris and Marseille. Everything overpriced and rooms at a premium, luckily Chevry catered to the media, providing my first press pass and comped two-star hotel. There were three primary hotels along La Croisette. The Majestic, near the old port, across from the elaborate concert hall and casino, hid the money and power players behind walled hedges. Further north, past the Palais convention center, the world famous Carlton welcomed music publisher / record company Presidents and celebrities. A long few blocks farther, The Martinez housed the independents and traditional nightly expense account bar menagerie. That first night I learned the importance attached to where you stayed when a couple denied accommodation, stripped and sat naked in the Martinez lobby. Management caved, confirming the French tendency to reward demanding behavior. In fact in France, respect coincides proportionately with one's arrogance and propensity to complain. The more you bitch, the better you're treated.

The first day was registration, La Croisette already lined with posters announcing albums, artists, and companies, dominated that year by Pink Floyd's *"Animals,"* with little plastic pink pig pins publicizing the premiere. As press, I skipped the long lines at the Palais, to La Maison next door for my all-access picture ID. Out of my element, hesitant to approach Joelle, the stunning press organizer, I simply watched her conduct a seminar in French *(all Greek to me)* and fantasized. French women seemed to innately accent their best feature, un-slaved by fashion with a flair for style. In Joelle's case her athletic body, held in a tight fitting knit. And age was irrelevant. If a woman believes she is sexy, she is. And in France they all still believe.

Opening night's red carpet gala was a black tie affair. Hosted at the Yacht Club, complete with ice sculptures, champagne, and my first taste of caviar *(not bad on a hard-boiled egg slice crostini)*, half expecting Princess Grace to drop in from nearby Monaco. *(Hard to imagine a little over a year ago I was living in my parent's basement)*. Armed with my 5"x 7" one inch thick *"MIDEM Guide"* the next morning I entered the Palais des Festivals for the first time. Originally built to house the Cannes Film Festival in 1949, a marble staircase let to each floor, lined with windowed rooms, each equipped with a sound system, turntable, and cassette deck, exclusively rented by MIDEM. An adorable staff of navy-blue-blazer girls bounced between floors offering guidance and assistance. Adjacent to the entrance an inordinately overpriced Bleu Bar Restaurant gouged attendees. On my first visit, simply asking for French fries, the waiter turned up his nose loudly proclaiming, "This is not a snack-bar!"

One highlight of my first MIDEM was meeting legendary Abba manager, Stig Anderson. When Russia wouldn't allow rubles out after an Abba tour, he set up a trading company, bought Russian tractors, and sold them in Africa at a profit. Now that was a manager! Set back off the street, he either owned or annually rented a full floor at The Grand Hotel, where I especially hit it off with his head of publishing, Anders Moren. Who, along with German publisher Rudy Holzhauer, introduced me to the Pompon Rouge. That night, past the see-through plastic dressed street-walker, down a narrow cobblestone alley, directly across from a secluded red light bordello, was the burgundy beret logo of the Pompon Rouge. A narrow wooden staircase led up to a suddenly bright laughing room of diners, the two gay owners bouncing between tables and the kitchen. The food fabulous, but no idea what was under the cream sauce. Punctuated with dessert when the blonde chef brought over a little statue and offered 'something special.' At my nod, a plastic penis popped out and pissed in my plate… a dinner to remember.

Site of the first MIDEM, attendees traditionally returned to The Martinez each night, vacuum packed into the bar until morning. After a full day at the Palais and a Margarita pizza on the Croisette, one evening, dressing for the nightly spawning, a knock at the door. Barreling through, a buxom German blonde I briefly flirted with that afternoon. Pinned to the bed, breasts bouncing through her open blouse above me, she looked down and asked, "You vant to fuck maybe?" I love German women! Later that night, lacking the energy to fight the crowd at The Martinez, I chose instead, the more subdued lobby of The Carlton. And there was Lee Zito, back turned, making a point to ignore me. When Leonard Feist, President of the National Publisher's Association, unknowingly tried to introduce us, instead of taking my outstretch hand, Zito began poking me in the chest. "You're gonna have to change the name of your paper you little wiseass! We had prior use in our British magazine long before you published. You'll hear from our lawyers." Then huffed out the front door, shocking poor Leonard more than me. The first thing next morning I called dad from the press office. Assured a heading in their magazine wouldn't affect my trademark, he'd have Sam take care of it. And once again, vengefully spending Billboard's money to no avail, Mr. Zito would look like an ass.

Back in The States a format war broke out when RCA introduced their first JVC, VHS based Video Cassette Recorder to compete with Sony's Betamax. Beta better quality, VHS recorded longer and cheaper. JVC's freely licensed system, as opposed to Sony's proprietary, would years later dominate the home market. Meanwhile, although not forced to change my publication's name, an electronics company litigated Midland International into Midsong Records, as Disco overtook pop culture and 'New Wave,' the underground. *"What's in a name?"* Who could hate bands like the Buzzcocks, The Cramps, The Nipple Erectors, The Slits and my favorite, The Sniveling Shits. With special mention to a newly formed UK Stiff Records slogan, "If It Ain't Stiff, It Ain't Worth A Fuck!" Almost enticing me to go out and listen to their Elvis Costello, who I assumed was a British/Italian Elvis impersonator.

To get even for initially sending them Punk, the British returned the favor with wimpy Disco. Big haired Leo Sayer's *"You Make Me Feel Like Dancing"* made me feel like throwing up. Mercifully wiped off the charts by the *"Car Wash"* movie theme; Popularizing the practice of ghetto kids smearing car windows at red lights for tips. Whether Disco's inter-racial dancing and dating a cause or effect, racial tensions seemed easing. Jimmy Carter appointed Andrew Young as Ambassador to the U.N. while mini-series *"Roots"* drew a record breaking 80 million viewers over eight consecutive nights on ABC.

Then came Studio 54. Formerly the home for such TV shows as *"What's My Line,"* *"To Tell The Truth,"* and *"Ted Mack's Original Amateur Hour,"* when CBS Studios consolidated operations at the adjacent Ed Sullivan Theater, Steve Rubell and Ian Schrager bought the 254 West 54th Street facility. Already successful at the Enchanted Garden disco in Queens, with Studio 54, closeted gay entrepreneur Rubell, and former college friend and attorney Ian Schrager, would carry the old Electric Circus concept to its logical conclusion. With cutting edge sound and lighting, floating artwork, trapeze artists and go-go dancers, moveable walls and painted sets, elaborate themes could change at a whim, even during the night. While Rubell famously screened the desperate entourage at the door for access to Oz, celebrities anonymously lost in the massive sexually charged cocaine cooked dance floor, occasionally slipping into the rafters for 'private sessions.' And Abba's *"Dancing Queen"* went to number one on the charts.

Back at Big 3, a *New On The Charts (NOTC)* subscriber called from Texas and another in Seattle, looking for information about a terrific song from a terrible movie of the same name, recorded by someone named Kasey Cisyk. After a few more inquiries, I brought it to Herman. Although I knew the songwriter Joe Brooks from the jingle business, he had a long-standing relationship and picked up the phone. Making a pretty substantial offer for an unreleased, unknown song and artist, Herman's real target was Joe's commercials, an 'incidental' addendum to the deal. Herman would later blame me for not knowing at the time, Pat Boone's daughter Debbie, was recording it for Curb Records. Resenting Herman's sneaky tactics, Brooks went elsewhere when *"You Light Up My Life"* became one of the biggest selling songs of all time.

Then a revelation *(as if there wasn't enough on my plate)*... why not an NOTC type service for the advertising industry? With each new national spot, list contacts for the Ad Agency, Director, Choreographer, Jingle House, etc. But where to start? From past experience, getting meetings would be difficult, especially remembered as a rep. First stop, the American Association of Advertising Agencies. With NOTC as proof of concept, they not only endorsed, but supported my efforts with a desk, phone, and letterhead. Soon, in the offices of top agency execs, the response was unanimous..."Hell No!" "If I discover a great new director and you list it, his price will go up." "Why should I reveal my contacts to the competition?" Reading Advertising Age should have been a tip-off, companies and clients bad-mouthing each other in print. Within days of my visit to Doyle Dane & Bernbach, a Sr.V.P. letter threatened to ban me from their building if I printed the name of anyone at their agency... So much for my great new idea.

Just as well, having recently extended my coverage to include the Top 100 albums as well as singles, and Lu Pollak shifting to full-time mom. I needed someone in the Broadway office. After a couple of misses, I found spunky, intelligently flirtatious Raleigh, with a dynamite little body hiding beneath her conservative business façade. As she took on the research and solicited ads on a commission basis, Lu reverted to just typing and mailing the last week of each month. Ironically that summer Donna Summer's *"I Feel Love"* was hailed as revolutionary, completely synthesized and forerunner to "Techno," five years after I lost my deal at Columbia for synthesizing a horn section. Also that summer, the city flirting with bankruptcy, nerves frayed by 'Son Of Sam,' the blackout on a sweltering July night touched off a powder keg... an explosion of looting and violence, areas of Brooklyn and the Bronx in flames, while I sat in the dark at The Bottom Line. With flashlights taped to their mic stands, NRBQ played on unplugged, an allegory for the recession proof music business in the midst of the country's financial depression.

A bloated, sequined caricature of himself, when Elvis died, an entire generation never saw the sexually charged Memphis kid that opened *"Heartbreak Hotel"* long before Vegas, and invited me in to rock-n-roll. Big 3 controlled Hill & Range, the catalogue of his early hits. So Herman rushed a commemorative songbook and tasked me with the opening bio. Afraid to embarrass him with her overweight appearance, when his mom died of a heart attack at age forty-six, Elvis never completely recovered. Years later, binging and popping pills, still haunted by (and perhaps mimicking) her image, two days after the anniversary of her death, his heart attack at age forty-two beat her by four years.

When negotiating exclusive catalogue and sheet music rights, even if outbid, as conciliation we'd usually get non-exclusive folio rights to individual songs. Traditionally this meant in a 'Greatest Hits' compilation, ten percent might be these non-exclusives. Researching the Elvis songbook, I noticed the definition of a 'folio' to be a collection including no less than six of our exclusive compositions. This minimum was usually irrelevant since we needed to recoup on songs we owned. But I had another idea… why not make dummy sheet music covers for four current hits we only had for folios and collage them with six we owned. Then put out a mini sheet-music booklet, selling at less than half the cost of the individual sheets. The trick was using our older singles with their new ones. Herman went for it and I started on the first *"Record Breakers"* compilation.

My artist dream drowning in a sea of Disco and Punk, lyrics and melodies relegated to Nashville, Billy Joel then tossed out a musical lifeline. *"The Stranger" LP,* including *"Movin' Out," "Just The Way You Are," "Only The Good Die Young,"* and *"Scenes From An Italian Restaurant"* kept the dream afloat, when out of the blue, a call from Lou Ragusa. He and Stan Vincent were about to launch Voyage Records and asked if I'd give up my cushy job to take a flyer on a new label. As V.P. of Music Publishing with the possibility of my own album, it was a no-brainer, but required secrecy until financing was in place.

The Metro North commute between Grand Central and Mamaroneck provided fabulous female fishing, especially on my way home. Walking the platform a few minutes prior to departure, checking each car for the best looking prospect before casually taking the seat next to her, made every night an adventure. Whipping out my *Billboard, Cashbox* and *Record World* magazines, while offhandedly opening *NOTC* to my picture, usually got a bite. One such catch was an impeccably suited financial analyst with a slit up the side of her tailored skirt. I'd seen her shut down come-ons in the past. The trick was dangling my lures and letting her cum for me. And she did... in my candlelit bedroom, kitchen and a blanket on the porch. Uncerermoniously interrupted by police banging on the door, responding to a complaint from the Italian grandmother with binoculars across the street. Another memorable pick-up was the *"Annie Hall"* dressed 'back rub girl.' Completely unresponsive on her back until, flashing on Parsippany Barbara, I turned her over. Within minutes, my knee firmly between her thighs, every backstroke had her moaning, grinding and soaking the sheets. Clutching the mattress with her outstretched arms, refusing to turn back over, my cock shoved in place of the knee launched a screaming bucking bareback ride. Her bottom bouncing up and down, sometimes side-to-side, shaking or simply vibrating and squirting. Gripping the mattress to stay on, praying the police didn't raid this rodeo, all I needed next was the fire alarm.

To grab attention in designing *"Record Breakers,"* I suggested an orange background, but not Halloween dark. Without showing me proofs, the production department printed anemic flesh colored covers that all but said 'please ignore me.' Initial sales barely enough to warrant another shot, the next in bright yellow did better, but not a 'record breaker.' Apparently fans would rather pay full price for singles they wanted, disregarding, or even turned off by, the extras they didn't care about. All water under the bridge I was about to cross, waiting for word from Lou and Stan. As George Burns puffed his cigar just like Herman in *"Oh God!,"* Bing Crosby took his last swing on a golf course in Spain, and anti-gay activist Anita Bryant took a pie in the face in Iowa. On that same day, the first Atari 2600 game system introduced Pong and video Blackjack. The fun and games ended a week later when a plane carrying Lynyrd Skynyrd crashed in Mississippi, killing Ronnie Van Zandt, Steve and Cassie Gaines.

Just as Ed Koch was sworn in as Mayor in Manhattan, *"Saturday Night Fever"* hit theaters and the 'Disco' Bee Gees became the biggest British import since The Beatles. Not to be confused with *"Saturday Night Live"* where, a few days later I finally got to see Elvis Costello, the first artist banned from the show for replacing the song they demanded with his music business protest *"Radio Radio."* Causing me to rethink my aversion to New Wave, especially in relation to mindless incessantly annoying Disco. Soon forced however, to eat my words, when Voyage Records later announced a distributed deal with RSO (Robert Stigwood Organization), the company that produced *"Saturday Night Fever,"* managed and recorded the Bee Gees.

They were eating more than words that afternoon at the ritzy Russian Tea Room. Larry's deal about to expire on Arista, wife Julie, four-year-old son in tow, demanded inclusion in the confidential discussions with Atlantic Records. Just as Tom and Vince were about to broach business, Julie whipped out her breast to nurse post toddler Julian. Extolling the virtues of breast milk, to the shock of posh clientele and staff, and the delight of Atlantic Chairman, Ahmet Ertegun. Within a few months, convinced she could now make the Atlantic deal herself, based on eye contact with Ahmet, Julie took over Larry's management. The Eleventh House fell apart, and Atlantic never happened.

With keys to Voyage Records in my pocket, this would be my last Christmas Party at Big 3. After a year of restrained flirtations, now all bets were off, along with some booze-loosened inhibitions.

Slipping into my office, big blonde Bonnie from production and tall red haired Maggie from accounting closed the door as they approached my desk. Unbuttoning as they slowly circled, my personal Christmas tree was standing when big Bonnie gave it a warm thigh hug, straddling my chair. Leaning forward with an ample hands-on test of Julie's breast milk theory, as usually shy Maggie allowed my free hand to slide up between her legs. My surprise at her unflinching soaked welcome doubled when she bent over and stuck her tongue in my ear. At that moment, with Bonnie's breast in my mouth, and Maggie's bush in my hand, the door opened... Beth caught in reverse surprise, early for our date to see *"Annie"* that night. It would be our last until a tentative reconciliation many years later. The price had understandably become too high.

The intercourse of 'sex,' 'love' and 'commitment' cum together differently for men and women. The female opens to allow the man completely inside, demanding a more intense commitment than the simple male injection. Not to mention the fact that, if impregnated, she must then carry for another nine painful months. *(Perhaps explaining why the female Praying Mantis eats the male before he can get out and do it to someone else)*. Historically also why it's easier for a man to separate 'sex' and 'love.' The Pill obviously made casual sex more 'female friendly,' as long as she didn't care about the injector, psychologically reducing him to vibrator status. But caring meant difficulty imagining him inside someone else *(not to mention seeing it)*. I would really miss Beth. To help soothe the loss, Bob arranged for Bonnie and Maggie to ambush me at a New Year's Eve party the following Saturday. Long after the ball and balloons had fallen, *'laughing all the way'* to my new offices at 1700 Broadway, the girls took turns on my personal vibrating noisemaker... *'And to all a good night!'*

XIII. (1978)
(The Voyage)

Everything about Voyage Records implied money... From the sleek modern 40th floor offices, to the heavy, four color ocean-green stationery complete with embossed gold logo. Entering through reception, to the right, a glass walled, deep pile carpeted conference room *(that I knew intimately)* and to the left, the only office without a window, designated for Raleigh and NOTC. At the elbow, a wall of panoramic glass offices, including mine, that led to Stan's luxury appointed glass corner suite. As the Copyright Act of 1976 went into effect, after years of signing practically unintelligible songwriter agreements, I made it my first priority to compose a plain English contract. With input from dad and Bill, I constructed a composite document, removing all the 'party of the first part' bullshit and clearly defining each point of the agreement. Then, my first taste of corporate politics... The company's high profile law firm, *(that shall remain nameless, since 30 years later a name partner would probably still sue me)* threatened to drop us as a client if we didn't exclusively use (and pay for) their contract. There's probably a law school course that teaches how to create problems to fight about, then charge for everything (including the phone calls).

Even before our official opening, demos came piling in. On the other side of the desk, it became painfully clear, there were a lot of bad songwriters out there. One bright spot though, was Philip Namanworth, a Jewish Dr. John type character with a raspy voice and distinctive piano style. Not as successful, actor Bob Gunton, complete with cowboy hat, pitching himself as a Country singer/songwriter. Meanwhile I began turning over more responsibility to Raleigh, planning to gradually phase out of the daily operation of *New On The Charts*.

Back at Big 3, covertly pushing Herman to retire, corporate brought in Harvard M.B.A., Steve Cotler, as his 'Assistant.' A charismatic closet screenwriter, we hit it off immediately, and were soon sitting in Herman's office after hours throwing around script ideas. Long past protest and disillusionment, we began *"RPM,"* the story of an Orson Wells type independent record company owner, holding out against the big guys. Something I could relate to... especially as I left for my second MIDEM.

As my airport courtesy car entered Cannes, copycat French kids clamored at car lights, with *"Car Wash"* cloths, wiping windshields... another case of American cultural exchange. *(They gave us French Fries, we gave them juvenile delinquents... a fair trade, both heart attack related.)* No longer a neophyte, at press registration, confessing my infatuation, Joelle blushed slightly in broken English and agreed to visit our yacht in the old port behind the casino. Oh yeah, I forgot to mention, Stan rented a live-in yacht coincidently named *'The Voyager.'* With a press conference scheduled the last day, Robert Stigwood set to fly in. I however, get seasick in a bathtub, and opted for the more private MIDEM provided room at The Canberra, a nice hotel just behind the Palais. But with a nightly locked lobby, late night liaisons limited, any date with Joelle had to end at her less restrictive residence. It took three such nights and several glasses of rosé to make it inside, after which she warned, if I didn't learn French in the next year, it would be my last such incursion. Understandable, since a little insecure with our age difference and her authority, it was probably not my best performance.

Voyage Records had two primary acts: Doc Aikens & Shields, a strong R&B trio Stan had been nurturing for years, and Euro friendly, experimental rock group Citadel. Along with NOTC, my responsibility was to make international sub-publishing deals, exclusivity arrangements with publishers in each major territory. On the strength of the material and pending deal with RSO, I raised substantial advances for the catalog, heavily promoting our upcoming press conference. Celebrating on *The Voyager* in the south of France, we had no way of knowing the disastrous commercial and critical failure of RSO's *"Sgt. Pepper's Lonely Hearts Club Band"* movie, had Stigwood struggling to stay afloat, and in no position to fly anywhere. Despite the champagne and brave smiles, the anti-climactic press conference left everyone in suspended animation.

It was business as usual back in New York, assuming everything would eventually *'Come Together.'* One addition to Stan's production schedule was the fabulous mistress of a reclusive mob boss. Demanding nothing but the best for her (arrangements, musicians, studio, etc.), with a side-deal never to release her record. The last thing he wanted was a spotlight. Linda Ragusa also should have been a star. When Donna Summer's manager offered and Lou chose to handle her instead, probably losing a deal at A&M, Voyage was now her last stop. A good Italian Catholic, she *'stood by her man'* and paid the price. The RSO deal fading, a change in course was debated. Either forge ahead as an indie, or convert to a production company and sell the masters to other labels. On the same day the new Pope John Paul I was elected in Rome, Voyage Records was launched. Not a great omen since in a matter of months both would be dead.

It hadn't been a good year, starting with Hubert Humphrey's death from cancer, just before Roman Polanski fled to France after sex with a 13 year-old girl. We then had serial killers Ted Bundy in Florida and The Hillside Strangler in L.A. to deal with when *'Hustler'* Larry Flynt was gunned down and paralyzed and the Flying Wallenda patriarch plummeted off a tight-rope in Puerto Rico. All preludes to the massive Love Canal disaster, 39 blocks of working class families living (and dying) above 21,000 tons of toxic industrial waste next to beautiful Niagara Falls. A moment of optimism peaked through when Begin and Sadat signed the Camp David Peace Accord, just before seemingly healthy Pope John Paul I suddenly died of a heart attack thirty-three days after his election. Whispers of foul play where disavowed but persist, especially as proof of Vatican corruption still unravels.

Shortly after the Mud Club opened in Tribeca, as an underground antidote to Studio 54, complete with gender-neutral bathrooms and a revolving art gallery, Sid Vicious stabbed girlfriend Nancy to death at The Chelsea Hotel. Norman Rockwell passed away along with his wholesome vision of America and anthropologist Margaret Meade left, probably still marveling at our collective stupidity; Graphically illustrated by the Jonestown Peoples Temple, drinking the Kool-Aid in a mass suicide... another tribute to organized religion, worshipping a Moses, Christ, Buddha, Muhammad, Joseph Smith, Jim Jones or Sun Myung Moon human manifestation of 'God.' A week later, Mayor George Moscone and gay activist Harvey Milk were assassinated in San Francisco, the original home of the Peoples Temple. And in New York, Voyage Records sank beneath a sea of debt.

When Voyage went down it sucked me under as well. Having personally guaranteed the subpublishing deals, some of the companies demanded reparation, completely wiping out my savings. With no income other than NOTC, I had to let Raleigh go and scramble to find office space somewhere in midtown. The city also financially strapped, I was luckily able to afford a converted hallway cubbyhole on the 23rd floor of the old Paramount Pictures building at 1501 Broadway. Now Beth, Raleigh and Lu Pollak all gone, I survived producing *New On The Charts* alone. Researching, ad sales, art & layout, newsletter leads, producer bios, typing with two fingers, stuffing, licking and stamping each envelope, that little room became my whole world. Standing on the ledge outside my window on New Year's Eve, I watched the Times Square ball fall across the street, the drunken mass of humanity waving below, and wondered what was coming next.

XIV. (1979)
(After-Math)

The new year opened with a bang, former V.P. Nelson Rockefeller dying of a heart attack while purportedly fucking his secretary and a lady lunatic opened fire at a San Diego school declaring, *"I don't like Monday"* (inspiring The Boomtown Rats' hit single). As former Attorney General, John Mitchell, skulked out of prison, the Shah of Iran did the same. I was able to avoid joining The Village People at the *"Y.M.C.A."* as they gestured on American Bandstand with January subscription renewals, and began NOTC training new mom Joyce Goldman at her home in White Plains.

Lou Ragusa floated seamlessly from Voyage to Infinity Records, Ron Alexenberg's new East Coast subsidiary of MCA, with apparent unlimited backing (and perhaps another chance for Linda). For me it meant a lucrative full-page four-color ad commitment for the year, finding a new printer who could handle color film separations, and another format change. The producer bios brought interest but no income. Record company A&R profiles, would not only generate ad support, but also get me closer to the players who could sign me someday. This meant more work, but with Joyce handling the research and typing it was doable. By targeting A&R, recording studios also advertised, inspiring my Studio Spotlight, listing their equipment and recent clients. The record label art departments created promotional black & white minis for each album. A collage of these on my cover worked for all of us…

www.notc.com

At MIDEM, Joelle greeted me in slow deliberate French, but when I confessed not yet learned, she took me aside wagging her finger... "No French, No Nookie," before turning back to the table with a teasing tail toss, refusing my advances for the rest of the week. The advent of the Sony Walkman was also a surprise kick in the financial balls to Bernard Chevry, when suddenly companies didn't need his overpriced sound systems to present their music. Officially banned from the Palais, it didn't affect the big companies that rented booths. But hunched in surreal corners and on the stairs, sneaky pushers offered free sound samples hidden in their raincoats.

That first rocky day closed even worse, discovering that I somehow dropped or misplaced my NOTC sign-up book with hundreds of dollars in subscriptions. In a case of unforeseen consequences, when the *MIDEM News* ran my picture and story the next morning, I couldn't have designed a better advertising campaign. The entire Palais suddenly knew me and *New On The Charts*, looking for my lost book. Eventually discovered in the booth of flamboyant, black caped, Michelangelo La Bionda who, with his bother Carmelo, were pioneers of Italo Disco out of Milan, and beginning a relationship that would last for years.

Manager Jim Halsey introduced Country music to MIDEM that year with the last live concert in the opulent and acoustically perfect Music Hall and Casino. Scheduled for demolition to make way for a massive new Palais des Festivals *(with pressure and purported payoffs to limit competition from neighboring Monte Carlo)*. Reveling in the Oak Ridge Boys' *"Elvira,"* and the solo artistry of Roy Clarke's acoustic guitar, clearly audible from the red velvet balcony, it seemed sacrilegious to be destroying such elegance and beauty in the name of progress.

Using MIDEM as a jumping off point, that year's detour would be a visit to my sister teaching in Israel. Huddling in front of a ceramic heater in her freezing Haifa apartment, picturing camels and desert, I had no idea Israel had winter. So, with an air mattress in the back of her Subaru, we headed south. Passing rows of trees in what was once desert, the beach town of Netanya was still too cold for swimming. Like my visit to Spain years before, the rifle-toting soldiers everywhere took some getting used to. Tel Aviv bustled with modern skyscrapers and condominiums along the coast in sharp contrast to the ancient marketplace stalls of partitioned Jerusalem another hour's drive inland. The cacophony of merchants arguing, gesturing, and berating each other's offerings, filled the meandering tented bazaar. More in keeping with my preconceived concept of 'the holy land,' but still colder than expected. That night, on invitation from a relative, we stayed at a nearby kibbutz, a noble experiment in pure communism. Gradually losing the next generation, opting out after mandatory military service, to the allure of 'Disco' capitalism.

Filling up with gas and water in Kiryat Gat, the sun began to warm as we headed south into the Negev desert. Topping off the tank again in Be'er Sheva just to be safe, within hours we were actually driving through my pre-envisioned sand dunes and occasional Bedouin on camelback, surprisingly dressed in counter-intuitive black. Apparently black not only absorbs the sun's rays, but also your body heat, with the right material and the slightest breeze, allowing that warmth to escape. With barely enough shekels between us, for gas, water, and one decent meal a day, by late afternoon we reached the modern (and expensive) resort city of Elat on the Red Sea. Overnight parking prohibited, we headed south into what would soon be Egyptian territory, to be returned to Sadat later that year as part of the recent peace accord. A few miles down the coast pulling into the open parking area of a German run holiday village called Neviot. The lot sparsely populated with an assortment of vehicles, pushcarts and tents, we watched an entire Arab family push in a brand new Mercedes they somehow acquired, but couldn't afford the gas to run. The resort was basically a horseshoe of shacks surrounded by meager vegetation with holiday lights strung throughout. Catering to diving enthusiast guests with a laissez-faire attitude.

That night, sitting in the sand next to the water, picking my guitar for the first time in a while, lights began to blink open around the parking lot. First joined by a fabulous Swedish guitarist who couldn't speak a word of English, then soon a wooden flute, sitar, squeeze-box accordion, tabla, and Arabian version of a violin, all communicating in one universal language. It then turned out everyone could actually sing the words to *"Yesterday"* phonetically. So there we sat, a Tower of Babble musical United Nations, in the desert sands of ancient Egypt, under a massive star lit Arabian sky, singing out across the historic Red sea, harmonizing to The Beatles.

In broken Hebrew, the Swedish guitarist explained through my sister (who didn't like or trust him) that he was a well-known artist at home. Forced to flee after continual arrests for driving to gigs without his license, revoked following marijuana convictions. One more arrest and they'd throw away the key, so with financial support from fans, he was now a traveling minstrel. His story struck a strange chord in my psyche and suppressed fear of ending up like him, foretold in *"Gotta Be Movin' Along,"* ♪ a song I had written years before. What was happening to my dream? Since *New On The Charts* and playing the businessman, although still planning to

♪ *Song available on iTunes & www.LEKalikow.com*

'make it someday,' I was barely a musician anymore and had written nothing new. The artist co-opted by the entrepreneur I thought was as a temporary role. No longer totally immersed in my music, it was seeping away.

On the beach the next day, in the distance a naked blonde perched on a sand dune, but before I could move, a dashing young Arab joined her on his camel. At first remaining on the animal, but soon sitting next to her in the sand. Eventually only the camel was visible, standing alone at first, then sitting. Later that afternoon, the two figures emerged, climbed on the camel and rode off together. Baking in the sun through the voyeuristic silent film, I was definitely ready to spend the night with the redhead German dive instructor who invited us to play for the village that night. Her muscular legs and underwater endurance made for an acrobatic, exhausting and wonderfully cathartic night of release that stretched to a late morning brunch, shared with my sister and Swedish accompanist. Who, despite my sister's uneasiness with him, hitched a ride as we headed back to Tel Aviv and my flight home.

On return, we detoured a bit, weightlessly floating on the salty Dead Sea before visiting Masada. The isolated self-contained rock plateau, where Jewish rebels once held off Roman legions for years, until 15,000 troops laid siege and eventually breached the summit, only to find the defenders' bodies surrendered in bloody mass suicide. We opted to climb the actual footpath once navigated by Roman soldiers, forgoing the tourist tram. My sister relating the story to our Swedish companion as we climbed. A desert breeze whispered through the archeological remains at the summit, tears welling in the jailhouse refugee, relating to the self-imprisoned souls who chose death over defeat on the once blood soaked ground beneath our feet. Standing together, eyes wet, we stared out into the biblical distance.

Back at 1501 Broadway, I continued working with songwriter Philip Namanworth and agreed to send out some of his songs for a royalty commission. This probably should have included co-publishing, but at the time more than half my NOTC subscribers were music publishers. As an impartial arbiter of information, I also, perhaps naively, felt it unethical to compete using their money. We thought one song, *"I Apologize,"* would be perfect for Sinatra, who's connections I made printing the *"New York, New York"* songbook at Big 3. With demos also sent to Tony Bennett and Wayne Newton.

Newton immediately wanted the song. The first time a composition is recorded and released is called 'the original recording' over which the publisher has complete control. After that anyone can 'cover' it, so that first recording is an important decision. Should we wait for 'The Chairman' or let Newton have it? Wayne was actually in the studio and needed to complete his album, so with no word from Sinatra, we agreed, eventually reaching Top 50 on the Adult Contemporary charts.

Still writing *"RPM"* with Cotler in the offices of Big 3 and on weekends at his home in Jersey, we were close to finishing when Herman finally accepted forced retirement. Suddenly Steve had his hands full, uncovering Herman's 'unorthodox' bookkeeping procedures. Steiger would print out royalty statements and cut the checks, but somehow forget to mail them until the next statement was due, filling a wall of metal file cabinets with unsent checks. If anyone called him on it, he'd produce the statements showing he issued everything in a timely manner, blame the accounting department for the fuck up, immediately sending all monies along with an extra advance (when he knew he could recoup), his sincere apologies, and a kosher salami… no problem.

Herman's concept of contractual 'gray areas' was more troubling. Since he believed the royalty advances he paid for printing a catalog were more than fair, it followed that if he hadn't recouped when the contract terminated, it was also fair to keep printing those songs until he did, despite the fact, in the eyes of the law, this was copyright infringement. On the few occasions a publisher actually went into a music store and caught it, Herman would be 'shocked,' claim ignorance, and promise to get to the bottom of the 'mistake.'

Then sit back, puff on his cigar for the appropriate time interval, before calling back. Apologizing profusely, assuring the 'idiot' in production responsible would be fired. Then a very generous offer to extend the contract a little longer, rather than pull the books from the shelves and go through the time and expense of dealing with lawyers... followed of course with the heartfelt gift of a kosher salami. Luckily we finished the *"RPM"* script before Barry Manilow's manager turned down the salami and hit Big 3 with a multi-million dollar infringement suit. Upset with his forced retirement, consulting to Warner Brothers Music, this placed Herman in the unusual position of testifying against his own misdeeds in litigation that would eventually bring down Big 3.

In a choreographed melding of art and life, the *"The China Syndrome's"* promotional tag read, *"Today only a handful of people know what it means... Soon you will know."* In the film a physicist proposes that a nuclear plant meltdown could render "an area the size of Pennsylvania" permanently uninhabitable. Less than two weeks later the 3 Mile Island Nuclear Accident, in guess what state? And topping the *Billboard* charts... Gloria Gaynor's, *"I Will Survive"*

A month later, questioning my own survival, staring over the pilot's shoulder in a twin-engine prop. With waves of motion sickness, tottering toward the runway, wrecks of previous attempts clearly visible in the shallow water. When I arrived at Joe Wheeler State Park for the Muscle Shoals Music Association 2nd Annual Record & Producers Seminar, Jimmy Johnson cracked up. "Nobody flies into Muscle Shoals," he laughed, "It's too fucking dangerous." Apparently everyone else knew to land in Huntsville and drive from there. The black and white poverty of this isolated rural community formed a cultural clay, when baked in a simple electronic recording studio, rose up with a voice that resonated through the bigotry of the times. The incidental mixing of talented white musicians marinated in southern black sensibility provided the backbeat for literally hundreds of hit records. Beginning with artists like Percy Sledge, Wilson Pickett, and Aretha Franklin, the Muscle Shoals contagion transfused mainstream, through everyone from Paul Simon to Duane Allman to The Rolling Stones.

The Muscle Shoals Rhythm Section of Barry Beckett (keyboards), Roger Hawkins (drums), David Hood (bass), and Jimmy Johnson (guitar) {dubbed "The Swampers" by Leon Russell's manager Denny Cordell} were the original session players for Rick Hall's Fame Studios. When Hall and Atlantic Record's Jerry Wexler had a falling out after a disastrous Aretha Franklin session, Wexler made the guys an 'offer they couldn't refuse.' With their own studio and a lucrative Atlantic production deal, they left Rick scrambling to fulfill his newly signed Capitol Records contract, an embittered rival. Now, ten years later, reluctantly together for this promotional event, the tension was still there, beneath the unfamiliar sweet scent of honeysuckle.

The facility, a three floor, wood frame motel on a deceivingly peaceful body of water that didn't advertise swimming, in deference to the hidden gators and poisonous water moccasins slithering through the surface. The 'Seminar,' really artist showcases, evolved into amazing downstairs dining hall, all-night beer-keg jam sessions. Probably the only time musicians from the two rival studios plugged in together, backed by the Muscle Shoals Horn Section, and encourage by local 'working girls' hand-picked by Jimmy to keep the party going. From the brilliant redhead poet/artist Mac McAnally to the astounding artistry of Travis Wammack, voice mimicking his guitar through the newly modified electronic vocoder, this was the ultimate *"Magical Mystery Tour"* taking me away from the insipid Disco Generation about to engulf the world outside. And on the ride back (to Huntsville this time), I couldn't help but notice my transition from participant to observer... Not grabbing a microphone or guitar like I might have ten years ago. Content to be perceived as the Editor and Publisher of *New On The Charts*.

Speaking of Disco, following Steve Rubell's loudmouth bragging about his income, Studio 54 was raided and charged with tax evasion. Howard Stein took the opportunity to launch Xenon to compete. A few months later, down on Avenue A, The Pyramid Club opened the East Village gay and drag queen closet, later to become an integral part of the Disco scene. Following punk's devaluation of the musicianship and poetry of the 60's, production centric Disco made artists as interchangeable as the jingle singers in commercials, producers and DJ's becoming the 'stars.' More 'club' than 'radio friendly,' record sales plummeted.

Seemingly oblivious to the changes taking place, at Infinity Records, former CBS 'boom time' promotion man Ron Alexenberg still believed that if you spent enough money you could sell anything. After signing irrelevant 'name' acts for records that did nothing, in the ultimate blind hubris, Infinity paid dearly to release an album by Pope John Paul II in his native Polish *(are you fucking kidding!!!)*. When most of the one million advance copies were returned unsold, MCA pulled the plug on Infinity (along with Lou and Linda Ragusa), and the remainder of my NOTC four color, full-page ad contract. The only Infinity acts retained by MCA were Spyro Gyra and Rupert Holmes, who's *"Escape (The Pina Colada Song)"* then went to #1.

With my recording career stalled and the music industry stumbling, a surprising call from the West Coast. Robert Harris was now President of Universal Television, and liked *"RPM."* Front balcony lined with cast iron jockeys donated by the hoi polloi when a speakeasy, the 21 Club sat between Warner Brothers, directly in front, and CBS on the corner. The dark expensive wood paneled walls lined with pictures of power brokers and celebrities. During Prohibition, a system of levers tipped the bar shelves, dumping liquor bottles through a chute when raided, a trick wall hiding the wine cellar next door, now housed patron's private collections. In from The Coast, Robert met me at the door, stopping briefly at coat check to borrow a tie to match my sport coat, required for lunch. In the end, we shook hands on a deal to option *"RPM"* as a Movie Of

The Week, and possible series pilot... and perhaps a new path for me?

Everything was changing... my dream, the music, the business, the possibilities. With *New On The Charts* on the desk of every major record company and music publisher, I was primed to take another shot when the music pendulum swung back. But would it? And when? And where would I be?

To sum up the seventies... I performed with everyone from Richie Havens, Eric Anderson, Tom Rush, Buffy St. Marie and Buzzy Lindhart to Edger Winter & White Trash, Van Morrison and Jefferson Airplane; had been through 3 major label deals that didn't work out (Chess, Capitol, Columbia) with 3 major producers (Birnside, Sherman, Ragovoy); 4 major publishing agreements (Birnside, Beechwood, Dick James, Arnold Maxin) and a major management situation (Krebs) and never got a record out or a song recorded and released by anyone; wrote and almost produced an off-Broadway musical *("Where Has All The Ivy Gone?")* that never happened; was the Entertainment Director for the first singles country club (Chateau D'Vie), that failed; then Administrative Director for a management and concert production company (Contemprocon) that eventually lost its primary artist and fell apart; repped music for advertising and recorded demos (with Don Elliot) that were never released; gave up a full time consultant's gig (at United Artist's Big 3 Music) to help launch a new record company that sank (Voyage Records). Got laid at least twice a week (over 1000 times in ten years, not counting blow-jobs), which meant my complexion was great. But there was still the rude awakening when college kids referred to me as 'sir,' that I had somehow slipped into adulthood.

As the humiliation of the Viet Nam sixties set in, having ripped the country's psyche apart, in the seventies we anti-bodies to stupidity just couldn't fight anymore as the body politic was overrun by reactionary corruption. Nixon's 'law and order' pretenders fouled the political machinery causing a breakdown in its ability to function and belief that it ever would. Capped off at the end of the decade with a near nuclear meltdown through corporate ineptitude, as we helplessly watched American hostages taken by Iran's Ayatollah, thumbing his nose at our emasculation. Stuck in a crippled system and unsure of the future, during my transition from altruistic artist to self-interest businessman, in the song *"Progress"* ♪ I wrote:

I'm not socially committed
    I don't know what to believe
All the people we've elected
    Have sewn pockets in their sleeves
And the food that we've infected
    With preservatives and greed
And the cities we've erected
    Not designed to let you breathe

Well so this is the price of progress
    Have we come so very far
From the days of horse and buggy
    To the days of jets and cars?
In our war with mother nature
    Every battle has been won
We've flown to the moon
    And clouded up the sun
And we've just begun

I do not know the answers
    'Cause the questions are not clear
And my eyes can see no longer
    And my ears can barely hear
And my heartbeat's growing fainter
    With the passing of each year
And I cannot help but wonder
    Where do we go from here?

I cannot hear
> I cannot feel
I cannot see
> Breathe free

So this is the price of progress
> Have we come so very far
From the days of horse and buggy
> To the days of jets and cars?
And though everything of value
> Must then surely have a cost
I cannot help but wonder
> Have we won
More than we've lost?

♪ *Song available on iTunes & www.LEKalikow.com*

Sex, No Drugs & Rock'N'Roll

The Soundtrack Album
Available on iTunes & Google Play

1. **Part Of It All** — Page 207
2. **Silhouette In A Negligee** — Page 230
3. **Corned Beef On Rye** — Page 232
4. **Subway Rider** — Page 234
5. **Ain't Gonna Look Back**
   (2 versions- Acoustic & Electric) — Page 241
6. **Midnight Woman** — Page 248
7. **Wish I Was A Lady** — Page 256
8. **It's Kinda Nice** — Page 270
9. **California Freeway Goin' South** — Page 307
10. **Gotta Be Movin' Along** — Page 331
11. **Progress** — Page 338

Produced and Performed by L.E. Kalikow
Engineered by Richard Corsello & Rob Freeman

All music and lyrics by L.E. Kalikow © 2016 Song Attack(BMI)

www.LEKalikow.com

www.ingramcontent.com/pod-product-compliance
Lightning Source LLC
LaVergne TN
LVHW041606070426
835507LV00008B/159